Jean Laplanche:

Seduction, Translation and the Drives

Institute of Contemporary Arts London

Jean Laplanche: Seduction, Translation and the Drives

A Dossier edited by John Fletcher & Martin Stanton

Translations by Martin Stanton

Psychoanalytic Forum

Institute of Contemporary Arts London

Institute of Contemporary Arts
The Mall, London SW1Y 5AH
Tel: +44 71 930 0493, Fax: +44 71 873 0051

Jean Laplanche: Seduction, Translation and the Drives
A Dossier edited by John Fletcher and Martin Stanton

ISBN 0 905263 68 5 (paperback)
ISBN 0 905263 73 1 (hardback)

The ICA is an independent educational charity financially supported by the Arts Council of Great Britain, Westminster City Council, the British Institute and the Rayne Foundation. The ICA's artistic programme is, however, primarily reliant on ICA membership, self-generated income, sponsorship and donations.

Produced by Graham Whybrow
Cover Design by Paul Khera

Printing and Binding by
W H Houldershaw Ltd., Rayleigh, Essex.

Contents

Publisher's Note

Jean Laplanche: Seduction, Translation and the Drives continues a new series of ICA Documents initiated by *Thinking Art: Beyond Traditional Aesthetics* – a collection of essays exploring the relationship between philosophy and aesthetics and based on the ICA's Philosophical Forum.

Compiled from interviews, transcripts of round table discussions and newly translated essays by Laplanche, this collection also had its origins in a conference at the Institute of Contemporary Arts, the first of a series which aims to reflect some of the most significant trends in contemporary psychoanalysis. Focusing on the main currents of Laplanche's recent thinking, it provides a unique insight into the developing philosophy of one of the most challenging and provocative figures in the psychoanalytic world.

Linda Brandon, Director of Talks, ICA

Acknowledgements

We would like to thank the following for their help in preparing this volume: the Cultural Service of the French Embassy in London for their assistance in funding these events; Dr. Robert M. Young and Free Association Books for permission to translate and publish 'The Drives and their Object-Source' and 'The Wall and the Arcade', and to reprint in revised form the interview with Jean Laplanche from *Free Associations* 23.

We owe a special debt to Linda Brandon, Helena Reckitt, Ragnar Farr, Graham Whybrow and Paul Khera for their hard work, enthusiasm and commitment to this project; Eileen Ashley, the Secretary of the Centre for Psychoanalytic Studies at the University of Kent, for all her work with the organization of these events and their transcription; the staff and students at the Centre for Psychoanalytic Studies at the University of Kent for their participation in the seminars and lecture; Richard Wells, ex-Director of the Freud Museum, for welcoming the Laplanche seminar at the Freud Museum; Helen Hayward for typing the initial transcripts; Jacques André for his help with the more complex nuances of French psychoanalytic terminology; Andrew Benjamin, Iain Bruce, Kate Farquhar, Maryse Fauré, Anne Lewis-Loubignac, and Meira Likierman for their help, support, and advice; and Nadine Laplanche for all her warm support and participation.

Note on the translations

Jean Laplanche's lecture 'Psychoanalysis, Time & Translation' was originally delivered in English. The English text was based on 'Temporality and Translation', which appeared in the *Stanford Literature Review* (Fall 1989, pp.241–259), and was translated from the French by Terry Thomas, though it was substantially revised by Professor Laplanche. I related this text back to the original French text (in *Psychanalyse a l'université*, January 1989), and discussed discrepancies with the author. The translations of 'The Drive and its Object-Source' and 'The Wall and the Arcade' are based on their most recent version in the new edition of *Vie et Mort en Psychanalyse* (Flammarion, 1989, pp.253–268, and pp.291–301). 'Notes on Afterwardsness' is translated from a transcript of a tape made in November 1991.

I would like to thank Professor Laplanche for all his help with the translations, and also John Fletcher for his invaluable criticism and help with clarification.

M.S.

Foreword

The English language reader will know Jean Laplanche as a critical archæologist of Freudian concepts, as in his best known work *The Language of Psychoanalysis* (1967), his influential essay on fantasy (1964) (both written with J-B. Pontalis), and his innovatory text *Life and Death in Psychoanalysis* (1970). These works represent a labour of recovery of particular concepts: the drive/instinct distinction, primary narcissism, *Nachträglichkeit* (afterwardsness or Strachey's 'deferred action'), *Anlehnung* (leaning on), and a re-situating of the death-drive. The elaboration of such concepts forms part of a symptomatic reading of the movement of Freud's thought as a whole – its repetitions, repressions, and impasses. It is a delineation of the Freudian problematic in order to 'attempt an interpretation of that problematic, which restores it to its most radical elements... [to] reconstitute a structure of Freudian theory beyond the successive forms in which it is embodied' (*Life and Death*, p.3).

This archæological work has also provided the conditions for an original theoretical project in its own right that has been developed through the 1980s in the *Problématiques* (1980/1987) and associated essays – now partly available to the English language reader in *New Foundations for Psychoanalysis*. This project continues with the current work in progress on time and translation. While plans are afoot for the publication of the five volumes of *Problématiques* in English, it will be some time before either they or the forthcoming book on time will be available. The present volume is intended to meet the needs of the English language reader in the interim period, as well as to provide a unique opportunity to study Jean Laplanche's work in the process of its elaboration. The material presented here derives from Professor Laplanche's visit to Britain in April/May 1990, and includes transcripts of a lecture, interview and conference at the Institute of Contemporary Arts, and seminars at the Centre for Psychoanalytic Studies, University of Kent, and the Freud Museum, London.

To supplement this, there are translations of articles and notes that present the main lines of Laplanche's thought in the principal areas of his recent work: 'The Drive and its Object-Source' contains an exposition of Laplanche's concept of the enigmatic signifier and its relation to drive theory; 'The Wall and the Arcade', taking off from Walter Benjamin's essay on 'The Task of the Translator', examines the importance of the translation model in the psychoanalytic process, and emphasizes the crucial function of de-translation and the 'word for word' (Benjamin's *Wörtlichkeit*); and 'Notes on Afterwardsness' explores the impact of *Nachträglichkeit* (afterwardsness) on psychoanalytic conceptions of time and temporalization, and pays particular attention to the differences between Freud and Laplanche's theorizations of this.

In an After Events section, these main areas are further critically assessed by some of the participants at the ICA Conference, who attempt to situate the importance and wider implications of Laplanche's theoretical contributions. Also included is a bibliography and brief biographical sketch.

Jean Laplanche: Seduction, Translation and the Drives

Interview

Jean Laplanche talks to Martin Stanton

MS: *The Language of Psychoanalysis* (1967), which you wrote with Pontalis, has become an essential source for anyone interested in psychoanalysis. Since then, of course, you have developed in your own direction, not least in translating Freud and extending research on Freud. It would be interesting to know, therefore, which parts of *The Language of Psychoanalysis* were written by you, and which were written by Pontalis?

JL: We constantly worked together. We each studied and prepared certain texts. One read out work and the other commented. So the book was constantly forged through discussion.

MS: Were both of you at this time influenced by Lacan? And if so, to what extent is this evident in the book?

JL: Yes, certainly, but Lacan did not like this project too much, because it was not under his direction, but Daniel Lagache's. Lagache and Lacan were already in conflict by this time. Nonetheless, there are many Lacanian concepts in the book. Lacan said it was too scholastic, but I don't think that is so: we developed a critical reflection on every concept. This way of posing major problems makes this 'vocabulary' (the original French title is *Vocabulaire de la Psychanalyse*) patently neither a 'dictionary' nor an 'encyclopædia'.

MS: Were you in fact translating Freud at this time?

JL: Yes, indeed I was. My first translation of Freud, in 1957, was of the text *On Narcissism: An Introduction* (1914), which I did for Lacan's seminar, so that people would have a French version to refer to.

MS: So you were very much involved with Lacan and the seminar at this time?

JL: I retain a great deal of affection for Lacan. He only ever did me good, so I have no personal grievance to bear towards him. Of course, I became more distanced from him as I disagreed with some of his thought and practice. I was in analysis with him for a long time, in fact up to 1963, at the time of the schism in the Société Française de Psychanalyse. So this finished – as it did for everyone who parted ways with him then. It was hard, but that is normal. He has never said anything to harm me, and I have never said anything to harm him. We met years later at a reception given by Edgar Fauré, and spent two warm and friendly hours together.

MS: You mention that Lacan advised you to study medicine. Does this reflect in any way on his views of lay analysis?

JL: Lacan was always in favour of medical training. He never took a clear position on lay analysis. In fact, he himself always remained very much a medic. All his family and close associates addressed him as 'Doctor Lacan'. At the time this was important, because he wanted access to psychotics. Me too, hence his advice to study medicine.

MS: When did you actually start to take a critical distance from Lacan?

JL: At the time of the Bonneval Congress (1960), when Serge Leclaire and I gave a paper on 'the unconscious'. This was not an open criticism of Lacan. We simply said: how can you say that the unconscious is structured as a language, when, in Freud, language is clearly associated with the pre-conscious? In fact, I think my theory of the unconscious is already very evident in this Bonneval paper. Lacan was above all a tactician. He did not want to hear the criticism. It was enough for him that his pupils were giving the paper at this prestigious congress. He was very much the head of a movement, like Freud. When someone was part of the movement, and participated in the glory of the 'cause', he or she could hold as many theoretical differences as they liked. But once you were no longer a part of the movement, you were excluded, no matter if you said exactly the same things as you had before.

MS: It is interesting that you observe that your theory of the unconscious was already evident then. Do you in fact have a conception of the development of your thought?

JL: Yes, it's the spiral model. Certain of my ideas are already there in *The Language of Psychoanalysis*. The seduction theory is also already there in the Fantasy article, and in *Life and Death in Psychoanalysis* (1970). Of course, these ideas are often embryonic; they are only more or less developed. By the spiral model, I mean we go back over the same themes but make some progress with them. If we don't make any progress, well that's just teaching (as opposed to research)! I don't actually contradict anything that I said in the beginning, I have just deepened it. The major emphasis of my work at the moment is the priority of the other. The implantation of messages is an old idea of mine, but the priority of the other's implantation of sexual messages is new for me. It doesn't contradict what I said previously, it is just a more profound perception. Anyway, for me, it is not possible to divide my work up into an early and late Laplanche!

*

MS: You evoke the distinction there between teaching and research. How does this apply specifically to psychoanalysis?

JL: This is a long question, because it must be posed in terms of both universities and training societies. These two have a mirror relationship to each other, and each one wants to be what the other is. My view is that psychoanalytic practice, and the training [*formation*] of analysts – which, for me, implies as its core, personal analysis – cannot and must not be institutionalized. It does not matter which kind of institution we are talking about, state or private institution, whatever. For me, psychoanalysis is not a profession. Once it tries to be recognized as such, it loses its soul. Why is it not a profession? Because it cannot have a *Zielvorstellung* [purposive idea]. Psychoanalytic practice cannot propose an aim, no matter what that is. 'Cure', for example, cannot be taken as the aim of psychoanalysis. 'Cure' is no more relevant an aim than divorce. Both imply the social adaptation of the profession.

Let's take the example of child psychoanalysis. One of the great problems here is heteronomy (subjection to an external law): that is, one brings you a child because he or she is not bright, or does not work well at school. And you are asked: please bring them back as good students. This is a major problem, because the analyst will start by saying to the child: 'all this is a joke, your parents want this, but we don't care, we will talk of other things, of whatever you want'. So psychoanalysis has to put all socially-adaptive aims – that is, the whole notion of self-preservation – in brackets. This is why it can never be a profession.

MS: Does this apply to training analysis, that is, adapting people to be psychoanalysts?

JL: This is even more true for so-called training analysis. The idea of undertaking a personal analysis as a learning or training procedure in order to become an analyst, or to take someone into analysis so that they may become analysts, really just amounts to taking some raw material and saying, 'in the end, I'll turn you into an analyst'. We know this does not work. The person on the couch only thinks of that – that the analyst has to make a report to the training body, saying, 'There you are! This person can or cannot become an analyst!'. It is the same thing as making a report to the National Health Service, saying, Mr or Ms so-and-so has made some progress, so let's continue the treatment you are paying me for. This is not psychoanalytic. Psychoanalysis cannot be heteronomous, and cannot accept any pre-established social aim.

MS: How then can people become analysts if there is no training analysis?

JL: In my psychoanalytic society, the Association Psychanalytique de France (APF), there are no training analysts or training analyses. It is one of the few societies in the world in which this is the case. People apply to us after their personal analysis. They can have been analyzed anywhere in the world, by analysts of any persuasion – a Jungian, Lacanian, or a member of our society. There is no question of starting an analysis under the auspices of the APF. Analysis is purely a personal question. You start it for whatever reasons there are in your head – fantasies, whatever... Even the fantasy of becoming an analyst: there is no need to leave this out of consideration, it has to be analyzed like everything else. It is not pre-judged as serious, realistic, or whatever. Analysis is therefore outside the institution, as it should be. Nonetheless, I should point out that this has been challenged for some years now within the APF. Some members want to go back to training analyses. But this will take us back to all those things associated with social adaptation. People will start talking of 'better' analysts – there will be selection, privileging our 'own children' (i.e. those analysts that our members train). This has to be resisted.

MS: So what about the other side of the mirror-relation you mention: namely, the role of psychoanalysis in the university?

JL: In my opinion, psychoanalysis can only be studied in the university at research level. Some of my colleagues disagree, but I think that students only reach the point when they can approach analytic thinking at the end of their studies. There is no point in teaching students to construct the main psychoanalytic concepts after high school, because they have nothing to go back over. Analysis is retrospective, it demands a return. It constructs in deconstructing. As such it is ex-centric to vocational studies. It cannot be learnt as a vocational technique, but needs to be approached at the level of research.

MS: Does this mean that there is no institutional or vocational link between psychoanalytic research and training? Is there, for example, any link between your department at the University of Paris VII and the APF?

JL: None. It's true that many members of the APF are university teachers. I founded a doctorate by research in psychoanalysis which people could apply for after what we call in France the 'professional training', or the level of postgraduate diploma (be it in clinical psychology or in psychopathology). So there is no professional postgraduate diploma in psychoanalysis in France. In any case, anyone who actually applies for the doctorate in psychoanalysis will already have a professional qualification in something else, so their needs will be different. To have a doctorate in psychoanalysis is therefore the same as having a doctorate of letters. No one thinks that a doctorate of letters entails the right be a writer. Similarly, a doctorate in psychoanalysis is not a professional qualification. It gives you no right to practise.

MS: Does this mean that psychoanalytic training bodies also have no professional rights?

JL: At the moment, anyone can put the title 'psychoanalyst' on the plaque outside the door. But I am against a certain 'integrationism', that is, the wish to conflate psychoanalytic theory and practice. Some institutes, for example, make the claim that they must carry out all research in psychoanalysis just as they carry out the clinical work. I do not accept this distinction between the clinical and the theoretical. Every discourse on the clinical is theoretical. This discourse can just as well be held in the university as in the psychoanalytic societies. Similarly, the theses I put forward are not just theoretical, but clinical as well. I think that all research in psychoanalysis touches on two or more of the following realms: the theoretical, the clinical, psychoanalysis outside the realm of cure, and the history of psychoanalytic ideas.

MS: This is very radical...

JL: I am very radical, but also very pessimistic. I think that the training institutes with their 'integrationism' will win. Even people like Serge Leclaire argue on the one hand that psychoanalysis is 'outside the ordinary', and on the other hand conclude that there must be a register of psychoanalysts. This is totally contradictory, and amounts to submission to social pressure to prescribe all forms of human activity. It must be shown that psychoanalysis produces results; whereas, in fact, it might not serve any specific purpose. It might even not help at all.

MS: What then if this register of analysts is set up?

JL: Well, we will have to call ourselves something else. In France, the registered term is 'psychanalyste', so perhaps we could use the term 'psychoanalyste' – which is never used! Unfortunately, you are not so lucky in Great Britain!

*

MS: Let us turn now to your work on the 'seduction' theory. You have powerful and original views on the importance of seduction for psychoanalysis. What differences do you observe between yourself and others on this subject?

JL: Well, I think it is important to note the distinction between seduction as fact, and seduction as a fundamental human situation. Masson, for example, limits himself to factual seduction. I am always amused by the subtitle of his book, 'Freud's suppression of the seduction theory', because it shows that he understands absolutely nothing of this theory. He thinks that the seduction theory amounted simply to the fact that seduction is real, and then later Freud suppressed it by saying that it was not real. It has been shown for a long time now that the seduction theory is much more complex than that. In *The Language of Psychoanalysis*, for example, we pointed out that there were various aspects to Freud's seduction theory: temporal, topical, and economic aspects, not to mention the evolution of sexuality. Freud moved from one factual scene to another factual scene, to the point where he concluded there was no final factual scene. He was obsessed by the notion of the real scene, but never managed to capture it. This comes from the fact that Freud relates to only two categories: the real and fantasy. If the seduction scene is just a fantasy, then it has no priority over other primal scenes, such as castration or return to the mother's womb. For Freud, the problem then gets relayed to pre-history, because if these primal scenes are not real, then real seduction and castration must have taken place at some earlier point in human evolution. So the problem becomes endless. Why endless? Because Freud never conceived that there could be other categories than factual reality and imagination, and he believed that imagination must be founded on some pre-historical or biological reality. This is where his seduction theory failed. Is this missing category that of the symbolic, which Lacan elaborated, and to which Pontalis and I related the primal scenes and the origins of fantasy in our article (1964)? I have basically distanced myself from this view, as you can see in *New Foundations*. I now call this third category the 'message' or 'signifier'. What Freud missed then is the category of the message. So, as far as the seduction theory is concerned, Freud gave great importance to the factual reality – which indeed should never be ignored – but missed out the message side altogether. We should therefore be careful to avoid the Freudian antinomy of either real seduction or fantasy, and look rather at the message side. Now, there is something unconscious that the most violent or perverse adult addresses to the other, even in the most violent act. This address or message, therefore, is a universal category. It is more vast than the category of factual or physical sexual abuse. Not all seductions are abuses. There is the implantation of an erotic message in the infant which he or she does not understand. Freud, indeed, was well aware of this. He noted that the infant picks up the erotic gestures between the parents.

Anyway, the basic points I want to make here are: first, that seduction is not to be placed on the same level as other primal fantasies; it is not a fantasy, but a communication situation. Secondly, this communication is neither bilateral, nor symmetrical.

MS: Is there no input from the infant at all?

JL: It is not interaction. It is a one-way action. It is one-way only on the sexual level. I do not deny the interaction on the self-preservation level: in feeding the infant, for example, one feeds and the other is fed, hence there is an interaction. But when the feeding message relays the sexual, it is one-way, it follows one direction from the feeder to the fed. From the beginning, one is active and the other is passive. But very quickly, the little human tries to turn this passivity into activity, that is, to make something of this message from the other. Still, there is this dissymmetry. This comes from the fact that the active one has more 'knowledge', more unconscious fantasies than the passive infant. The adult has more, because he or she has an unconscious. His or her gestures have more because they are impregnated with 'symptoms' (in the sense of the psychopathology of everyday life). So even the slightest gesture for the infant will carry something enigmatic.

MS: How is this perceived by the infant as enigmatic?

JL: I distinguish the term 'enigma' from other terms like 'puzzle', 'mystery', or 'problem'. For example, black holes in the universe are a problem, not an enigma. An enigma is necessarily something posed by someone, and not something just difficult to understand. It is also posed by someone who is not conscious of the essential, and who does not have any solutions. So it is not a puzzle.

MS: How does this relate to the Lacanian signifier?

JL: Lacan had the great merit of showing that the categories of the real and the imaginary were insufficient. On the other hand, his third category of the symbolic is misleading. He overestimates the role of language. The unconscious is not structured as a language. The third category for me is the signifier, or message, which I do not locate in the same way as he does. Both of us stress the priority of the other, though his other always remained a thought of the subject. He also tended to mystify that priority by introducing the notion of the 'Big Other'. For me, the priority of the other is the priority of the message from the other on the sexual level. In short, the difference between us is that he was never interested in the implantation of the other's message in the primal scene; he was not interested in the theory of seduction.

*

MS: If we may move on now to the issue of moral values. You state quite forcibly that moral values can be transmitted and persist in individuals without ever entering consciousness. They remain, as it were, enigmatic: they are never decoded nor subjected to contextual analysis. As such, they persist as psychotic enclaves that can dangerously disrupt individuals and societies. Is this not somewhat over-pessimistic?

JL: No, it is not pessimistic. I am struck by the immutable character of moral imperatives, even in psychoanalysis, and indeed, even in Freud. Freud remained very rigid here. When he discusses moral issues, they remain very much self-enclosed, in enclaves. There is no fundamental interrogative work, for example, on either taboos or moral imperatives. In his discussion of narcissism, though, Freud does relate the moral imperatives of the super-ego to paranoid observational delusion. The phrases, as it were, of moral imperatives, like those of observational delusion, are introduced whole – they remain like unworked chunks, just as unworked sentences in dreams. Moral imperatives remain in the super-ego like that. Just like the sentence – 'Which is the way to the cathedral?' – which was said in the shop yesterday, can enter into a dream with no obvious connection. This conveys the idea of a message that is not metabolized.[4] Still, I do not consider this pessimistic.

MS: How does this relate to the practice of psychoanalysis, particularly your view of what happens in the psychoanalytic session?

JL: Given the primary meaning I give to seduction – that is, not in the factual sense of sexual abuse but rather, as the implantation of the message of the other – the psychoanalytic session could be said to reproduce the primal situation. It reproduces it in so far as the analyst is supposed to 'know' more than the analysand, just as the adult 'knows' more than the infant. People who come into analysis generally say: 'Doctor, what have I got? Tell me the truth about myself. You know more about myself than I do'. This 'you-know-more' aspect is captured in the Lacanian formula that the analyst is the 'subject who is supposed to know'. This is a beautiful formula... but I have tried to find more about it in Lacan's work, and, unfortunately, there is little more than the formula. So it remains an 'enigmatic signifier' for me! Still, I would like to mention two important aspects of the session in the light of my theory of seduction. First, there is the traumatic element – or, better, micro-traumatic situation – of the subject faced by the enigma posed by the other, who, in this case, says nothing. As in all trauma, 'energy' is created this way. This is quite abstract, and it is probably not the place to go into this here. My second aspect concerns the difference between what I call 'hollowed out' transference and 'embossed' transference (*transfert en creux et transfert en plein*). Whether explicitly or not, all formulations of transference continue to say that the subject on the couch continues to relive past events in relation to the analyst. The analyst is sufficiently neutral to allow these experiences to modify and elaborate in their own way. In this view, the analyst is in a 'hollowed out' position. If, though, the analysand projects into this hollowed out space the fullness of associations related to an imago or unconscious image of a former object, he or she will fill it. This is what I call an 'embossed' transference. I do not know how you translate that in English.

MS: It is actually translated as 'hollow' and 'full' transference (1989, pp.160–2), which I do not think conveys what you want to say.

JL: No, that is no good at all. In sculpture, for example, you draw a picture of St. Thomas à Beckett, and you model it either 'en plein', that is, it becomes embossed and stands out; or you can do it 'en creux', so the image is cut into a flat surface. The notion is in fact very simple. There is a hollowed out transference in the infant's relation to the enigma. The subject can bring this back into the psychoanalytic cure, and so does not elaborate through embossing material, but rather continues the infant's work of hollowing out, or metabolizing the enigmatic signifier. So the essential in all this is that we do not only or mainly re-live in analysis painful experiences of people who were cruel to us (and so forth), but rather an enigmatic relationship – what could that have meant at that time? This is reiterated in the question – 'Doctor, what do you want of me?' This is what I call 'hollowed out' transference.

MS: So the transference is articulated through these two modalities. There is no question of analysis removing the transference...

JL: The core of transference is not an illusion, so it cannot be dissolved. It is not a question of someone saying, 'you thought it was like that, well, in fact, you see it is like this...' The only way out of transference is the transference of the transference. Here I refer again to my image of the spiral: there is a moment when you are going round that you can spin out from one orbit into another.

MS: If I may bring in another interesting concept that you use in this context: translation. You use the term 'translation' both in the specific sense of translating from one language to another, and in the more general sense of what the child does with the enigmatic message or signifier, and what also goes on in the analytic session – only here you talk of de-translation and re-translation of messages. Is there in fact a link between this specific and general sense of translation?

JL: You are pressing me to go into a point that I have still to elaborate. The question raises two related issues: first, my own tasks as a translator of Freud's work into French, and secondly, Freud's own use of the term 'translation' to describe human existence as a series of translation attempts. In this latter sense, of course, it is not just words that are translated. So I do not want to jump into making a synthesis of the two senses here: rather, to put them both in their own perspective. They are both quite separate, and one has to say that there can be theoretical conflicts involved in trying to create a synthesis. In both cases, though, that is, the activity of the analyst and that of the word-translator, both must beware of interpretation (or 'constructions' in analysis). Both also indicate that de-translation is essential to translation.

To talk first of my activities as a translator of Freud: over a long period, I have come more and more to an objective stance which will leave the reader as much space as possible to intervene. This applies both to terminological and stylistic issues. For example, if you translate *Nachträglichkeit* by 'deferred action', you are certainly interpreting. Equally, if you re-model a phrase, you are also interpreting. There is also a will to non-interpretation on the stylistic level, that is, to keep, despite the different structures of languages, something which renders the rhetoric of the author as it presents itself – that is, the order of terms, the way in which ideas come one after the other. It may even be a deceptive rhetoric in which the author seeks more to seduce than to convince the reader. In the present discussions on Freud translation, notably on Strachey's English translation of Freud, Axel Hoffer has given a paper in which he says 'there is no translation without interpretation'.[5] When you say this, you arrive at the following conclusion: Strachey is an interpretation; a new translation will be another interpretation; so let's keep Strachey. This is sophistry. I am not a utopian, and I am not saying that we can translate without interpreting at one moment or another, but we are talking about limits. An ideal of translation is to avoid interpretation, that is to say, one leaves readers with their capacity to interpret.

MS: You have been heavily criticized in France for your use of neologisms in the new French translation of Freud. For example, your choice of *désaide* to translate *Hilflosigkeit* (Helplessness): critics say *désaide* is not a French word. Similarly, you are proposing the neologism 'afterwardsness' in English to translate *Nachträglichkeit* (as opposed to Strachey's 'deferred action'). What motivates this use of neologisms, and how would you reply to your critics?

JL: The translation of *Nachträglichkeit* by 'deferred action' imposes an interpretation and blocks the reader. We are looking rather to open up possibilities for the reader to interpret. 'Afterwardsness' does precisely this, and better conveys the original. Still, there are good and bad neologisms. Strachey's Greek or Latin neologisms in English are bad. These don't belong to the language, so appeal to no continuity and have no real resonance in the reader.

'Cathexis', for example: the verb 'to cathect' says nothing. The good neologism must be, so to speak, 'hollowed out' – that is, allow a hollowed out transference; it is implanted in a certain way in the language in which the text is translated. It is a word which derives from the normal rules of English or French and which is plausible and understandable with a little effort. This neologisation belongs to the life of all languages. All languages live through neologisms, also through usage, because neologisation also includes new uses of a word with a different meaning. I'll give you an example in French: *initier* (to initiate) means in French to introduce someone into a religious sect. Now one begins to use it – perhaps under the influence of the English – to mean to start a proceeding. Another example that I give in *Traduire Freud* (1989) is the word *sélection*: this is a neologism in French which was introduced by the French translator of Darwin. No one thinks of it as a neologism today. A final example: the word *civilisation*. This was introduced at the beginning of the 18th century to designate the transformation of case procedure from penal to civil courts. It was a legal term. One said: 'he has 'civilised' the case'. Then suddenly, Mirabeau's father introduced our present sense of the word. So, to repeat: neologisation is a living process of language. Until now, everyone has said that everyone has the right to use neologisms; Proust,

Gide and Lacan had the right to neologize, everyone in the street has the right to neologize, but has not the translator the right? The translator would have to search the dictionary for the most banal term. This is wrong. Languages are enriched by neologisms, and much of this enrichment has come from translators. The translator has fully the right to create.

MS: What role do neologisms play then in discriminating between good and bad translations of psychoanalytic terminology?

JL: Neologisms become necessary when the term is untranslatable. To return to the famous *nachträglich/Nachträglichkeit*: if you look in Strachey or Masson even, you find 'nachträglich' translated sometimes as 'later', sometimes as 'belatedly', sometimes by 'subsequently', and sometimes by 'in a deferred fashion'. This means that the unity of 'nachträglich' is lost. My position as translator is that the reader must be able to follow the continuity of a word by the same translated word; that is, to follow something that often, in Freud, has its origin in common language, but which becomes a concept. In Freud, *nachträglich* becomes a concept, and he uses the substantive *Nachträglichkeit*. So to translate this, we have to find a word that will be in keeping with common language but will convey the conceptual unity. In French, we have *l'après-coup*, which is not a neologism. But in English, you have no equivalent, so I suggest a neologism, 'afterwardsness'. This reveals these qualities of the original language. I think it is interesting that German readers of Freud never paid attention to *nachträglich* before the French started to insist on *après-coup*. Rudolphe Loewenstein[6] proposed this translation first, but not in a systematic way; Lacan displayed its unity, and in fact brought out the conceptual meaning of the term. One could say this was an 'afterwardsness' effect on the original German.

MS: Perhaps, as part of the 'afterwardsness' of this interview, I should ask you about the future direction of your work. I believe you are working on a book on the subject of time?

JL: Yes. Perhaps I should explain a little where this book comes into my work. My written work can be seen as a series of developments and contractions. This will not be evident to English-speaking readers, as some of these books have not yet been translated. There was *The Language of Psychoanalysis*, which was a broad exploration, then a contraction in *Life and Death in Psychoanalysis*. Then there were the five volumes of the *Problématiques*, which were conceptual explorations based on my lectures. The *New Foundations for Psychoanalysis* was a reflection on some of the themes raised in the *Problématiques*, and really cannot be understood without them. The decision to write a book on time therefore entailed not so much a contraction; it means, as it were, a return to philosophical reflection, a philosophical reflection on the psychoanalytic process. I have already discussed the three or four concepts that form the basis of this reflection: first of all, afterwardsness; then, translation, which, as I've said, is the only way to approach the temporal form of afterwardsness, because it is a movement forward in time through first going backwards; the third concept is seduction; the fourth is the priority of the other in the constitution of human time. Within this term, 'human time', I would also like to draw a distinction between its process, that is the movement of interrogation of the enigma that I describe in my theory of seduction, and, secondly, the motor of time, which is the other person, or the adult. The other person is at the very origin of the human subject's questioning. This is distinguished from the internal other, the other thing, finally, the unconscious, which is the residue of the movement of questioning. So there are two temporal motors, which, after all, involves me in something of a return to Aristotelianism. In Aristotle, God is the immobile motor of the movement of the spheres, and I think that the other is the immobile motor of the movement of temporalisation.

MS: Time to end...?

JL: Time certainly for lunch!

MS: Well, many thanks for your time for this interview!

Notes

1. Serge Leclaire is a prominent French psychoanalyst who is relatively unknown in the English-speaking world. He was a close associate and pupil of Jacques Lacan and led the

negotiations between the Lacanians and the IPA during the 1963–65 crisis. He is author of numerous books, including *On tue un enfant* (1973), *Démasquer le réel* (1971), and *Psychanalyser: un essai sur l'ordre de l'inconscient et la pratique de la lettre* (1968). Since Lacan's dissolution of the École Freudienne de Paris in 1980, he has distanced himself from affiliations with major training bodies, but assumed an important if individualistic role in the debate on establishing a French 'register' of psychoanalysts.

2. Daniel Lagache was a crucial figure in the development of psychoanalysis in France. He obtained doctorates in philosophy and medicine (like Laplanche), and pioneered the teaching of psychoanalysis in France within the psychology department of the University of Strasbourg. He was a friend and ally of Jacques Lacan, until the crisis of 1963–65.
3. Jean-Bertrand Lefèbre-Pontalis met Jean Laplanche during the preparatory class for the ENS. Pontalis later became a philosophy teacher in Cairo, but they met up again in Paris through Lagache, and collaborated on *The Language of Psychoanalysis*. Since then, they have followed their own ways. Pontalis is presently an editor at the Gallimard publishing house.
4. Metabolization in Laplanchian terminology combines both forms of transformation of the signifier, that is, metaphor and metonymy (cf. Laplanche, 1989, p.131–3).
5. Axel Hoffer, 'Can there be translation without interpretation?', Proceedings of the Congress of the International Psycho-Analytical Association, Montréal, July 1987; cf. Axel Hoffer, *International Review of Psycho-Analysis*, pt.1, vol.18, 1991.
6. Rudolphe Loewenstein was a Berlin-trained psychoanalyst who settled in Paris in the early 1930s, and trained many of the first generation of French psychoanalysts, including Jacques Lacan. Loewenstein fled to the United States to escape the Nazis, and in the 1940s and 1950s became a prominent figure with Heinz Hartmann and Ernst Kris in the development of 'ego psychology'.

Events

The Kent Seminar

1 May 1990

QUESTION: What do you mean by the enigmatic signifier?

JEAN LAPLANCHE: The division of the individual between conscious and unconscious doesn't exist at birth, it comes about through repression. This is the first point in my thought that would not be accepted by all psychoanalysts, many of whom would think that there is something biological and primary that is unconscious, which I don't believe because it would have to come from phylogenesis, which I reject as a doctrine. So there is a major difference between the adult and the infant which is that the adult has an unconscious, or his unconsciousness is split between the preconscious and the unconscious which is repressed. What he has repressed is mostly sexual. Now one of the main discoveries of Freud is that this sexual unconscious pervades all our actions, not only our dreams. If you take the *Introductory Lectures* (1915–17), you see that Freud does not begin with dreams, where the unconscious comes out more obviously than other places. He begins with parapraxes – bungled actions such as slips of the tongue or pen, forgettings and so on, the everyday life manifestations of the unconscious. That is very important because any of our acts leaves in its splits and fissures a place for something unconscious.

So what do I mean by enigmatic signifiers? The adult addresses himself to the infant, addresses to him gestures and not only speeches (at first only a few words not language as such). I am not Lacanian when I speak of the signifier – I do not speak mainly of the verbal signifier. I mean every gesture of the adult is a signifier for the child. This signifier, like any of our gestures, has two meanings. It has an adaptive meaning and it has an implicit meaning which is impregnated by something sexual. I take the example of giving the breast. This is only an example after all, because we might think of future societies when the child won't know anything of the breast any more. For the Kleinians the breast is an object qualified, through projection of the infant's drives, as good or bad. In general no analyst takes into account the fact that the breast for a woman is an erogenous zone; that is, in giving the breast, you cannot split completely the question of giving milk and nourishment from the fact that, for the woman, it has a sexual meaning which is latent. She experiences an excitation in the breast which is given to the child and is also given to her sexual partner, and so on. So what I mean by signifier is that a thing like the breast is not only an object, it is a message presented to the child. But, in the enigmatic signifier, there is not only an explicit message, but also an implicit message, and the child cannot but understand that there is something hidden in it. He doesn't understand it exactly, has no idea of what the fantasies of the mother are (about sexual pleasure in the breast and so on), but it is impossible in this relationship that something is not perceived of that 'normal parapraxis'; what is perceived is that this gesture has something of another meaning, another meaning which is even unknown to the mother herself. That is the most obvious example of the enigmatic signifier. Any gesture is usually materialised by a thing but a thing having a meaning. It is not just an object, it is a part of the body which has much meaning. So it is impossible to think of it without taking into account its divided situation; it has more meaning for the adult than for the child, the more being precisely the sexual part of it. We could say that behind an enigmatic signifier the child perceives that there is a hidden message. Some people say that any signifier is in itself enigmatic. That may be true if you want "enigmatic" to be an equivalent of "polysemic": you can give several meanings to the discourse of the other person, it is always intrinsically polysemic; you have to translate, to interpret it and it is open to new interpretations. But the the enigmatic signifier is doubly enigmatic, not only in the usual meaning of puzzling or interrogative, rich in meaning, but also enigmatic in the precise sense that the meaning remains hidden, not only for the one who receives the message but also for the one who sends it. Take, for instance, the enigma of the Sphinx: you cannot think that she already knew the answer to her enigma, because the enigma was such a problem for her that when it was solved by Oedipus she killed herself as it was something unbearable to her, revealing to her something of her unconscious.

Another example of the enigmatic signifier would be what we call the primal scene. We don't think that every child has actually witnessed a sexual scene between its parents, but one way or the other he has perceived something of it. The impact of the primal scene is also an enigma: what does this pleasure mean which I perceive? Another very important point is that you cannot think of someone giving to the child some kind of spectacle of making love with their partner, even if it is in the other room, without the intention to have it perceived: it is given as a message some way or another. Abstention is also something active, the abstention from making love so that the child cannot perceive it, which is after all impossible, but this abstention is also something positive. The parents can't be completely unaware that they are saying something to the child, because they cannot hide their relationship – they show it more or less. It is consistent with what Freud said about sexuality: the parents are not completely aware of what sexual pleasure means for them, of the sexual fantasy behind their own intercourse.

ANNETTE KILCOOLEY: Is the enigmatic signifier conflict-free?

LAPLANCHE: No, absolutely not. I think it is conflict-full, conflictual, because it is enigmatic, unknown, hidden, it involves the repressed. It is like the example of parapraxes, slips of the tongues and so on, in which it is the conflicts behind them which make them slips of the tongue. We always make "slips of the tongue" in the broadest sense of these words; our conscious messages are infiltrated by unconscious ones which remain unconscious because there is conflict.

I want to return to the question of the impact of the enigmatic signifier on infantile sexuality. I really think that even if there are some biological aspects that could relate to the hormonal metabolism in the infant, nevertheless human sexuality (sexuality with fantasy) is not internally generated, it is implanted in the infant. To be sure, the abstraction of "the infant" is not possible in any observation, since from the very beginning you have a child in the adult environment; but abstraction is always possible from a scientific point of view, that is when you try to separate independent factors, and from this point of view an infant by itself exists on the level of self-preservation, not on a sexual level. Sexuality comes into him from the adult implantation and something occurs for the succession of phases as Freud described them – oral, anal, genital – to happen. It seems crazy to me that they should be explained from a biological point of view, that internal sexual excitation should first go to the lips, and then to the anus after a few months and then to the genitals after another two years, and so on. This migration is inconceivable; the only way to conceive it is that in the self-preservative process there are successive zones or places of the body that take more attention from the parent, and after all it is more the parents or the culturally determined attention to the preservation of the child that takes care of nourishment and excretion. It is through the interrelation of the parents or the carers to the child that sexuality gathers, passes as if through a conductor; it is conducted through the care given to the child. That is why those exchange zones – exchange of products, of food mostly – become erogenous zones. It is almost a concrete image to say that the enigmatic signifier is implanted in this or that part of the body; as almost the whole of the body is able to receive messages, it is those parts related to the preservation of life which become the places for the main sexual excitation and fantasy.

BRAD SIDEY: Would that coincide with what you call the birth of the unconscious, where the unconscious is made up of the untranslatable aspects of the primal seduction? You call the unconscious sexual through and through. Does the birth of sexuality in the infant equate with the birth of the unconscious?

LAPLANCHE: The unconscious grows from different types of messages. But metapsychologically, I don't say that the unconscious is made up of enigmatic signifiers, as such, which would mean that the unconscious of the child is the unconscious of the mother. Instead, there is an active part played by the infant which is repression; that is, the infant doesn't take the whole of the message, but tries to understand it and the parts he understands do not become unconscious. The parts that are not understood become unconscious. The unconscious grows and grows, not in an organised manner, but side by side with those different types of relationships with the carers which are interrelations of self-preservation, but which from the point of view of sexuality are only one-way relations (from the adult to the infant). In my description of repression I fully agree with the idea of the transformation of passivity into activity. At first, at the sexual level there is passivity, but the child tries to integrate it actively and it is the part which is not integrated that becomes unconscious. Towards this part the individual remains passive, that is, the passivity towards the adult in the beginning becomes our passivity towards our unconscious. We are deeply passive in our relationships to the remainders of the adult messages, to what I call "objet source", i.e. the source-objects of the drives, those relics of the adult messages. There still is a passivity to what yesterday I called the other. Freud uses the terms *der Andere* and *das Andere*: the other is either the other person or the other thing (*l'autre personne* or *l'autre chose*). There are two others: the other person from whom come the messages and then the other thing which is the remainders of the messages of the other person.

QUESTION: So there is no inherent sexuality in the child?

LAPLANCHE: I don't think so. I would not argue against the ascertainment of reactions in the sexual organs, but after all we know that what Freud called infantile sexuality was not mainly genital sexuality. I would not make a big thing of erections in the male organ at two years, two days or two months. That is not for me the real problem, which is sexual fantasy. As Freud pointed out, those fantasies are not at first genital but oral and anal. The new-born infant doesn't have what is characteristic of human sexuality, that is, sexual fantasies. Sexuality in human beings is bound to fantasy. As soon as there are no representations, there is no human sexuality as such – any kind of representation, even the most primitive. Even penetration is first a fantasy.

QUESTION: If the adult has a preoccupation surrounding oral or anal sex, is that a regression to attain the sexual messages that are coming from the mother?

LAPLANCHE: Not only from the mother; any adult. We take the mother as a prototype: what I am trying to explain is that although the mother is the main source of messages in our civilisation, the problem is not bound to the female sex. When you have a regression it is certainly a regression to a certain type of infantile sexuality, and infantile sexuality going back to a sexual type of messages: an overemphasis on such and such a zone and on such and such process – excretion being valorised or not, or retention being valorised. But when excretion is valorised, it is first valorised by the adult.

MICHAEL GRANT: Can one speak of temporalisation in respect of the unconscious?

LAPLANCHE: No, I don't think so. I stand by Freud's general formulation about this. I only try to explain what it means. Freud said there is no negation in the unconscious, there is no time, there is no doubt nor certitude. It means there are no bounds, no thought; and time means binding. Time or temporalisation means binding events together to make a line, to make a discourse in its widest sense. We think of the unconscious as remainders of messages, remainders of bindings but without binding. In that respect I am completely against Lacan's formulation that the unconscious is structured like a language, which means that in some way it is temporal too. I think it is completely atemporal.

MG. How does this affect the nature of the dream? Presumably there must be a mechanism whereby the atemporality of the unconscious material is equipped with or becomes possessed of a syntax in order to constitute the manifest dream. How are we to envision the transition from the atemporality of the unconscious to the temporal structures of the manifest dream?

LAPLANCHE: Time in dream is a very special time and we don't know so much about it. We don't know when we have dreamed, what came before and after the dream and so on. You have a feeling of temporality in dream, but I should say dream is an attempt to translate something, to move into time, what is atemporal. When we talk about the unconscious we must know that there are different levels, and that there are many things that are unconscious and yet are not *the* unconscious. That is what Freud tried to express, saying that the primal unconscious attracts fantasies that become unconscious. Those fantasies could have some kind of temporal development, so what Freud says about the atemporal unconscious would be true only for the core but not for the more and more superficial levels of it. Usually with dreams we cannot say that any dream goes back to the deepest unconscious; you have many dreams that remain on a somewhat superficial or at least first level of desires. That is a question of levels. The ultimate matter is itself atemporal and even the dream is an attempt to bind it; the dream is not the unconscious, if you think of the unconscious as unbound, that is no bindings between representations. All you know of a dream, not only its secondary elaboration which allows the dream to be put into a narration, but the dream in itself, when we dream it, is trying to introduce interrelationships and to temporalise something that is not temporal.

MG: There is a dream that Freud discusses in which the child says, "Father! can't you see that I am burning". In Lacanian writing this takes on importance as a locus for the intrusion into language of the child. Thus the reality of the dream appears to introduce into the dream structure the reality in some sense of the death drive. As though this particular dream were a manifestation of the underlying structure. Therefore that particular dream seems to give a kind of enactment of the transition from the atemporal unconscious into the actual representation itself. That is to say, the subject dreams the process of its own subjectivisation: the dream is a manifestation of what constitutes that dreaming subject. Would you accept that kind of view?

LAPLANCHE: Yes, maybe... I should go back to that dream, but I am not attracted to it and I will tell you why. There are some dreams in Freud that give rise in the commentators to a mystical view. "Father! can't you see that I am burning?" – it is so dramatic that it lends itself to this. I am also very cautious about Freud's dreams because as you know Freud doesn't give one third of the associations he had. Usually he gives those dreams only to exemplify one part of his theory and he just cuts the associations at the point where they become too deep, at the point that they become sexual, or at the point he thinks it has no longer anything to do with what he has proven at this particular moment. At the beginning of the wish-fulfilment section [of *The Interpretation of Dreams*], he begins with this dream and asks, "Well, how is this is a wish-fulfilment?". People have made many romances about such things but I am not too romantic about that kind of metaphysics. This is really beautiful to put in a film or picture or theatre, but, as long as we actually don't have the whole of the associations, I think it is too much commented on.

MG: Of course, what is peculiar about that dream is that Freud had it, as I remember, from one of his patients, who had herself heard it from a friend, who had in turn heard it.

LAPLANCHE: As for the death drive you talked about, I have a very particular conception of it. Just because death is present in the manifest content of the dream as in many others, it doesn't mean that the death drive is manifesting itself at that place. For me the death drive is mainly the destructuration tendencies in the psychic apparatus; especially repression is an example of the death drive, that is putting a representation apart from its affect and de-binding it. I don't see a striking example of de-binding or un-binding in that dream. Perhaps I am a little unfair as there are some pieces of Freud that are attracting so much pathos.

JOHN FLETCHER: I would like to go back to the enigmatic signifiers, and how you understand the process of primary repression. Freud gives an account of it as an anti-cathexis or expulsion of psychical representatives from consciousness which fixes them. How would you relate this to the metabolas, the algebraic diagrams, where the S1, S2 signifying chain substitutes for the original signifier which is pushed below the bar of repression and assumes the status of an unconscious signified.[1] The signifiers that substitute and stand in for the primal repressed, are they the child's attempts to answer the enigmatic question? To feed in more signifiers? Are they fantasies?

LAPLANCHE: They are the child trying to understand, to bind, that is to give some account of what is coming to him, that is substituting another message, another meaning, another text, for that original signifier. But it is not a pure substitution, because if it were a pure substitution then the message would be completely understood and translated, and it never is. So the part which is not translated comes down under the bar.

JF: So it's the child's elaboration and fantasy that seals the primal unconscious, because it excludes the original signifiers?

LAPLANCHE: Yes, yes. You talk of anti-cathexis. Once, in the old text on the unconscious with Leclaire,[2] I used the metaphor of the design in which something is hidden. Napoleon's hat, exactly. I think this is still a good model for anti-cathexis. There is a drawing of a tree, and in the tree you have hidden a small Napoleon's hat. The anti-cathexis is the completeness of the story that is told that prevents one perceiving a small part of the design – the hat. It could be a model of anti-cathexis, that is, any mental organisation has an effect of repressing, anti-cathecting what doesn't fit into it. It would be another way of putting it, nearer to Gestalt theory.

JF: You don't think that puts the realism of the unconscious at risk by making it a phenomenological question of perception? If you look at it this way it looks like a tree, if you look at it that way it looks like Napoleon's hat. Doesn't it deny the two different sets of representations or signifiers – Freud's problematic of the double inscription with representations at different levels, in the unconscious and the preconscious?

LAPLANCHE: I don't think so, because each signifier is equally present: Napoleon's hat is really present, it is not just a point of view. Well, there are two different points of view, but both are real.

JF: So it is the attempt to elaborate that excludes? And there is no direct transmission of the parental unconscious, or the excluded signifiers to the infant?

LAPLANCHE: Yes, exactly, it is the attempt to elaborate that excludes. That is an important question, because this idea of the transmission of the unconscious comes to something imaginative, the kind of interpersonal unconscious that would operate from one to the other. I think that after the repression has taken place or in the same movement, the person becomes closed to the other, not completely, but there is a movement of *fermeture* – closure – one which has something to do with Hegel. The inter-personal unconscious is one of the Lacanian conclusions; I wouldn't say it is Lacan exactly, because Lacan said different things. Maud Mannoni used to go very far on this; in some of her books you had to analyse the parents. But then why not the grandparents and so on? Who is the one to be analysed?

JF: This becomes crucial with the notion of the phallus, and what that signifies for the mother, and how the infant acquires the fantasy or signifier of the phallus. Lacan and Mannoni seem to suggest it is from the mother, as if there is a direct transmission.

LAPLANCHE: I think so, and I disagree completely.

JF: So you wouldn't see the phallus in the Lacanian sense, as an enigmatic signifier?

LAPLANCHE: Maybe sometimes, but I won't give it absolute priority. I think the phallus is bound to the question of castration, and what I try to say is that, even if the castration complex is very important in our society, it is a secondary way of binding. For me it is not as primary as for Lacan, and even for Freud, because I think they are both on the same track. I would say that as fundamental as they may be, the Oedipus and castration complexes are ways of secondary elaboration of the primary messages which are much more unbound than that; they are ways of binding. I said once that Oedipus was the first criminal through the feeling of culpability – that is, the feeling of culpability is more primary than the elaboration in the complex. And as Freud sometimes attributed to Klein: "You are not guilty because you killed your father; you killed your father because you were primarily guilty", that is, confronted with something even more awful than killing your father. The Oedipus is a way among others; it is the main way, in our civilisation, to bind.

JF: It sounds like Sartre's account of Genet, who is made a criminal before he commits a crime.

LAPLANCHE: I think Freud would not agree that the Oedipus complex is a way of responding to culpability.

JF: The other question I wanted to ask is about sublimation. In yesterday's lecture,[3] you cited points of view that are different from your own, Jung and Ricoeur, and the idea of assuming a future, a movement towards the future which abolishes the past, which subsumes the *arche* into the *telos*. Ricoeur does it through invoking the notion of sublimation, and sublimation is such a problem in Freud because it is underdeveloped as a concept. My question is about time and the orientation towards the future, and what you would say of sublimation in relation to temporality and the movement towards the future. Sublimation seems to suggest some movement beyond the *arche*.

LAPLANCHE: I have discussed sublimation in one book,[4] and it is one of my most incomplete developments. The way I tried to trace sublimation was to say that sublimation should be understood in relation to what I called the neo-genesis of sexuality. For me, sublimation cannot be attributed to any human activity; they are mostly cultural activities, especially many artistic or intellectual activities. Sublimation is not just a transformation of a ready-made drive, for there must be some new incitement for the drive in the work itself that comes to sublimation. That is a kind of new source put into movement at the time of the sublimation. It comes back to the Freudian idea of the conservation of sexual energy, which I am against, a certain economic quantity that remains the same; it must be in sexual activity at the beginning, then you find it the same in the activity of painting – which is false. Freud himself in his book on Leonardo said, "How can you say that a man who paints has less sexual activity?"; it is a very crude idea and it is not true of artists or of many creators. Some have more of this and less of that, but mostly it doesn't work this way. So you have to think of sublimation in a less transformational and so-called mathematical way than Freud thought of it, which is of inhibited and desexualised drives and so on. We must try to think of sublimation as new sexuality; it is something new, maybe coming from the message, from the work itself. It is a kind of new excitation, new trauma coming from the sublimated activity itself, and through this new trauma comes new energy. I try to connect the idea of sublimation with the idea of research or trauma, and I coined the idea of traumatophilia.

JF: So sublimated cultural activities, whether it is theoretical research or artistic production, are in some relation to a trauma or an enigmatic signifier being reworked?

LAPLANCHE: Being reworked and reproduced. And maybe you reproduce something of the trauma in your own incentive to research or to paint. I add in one of my articles I have just begun that when you put the words "dream" and "trauma" on the page, it becomes traumatic to you. Before you have read the first lines, you auto-traumatise with those terms and say "ah!", and then you try to bind it. And I think in any creative adventure, there is something like that. You push forward things that traumatise you.

JF: In Hoffman's short story, 'The Sandman', which Freud talks about in his essay on 'The Uncanny' (1919), there is a latent theory of literature, of writing as trauma. Hoffman talks repeatedly about the narrator and the protagonist, Nathaniel himself, who produces lots of poems and stories, as having some power to penetrate with fiery beams into the heart and to produce a trauma in the recipient. Hoffman has an account of the transmission of an almost fantasmatic energy which is traumatising. The one who produces the story, whether it is the narrator or Nathaniel himself telling the story again and again, is, as it were, releasing a trauma which then has a life of its own in the recipient. But if it is a trauma, it must also be a seduction.

LAPLANCHE: We have to find a way between seduction and trauma at that point. After all, even when we think we are creating, we are always being worked by foreign messages. It makes me think of the messages you don't want to receive because you hate to agree. I say I don't read Ferenczi because I don't want to find my ideas in him, and Freud said he didn't want to read Nietzsche because he wanted to auto-traumatise, rather than be traumatised by Nietzsche.

JF: The Russian linguist and literary critic, Mikhail Bakhtin, has an account of the word where the writer has to take words that are already saturated in messages: he can't take a clean word or an empty one. It is always already saturated in advance, and he has to negotiate or struggle with those pre-given messages within the language or the material he uses in order to wrest his own meanings out of them, and is therefore going to be in some sense possessed by them, by the very fact of language being pre-existent. Bakhtin elaborates a theory about the alien word, which seems very similar to what you are saying about the signifiers, the extent to which they are blocked out or the extent to which they are accepted or integrated.

MG: You mentioned the uncanny, and Hoffman. Now Todorov, in his treatment of the fantastic, describes a hesitation between the marvellous and the natural explanation of the story's motivation, the setting-up of a double articulation around hesitation. This seems to me to be similar to what you have been saying about temporalisation: as you move into the past you move into the future , and as soon as you are in the future you are in the past, in a kind of double deferral. In novellas such as 'The Sandman' and 'The Turn of the Screw', Todorov argues that this development (the suspension of hesitation) is something which is very close to Freud's account of the uncanny. What is essential for the effect of the fantastic is for the text to hesitate between two moments of explanation, two foundations of motivation, one supernatural or religious and the other scientific or psychological, and the resolution of this never comes in the text. It has been argued that what one sees here is an early attempt to define in literature the play of *differance* as a temporal structure of deferral. Would this be a legitimate extension of your thoughts on time and the double articulation of time, applying it to literature or film?

LAPLANCHE: I think that a legitimate extension would be to find out behind the narratives, or behind the two motivations or two explanations, something in common which would be less elaborate than either explanation – that is, some more elementary signifiers. Behind the two explanations in conflict that play to each other like two aspects of the same thing, one should analyse the something behind that moves it. Maybe we can't touch it, but in analysis we try to touch it; it is a way of temporalising, starting from those unarticulated elements. But this usually cannot be done, and maybe should not be done in literary analysis, because we don't have the whole material, we don't have the method for it. I stand very much by the point of view that analytic method is bound to free associations, and for free associations you must have the subject to associate.

MG: Do you think that the application of psychoanalytic concepts of this kind, to literature and to film, is legitimate in general?

LAPLANCHE: I try to think of this not as applied. I hate this word 'applied'; applied means you find all the information somewhere and you just apply it like you apply something to skin, or you say 'applied physics' that is just building a bridge. Applied is merely derivative, but what I call 'extra-mural psychoanalysis', psychoanalysis 'outside the walls' or outside the cure, should have the ambition to have findings of its own: that is, to find other methods, for as I have said, the main method you don't have, because you don't have a person to give you free associations. But you have many other ways: for instance, trying to define the effect of the work. The creation is much more difficult because you don't have the creator on the couch. Sometimes the creator is on the couch and says something, but in the way of the effect, not in the way of the production. Freud's book on *Witz* [*Jokes and their relation to the Unconscious* (1905)] is an essay on the *effect* of the joke not on the *production* of the joke; his analysis focuses on the way the joke acts on the listener. The way is wide open for studies of the effect, rather than the production, of the work. I have had a student writing a thesis on the insult-effect; not the way you produce an insult – it would be very easy for a Kleinian to discourse about that, bad objects etc. – but on the effect of the insult, the different types of insult, on the mechanism of the effect: what is the goal, what are the means? This is not just applied, because after all you have to invent.

MARTIN STANTON: I want to ask about your notion of the psychotic enclave. What I find frightening, and even ominous in *New Foundations*, is your argument that moral values might actually be transmitted as psychotic enclaves, so that they may remain unmetabolised, unsubstituted for, without ever being translated. You say this is one of the things we may have to face up to in the future.

LAPLANCHE: Yes, and it is trauma for me too – as yet unelaborated!

MS: What then are the limits of psychoanalytic treatment?

LAPLANCHE: What is unable to be metabolised. Let me give an association about that from *Totem and Taboo* (1910). It is interesting to see the position of Freud on the totem, about which he says many things, especially things that have nothing to do with what he says about the mother or the father, which, after all, is only one chapter. At the beginning he says that the taboo is different from morals, in the sense that the moral is systematic and the taboo is not. Then a few pages later, he says that the taboo is at the origin of the categorical imperative, which then means that what he said first of morality – that it is a system – he cancels a few pages later by saying that the taboo is absolute, and the categorical imperative is absolute. There is no symbolisation possible, there is no way of explaining or fantasising or theorising about it; it just must be so. The taboo looks a little like a collective psychotic enclave, something that prevents the work of mourning. He says the taboo is a closed space where you cannot enter; it is a closed-off area in social space, because you are limited from such and such places, and it also has a time because after a taboo is finished, it is finished, and you go back to your activities. It is an enclave that is outside of elaboration. The relationship between that and the moral is made by Freud, in a certain sense; in a double sense of opposition and non-opposition.

JF: It is a suggestive, but rather disturbing, remark you make in *New Foundations* about the superego and the psychotic enclave; how does that relate to the Lacanian theory of foreclosure, of the repudiation of the paternal signifier? In a footnote, I think it was to your 1964 paper on primal fantasies with Pontalis,[5] you said that it was unclear whether Lacan's theory of psychosis is really a theory of the super-ego, or the other way around. There is some ambiguity about how they are related.

LAPLANCHE: I don't remember that note but, for me, foreclosure is to be ranged amongst all the ipsocentrist mechanisms. Ipsocentrist means that you can make the subject into the subject of the mechanism, that is, "I introject", "I project", "I deny", "I repress", "I foreclose"; all those processes are ipsocentrist, centred on the person. Even foreclosure, which is meant to set something completely aside, but it is set aside by someone who sets it aside. What I am trying to introduce are mechanisms where it is the other who is the subject of the mechanisms. When I say implantation, you cannot say "I", or "Sigmund" is the subject who introjects or who does project, or does foreclose; when I say implantation, I say the *other* of Sigmund does implant in Sigmund. When I talk of the categorical imperative, it is the other that implants the categorical imperative.

JF: How like – or unlike – is that to the Kleinian concept of projective identification, where the subject splits off and puts part of himself in the other?

LAPLANCHE: But he does it himself, he projects part of himself outside. It is a question of the chicken. There is an old psychiatric joke about the man who is a paranoiac and enters the hospital because he is afraid that he is going to be eaten by chickens. He is a grain, and he is going to be pecked up by chickens. He has psychotherapy for a few months, sees a doctor and says, "I know I am not a grain". A few days later, again he criticises the doctor and says, "Well I am not a grain, I am sure of that. Let me leave". The doctor releases him, and just as he goes through the yard of the hospital, the doctor looks out. It is a country hospital, there are some poultry in the yard and the man begins to run. The doctor says to him, "But you know you are not a grain!", and the man replies, "Sure I know – but does the chicken?" What I am trying to say is that, at the bottom of projection, there is something that is not projection – that is, a question: what does he want from me? Sure you can analyse this projection and cure it, but you must bear in mind that under this everyday projection there is something true, that is, a question not about what I am introducing in the other, but that something comes from the other. That is the point I am trying to introduce, which is, I think, new.

DUNCAN BARFORD. If we could return to the enigmatic signifier for a bit. As I understand it, in the analytic setting, the analyst represents to the analysand an enigmatic signifier which is a to-be-translated, which sets going the process of self-translation or de-translation. Does it matter what is said in that case? There seems to me to be two things that are capable of translating in this process: one is the transference and one is the interpretation. So how do the two relate?

LAPLANCHE: I wouldn't agree that the analyst is a signifier. I would say he is, as Lacan says he is, *le sujet supposé savoir*; 'the subject supposed to know' is supposed to have more knowledge than the analysand has to send enigmatic messages. That's what I think Lacan meant, at least, that is what I mean in using Lacan's formulation. The analyst, does it matter what he says? You must understand that through the process of detranslation and retranslation. I think he must refrain, as regards the analysand and himself, from knowing more than the other; he is supposed to know but he has to refrain from knowing. So what he says must not be in the way of retranslation: the retranslation is the work of the analysand. But this doesn't mean he has nothing to do, nor nothing to say. Outside of the transference is still another problem. He has to help detranslate but not retranslate. Let me take an example when Freud talks about interpretation and construction; it's a famous text, 'Constructions in Analysis' (1937). In this text, Freud comes to a very new idea, which is that interpretation is just making relationships between terms and what we first called interpretation we have to call construction. He gives an example that this image in this dream is your mother; he puts it in relation to signifiers, but he doesn't construct any story, any fantasy; he just points out that he helps the analysand to enter his associational paths, and even the crossing of those paths at certain points. He helps deconstruction work. And also, he says, there is a construction. The example he gives is construction in childhood: at the age of four you were the favourite of your mother, then came a small brother and you had the impression of being abandoned. That is a construction and not an interpretation; but actually I say it is a re-construction of an old construction. He points out the construction the child himself had made, that is, the theorisation the child had given to himself of what was signified to him by the mother, when giving birth. Giving birth to a child is a type of enigmatic signifier: what does she mean to me when giving birth to a small brother? He made out of that a history, an interpretation that she prefers him and hates me, which is a construction. Now, what Freud says is a construction is in fact the reconstruction of an old construction, which again the child has to deconstruct again and again. So my answer is that, yes, it is important what the analyst says, but what he says (as little as possible) should not go in the direction of reconstructing the patient; the patient reconstructs with the elements the analyst helps him to find in the past. So the way of analysis is to analyse, to destruct, in the way of the death drive. He works in the way of the death drive in that sense, but also there is the problem of holding, containing also. So, yes, it matters, to answer your question, but I am not in favour of the overly synthetic intervention of the analyst, except to help re-construct old constructions and help again to deconstruct them. When we construct the fantasy that happened at five, it is to go back to the elements, because that was a fantasy then, and then to go back further and further.

QUESTION: Is the enigmatic signifier in any way resolvable?

LAPLANCHE: No, it is not. The unconscious is as much unresolvable as the enigmatic signifier is. That was an illusion of Freud's at the beginning, at the time of the seduction theory, that the unconscious was resolvable.

JF: I understand that is your position, and a necessary position, but some of the formulations you use at times, when you talk about the economic factor in the drive: that it fluctuates, is only relatively constant; or that the symbolisation in the analytic process can reduce the compulsions, reduce the drive energy, and the drives can be re-energised or re-stimulated by a repetition of the experience of seduction; doesn't this make the drive energy pathological? Doesn't it move the concept of the drive energy in the direction of the pathological, which is something that may not absolutely be reduced by analysis, but there is a tendency towards its reduction or its elimination by the analytic process? Doesn't that make the drive energy itself seem pathological, a symptom? Is the drive a symptom?

LAPLANCHE: Yes, a symptom of the human being. We can be existentialist on that point. I could take Sartre's formulation (who is not one of my best friends!): man is a useless passion. On that point the difference between pathological and the normal is to be kept. That was the main mistake of Freud in his seduction theory, he thought he could reduce pathology, reduce the situation of seduction.

JF: So you are saying pathology is constitutional?

LAPLANCHE: It is constitutional of the situation, not biologically. Structural if you want, in a sense... That is what Freud says in the *Three Essays on Sexuality*, that human sexuality is pathological.

Notes

1. Laplanche discusses the mapping of psychic processes as semiotic operations at some length in Jean Laplanche and Serge Leclaire, 'The Unconscious: A psychoanalytic study' (1960), trans. Patrick Coleman in *Yale French Studies* no. 48, 1972. A briefer, more recent discussion appears in Jean Laplanche, *New Foundations for Psychoanalysis* (1987), trans. David Macey, Basil Blackwell 1989. It is also discussed in Stephen Melville's contribution to the ICA Round table discussion in this volume (p.76 et seq., below).
2. See Laplanche and Leclaire (1960), ibid.
3. See Jean Laplanche, 'Psychoanalysis, Time and Translation' in the present volume, (pp.161–177).
4. Jean Laplanche, *Problématiques III: La Sublimation*, Presses Universitaires de France, 1980.
5. Jean Laplanche and Jean-Bertrand Pontalis, 'Fantasy and the Origins of Sexuality', in *Formations of Fantasy*, eds. Victor Burgin, James Donald and Cora Kaplan, Methuen 1986.

The Freud Museum Seminar

3 May 1990

MARTIN STANTON: As I am sure you know, there has been a debate about the new translation of Freud that Jean Laplanche is at present chairing, especially the use of neologism to translate some of Freud's terms that have formerly been translated otherwise. We got into a debate earlier about the nature of neologisms, and were discussing whether the term 'afterwardsness' would serve to translate *Nachträglichkeit*, as opposed to less satisfactory translations, such as retrospective attribution (recently proposed by Helmut Tomä).

PROFESSOR LAPLANCHE: I could introduce that point instead of making a general speech about my conception of translation and of translating Freud and works of thought as a whole. The word *Nachträglichkeit* in Freud's German is very important. First of all, it is a word from the common language, that is, *nachträglich* is an adverb and an adjective that is very much used; so you may use it as in "afterwards I thought that" or, "this house was not built as it should have been and afterwards it fell down". So 'afterwards' is the after-effect but it is also something going back to before. I am going to argue that this word like all words in Freud is taken from the common language – as many people have stressed – but the other thing people don't see is that it is first taken from the common language, and then becomes elaborated as a concept, that is deliberately and not spontaneously. Freud constructs concepts out of these common words. The second aspect is *Nachträglichkeit*: when *nachträglich* becomes a substantive it becomes more abstract. *Nachträglichkeit* means many things in German; it means the fact that something comes afterwards; it means also something like revenge or bearing a grudge, when you take revenge because of something that took place before. This is, therefore, a very good example of a word from the common language, from the *Sprachgebrauch* as they say in German, that becomes a theoretical term. I made a very precise history of this term from the first letters to Fliess up to the case of the Wolf Man.[1]

When language doesn't have a single term to translate something, it is diffracted into several possibilities. What happened in the English translations of Strachey and Masson was that, according to context, sometimes it was translated by 'later', sometimes by 'belatedly', sometimes by 'deferred action' or 'subsequently'. Strachey, not having the right term, must use several English terms; it is diffracted in different contexts and it gives the illusion that there are several meanings. Actually there are not several meanings. It is only the effect of diffraction in another language that gives the appearance of several meanings. A German wouldn't say these words were homonyms. There are not several *nachträglichs*, but only one in German, whereas in the English translation it looks as if there were several. In French we have one word, that is *après coup*, as suggested by Loewenstein in his translation of the Wolf Man case study; afterwards Lacan stressed it. Loewenstein did not use it consistently, however, he suggested it in French, and Lacan was the first to say it was an important term in Freud. So that is what I call on one side diffraction, when one language doesn't have a single term, and on the other side refraction. Why refraction? Because *après coup* is not exactly *nachträglich*: in German you have the idea of 'tragen' to bear or carry, also to bring to fruition, 'nach-tragen' to carry after or behind, and in French you have the idea of 'coup' that would be stroke or blow, hence *après coup* – after stroke. So it is not false to translate *Nachträglichkeit*, afterwards or afterwardsness, by *après coup*. This is a very good example of the evolution of one term in Freud from the common usage into the conceptual use. As an example of the common use, Freud says: "Phantasien sind Gehörtes und nachträglich verstandenes", that is "Fantasies are heard things, understood afterwards".

That is the common use, but you already feel the idea of afterwardsness, and at the very end he comes to a formulation that looks awful for someone who is not a scientist: "*Der betrag der Nachträglichkeit ist vermindert?*" – that is, "The amount of *Nachträglichkeit* is very much diminished". He talks of *Nachträglichkeit* like something that you can have a quantity of, as if the amount could be put on the scales and weighed. People who say there are no conceptual terms in Freud are completely wrong, and people who say that he invented conceptual terms from nothing are also wrong, because he invented conceptual terms from common usage, very gradually, with dialectical steps towards the concept. The other point I will make about the usefulness of translation in understanding Freud's concepts is that, if you look at the indexes of the German edition, you scarcely find *Nachträglichkeit* at all. You will find *nagträglichgehörsam*, which means after-obedience, a lateral meaning of *nachträglich*. I think this was used in the context of hypnosis, meaning obedience to the hypnotist after you have been woken. So in the indexes of the *Gesammelte Werke* (the German *Complete Works*), in the indexes of the *Studienausgabe* (the German study edition) which are taken from the English Standard Edition, you have no German record of *Nächtraglichkeit*, not to mention the concordance of the Strachey's Standard Edition in English where you have no single translation. The Germans, and Freud himself when he published his work, were not aware of the importance of the concept he had put forward. That is true for other concepts: there are concepts which are important in Freud of which even Freud or his disciples forgot the importance or meaning. If you look at the Standard Edition indexes now, you find very few references, and this is because they don't have the one term. So it is only through the test of foreignness, that is, going out into the foreignness and the strangeness which is outside of the *patrie*, the homeland, the native tongue and coming back; it is only this movement of translation that comes back to the work and makes the German people today aware of the importance of *Nachträglichkeit*, which they would not be aware of from just reading the German text. So that is an important example of our approach to the conceptuality of Freud, and it is a reason for our insistence on consistency in the translation. This doesn't mean that any word would be translated by the same terms (there wouldn't be any translation), but for all the terms that have a conceptual evolution and meaning, even a latent conceptual significance, then we try to find the right term and we translate it in one and the same way. That is the reason why now, as I have a paper to be translated into English: "*Nachträglichkeit dans l'après coup*," that I'd prefer it to be translated into English not using the French phrase. Let's have an English term now. I propose 'afterwardsness'.

MS: The examples that have been challenged in France include the translation of Freud's *Hilflosigkeit* by *désaide*, that is, the creation of words which sound strange to the French ear. The argument has been that this isn't really the true function of a translator, to create neologisms. Whereas Professor Laplanche's approach has been to refuse to impose an interpretation through his translations, to overtranslate, but rather to translate without interpretation and therefore to give the reader as much freedom to interpret as is possible; and so, for example, not to follow Lacan's translations of Freud, which are interpretations. In *L'Ane* a debate has raged through several issues demanding why the new French translation has not followed Lacan's brilliant translations.[2] The reply has been that they are interpretations and not translations. For example, Lacan translates *Zwang* by obsession as opposed to *contrainte*, which is a much more open word, conveying much more accurately the idea of restriction and constraint than obsession.

LAPLANCHE: I might add a few things about Lacan. Lacan was a very good reader of Freud; he pointed out the importance of many Freudian terms and presented us with "après coup", unlike Loewenstein who just translated it but never interpreted it. So I give homage to Lacan for that and also for a second point. Lacan says that there is consistency in Freud's language, although he doesn't always follow this consistency in his own propositions for translation. For example, two opposite instances: in one instance there are two terms in Freud, ideal ego and ego ideal, so everyone says they are the same thing. Lacan says maybe we don't understand exactly, but Freud's use is always watertight, so if there are two words in Freud, there must be some difference. Actually he was right, and when you read 'On Narcissism, an introduction' (1914) you find the difference between Freud's use of *Ichideal* and *Idealich*; it's misleading to translate it by one word. Here Lacan said: two words, they should be translated differently. The other instance was when he talked about *forclusion* (Fr.) that's *Verwerfung* [usually translated into English as 'repudiation']; I don't say this is the right translation. There was an argument against him, which was that you use *forclusion* for *Verwerfung* and you mean something furthest from consciousness, but Freud also used *Verwerfung* for the most conscious judgements. Lacan replied that there must be something in common between the two, and even there, in the conscious judgement of condemnation – *Urteilsverwerfung* – there is something of *forclusion*. Lacan was stressing consistency and we are following the same path, that is, attention paid to the signifier and not only to the supposed meaning. If the same term is used by someone who uses language very consciously and deliberately, then there is some reason for using the same term. Now Lacan is not always consistent on this point, and those people who attacked me were not Lacanian in that sense. They said that, according to context, you had to translate the *Ich* sometimes as the subject, *le sujet* and sometimes the ego, because sometimes it is the bad *Ich*, the ego – in Lacan the place of alienation etc. – and sometimes it is the subject of speech, *le sujet de la parole*, and then you have to translate *Ich* by *je* or the subject. This is opposed to what Lacan said about Freud, because if it is watertight then it should not be leaking at that point, so that sometimes you translate it by the subject and sometimes by ego. Lacan gave a very good direction as a whole, but himself – and much more his disciples – are not Lacanian in that sense. What they advocate in this article is against what they always say, which is understanding first; whereas Lacan said, don't hurry to understand, stick to the words first and don't try to understand from the very beginning, because if you just begin by understanding you will project something of yourself.

JACQUELINE ROSE: Will you say something more: if there is no distinction between the bad ego and the subject of speech in linguistic terms, how do you see that affecting the conceptual distinction? Would you conclude from that, that the conceptual distinction between the "je" and the "moi" is illegitimate?

LAPLANCHE: No, I think there is a dialectic between the two. I cannot give an exposition of it now, but just read our article in *The Language of Psychoanalysis* – the most important article in the whole book.[3] In this you will see how both are linked together. Most people, Hartmann etc., say that from 1895 to 1920 Freud spoke of the ego as a whole personality, and from 1920 onwards he spoke of it as an instance, as an agency – which is false from the beginning. There are not two separate *Ichs* in Freud. If you go back to the *Project* you will see the ego as an agency already, an agency taking over the whole of the personality. As in Marxian dialectics where you have the whole society and one class which takes representation of the whole and says, "I am the whole", or the Marxian theory of Bonapartism whereby the Bonapartists say, "I am the whole of the society", when in fact they are only an instance or agency, a part of the whole. You find this dialectic in Freud, and you also find this dialectic between the ego as a subject and the ego as an agency, even in Freud's phrases. But how can you show a dialectic if you separate the two terms? If you separate the terms there is no more dialectic. There are two terms, that's all; the ego and the subject. That is easy to understand; either I am alienated into an agency, or I am the subject as such. But to show how "Wo Es war soll Ich werden", that is a dialectic. There is a dialectic in this phrase. You will see the trick of Freud in this phrase; it is a little like *Nachträglichkeit*. He takes a pronoun "ich" (it is not a substantive) and he transforms the pronoun into a noun. In German you have two ways to transform a pronoun into a noun. First, to put an article before, "das Ich", the I, and the second way which French and English don't have, is to put a capital when you have a substantive. That is not a question of dignity, that is a question of a substantive. All substantive nouns in German have the capital. So that there is a transformation from the common language, from 'ich bin', I am, 'je suis', to the 'das Ich', 'le moi' or 'le je' (I won't argue this in French at the moment). Now, in this phrase, which is a *Witz*, a play on words, he has cancelled the article. He doesn't say "Wo das Es war soll das Ich werden". He has cancelled the articles but he has not cancelled the capital, so he keeps capitalising "Es" and "Ich"; there is something remaining of the agencies, the *Instanz* which he talked about all through the book. This is a device, a way to show that what is an *Instanz*, an agency must become a subject. That's the interpretation of Lacan which is not so wrong. But how can you show this dialectic if you translate it in a different way?

I am using these simple examples because the question of neologism is only a detail, it is not the main point. You only make a new word when you don't have one and it is necessary to have one single word. For instance for "Hilflosigkeit" you have the one word, helplessness, so in English there is no problem. It is the opposite of *Nachträglichkeit*: in French we have *après coup*, but in English you don't have a word. In English you have 'helplessness', so there is no need for a new word, just consistency: every time you translate *Hilflosigkeit* use 'helplessness', for *Hilfe* use help. So the making of new words is only the problem of any translator of a work of thought. For instance, Chateaubriand, translating an English poet, says in the preface that people will say he doesn't speak good French but that he will use expressions and create new uses of the French words. But this is in poetry. Chateaubriand is someone who said, "Why should the translator be just the servant of the work"? Any writer, as the writer, has the right to create new terms; why should the translator be a servant? If he is a servant, he would be a servant of the petrified state of his language; a neologism today is going to be in the next *Petit Robert*. For instance, *pulsion* (drive) is now referred to as a word in French and is cited in Robert as "psychoanalysis 1940", or whatever. Now everyone says *pulsion*. If you dial *pulsion* on what we call the pink computer in France, you get a young woman talking to you about sex; so *pulsion* has become an ordinary word.

JOHN FORRESTER: I would like to ask a question about the strategy in a large-scale translation of Freud, because the idea of translating the complete works of Freud already commits one to certain choices as a translator. If you are translating one poem your commitment is to that poem. You might also say if you are translating *The Interpretation of Dreams* that you might start off with a commitment to that work. If you then move up a stage and talk about the *Gesammelte Werke*, you have a much bigger commitment, but it is still a commitment to a single author as a binding, unifying factor. But at the earlier stage, when you are dealing with a poem or with a single word, some of the decisions about translation might move laterally, they might move away from the linguistic issues raised by particular terms or phrases used by one author towards the linguistic milieu, towards the kind of language spoken and written around that author, in order to try to communicate the resonances of the work to the foreign reader you are addressing as a translator. This kind of consideration has led to some interesting examples in recent thought about translating in Britain, say, for instance, the word *signifiant* in French, which the translators of Saussure want to to translate as signifying, and to get rid of the word signifier on the grounds that *signifiant* is a gerund form. In French you have the terms where *signifiant* is used in a verbal form, and then you have *le signifiant* as used in a noun form; and you lose the homophonic element there which may mean moving towards homonymy for some occasions. I am interested in this because I translated the Lacan of 1953, and it is never clear when Lacan is writing in 1953–4, whether, when in talking about *signifiant* he has a Saussurian reference in mind or if he is referring to the general activity of signifying. [Laplanche: No, he is referring to Saussure].That is a decision one has to make. In order to make this decision you are going to have to refer to the intellectual milieu of the context; whether he had read Saussure, whether he had read Hegel, Heidegger, and so on. When one takes on the *Gesammelte Werke* of Freud is one going to lose sight of considerations like that, given the enormity of a problem of tracking terms, from 1900, to 1905, to 1920? Because then one is not going to be as concerned with problems like the linguistic milieu or the linguistic contexts. For example, the resonances between the *Three Essays on the Theory of Sexuality* and Weininger, questions which an intellectual historian would address and, in a work as exact and as scholarly as a new translation of Freud, one would also want to take on board. So does translation depend on the specification of the context for all terms? Is it the complete works of Freud or is it psychopathological literature, Vienna 1900?

LAPLANCHE: There are ten questions in what you say; it is very exciting. I go back to the signifier first, as an example, because when I heard Lacan in his Seminar, it was absolutely used as a reference to Saussure. There must be a consistency anyway between Saussure's use and his use; I won't choose for the English between signifier and signifying. I use signifier because people said it was okay. I think it is a question of context; actually the context for Lacan is the context of Saussure at that point, as he was taking concepts from linguistics even though he makes use of them in his own way.

Second point. I should say that Freud uses many terms of his milieu, but I would think of Freud's work as something more closed to influences, or more transforming influences into his own conceptuality than Lacan. I think there is much more of Freud's conceptual system that could be translated without taking too much care of what has been said, for instance by the psychiatric and physical sciences. For instance, the way he takes over the notions of *freie gebundene Energie* from physics, which he transforms and uses in his own way. So I think it is much more legitimate to take Freud's work comparatively, as an island or peninsular, more than for Lacan.

Another point would be the difference between poems and the work of thought. I think there is a big difference between the work of thought and a poem. I try to take this metaphor in translating Freud: the author of thought takes his own language as a big palace, a huge building, but he inhabits only a part of it. He leaves parts almost completely empty; he uses some passages and doors more than others. So there is a way in which an author of thought uses his language. A poet tries to use his language as a whole, he tries to inhabit as much of the palace as possible; going from one place to the other, he uses new meanings of the words and new resonances. That is one reason why you cannot think exactly of Lacan's work as a work of thought, because it is a little between a work of thought and poetry; he twists words and expressions and uses it as an argument, as a way of convincing. This is something Freud does sometimes, but not always. For instance, "Wo Es war soll Ich werden" is an example of Freud making a kind of joke, twisting words to make a convincing message for the reader.

Now, the question of the difference between the individual work and the *œuvre* as a whole. For the work of thought (and although we are talking about Freud, we could also be talking about Kant or Hegel or Descartes), taking a small article, or one work, ignoring the other works, is a little like taking it as a poem. It is common for a translator who translates a single text of Freud into French, such as 'The Medusa's Head' or 'Negation', to take the whole of the German language as a context, rather than the whole of Freud's work. For myself, with an author like Freud, the context of Freudian language – Freudian thought – is more important than the context of German.

Hilflosigkeit is an objective state for Freud, much more than a subjective one. For the ordinary German *Hilflosigkeit* means distress and tears, whereas in Freud it does not have this pathos. So this illustrates the idea that the author uses only a part of this big palace of language. That is what I try to convey through the expression, translating Freud not into a German French (which would be stupid), but into a Freudian French, which means that there is a Freudian German too. If there is a Freudian German, it is the way Freud inhabits his own language, so there may be a way of inhabiting the French language in a similar way. This involves trying to trace the same passages, to use more this living room and dining room than the other one. This would be an analogous way to inhabit the French language as Freud inhabited the German, and this means that we always give the priority to the general context of the work against the particular context of one article, and in one article or book priority is given to the general context of the book against this phrase or this page; that is always to take into account the whole of the writer's *œuvre* and its evolution.

If you turn to *Hilflosigkeit*, you cannot translate it from the text of 1926 (*Inhibitions, Symptoms and Anxiety*) alone, you must go back to the *Project* of 1896, where he uses it for the first time. Here he talks about *fremde Hilfe*, foreign help, for the first exchanges between the child and the parents. The child needs foreign help. That is why, translating *Hilfe* into French by *aide*, we said it is impossible to have a French word for helplessness that would not have the root *aide* in it. That's why we created *désaide*, not to be funny. If we had used *détresse*, we would lose the continuity between the *Project*, where Freud talks of *Hilfe/aide* and the texts where he talks of the absence of *aide* that is *désaide*.

J.F.: To take an old chestnut in translating Freud into English: 'das Ich', the ego. Someone like Bettleheim didn't understand – or even know of – the German philosophical tradition in which 'das Ich' is a standard concept as in

Kant's *The Critique of Pure Reason*. It leads to all sorts of problems in the interpretation of what Freud is up to, but one of the things that is clear is that its very straightforward translation as the ego resonates with all the 19th century translations of German philosophy. *Das Ich* is always translated as the ego. If one wants to build on the fact that Freud has repudiated philosophy and there is something else going on, and yet he allows himself to use this very mainstream philosophical term suddenly in the middle of 1923, then you may want to move to some other translation such as the I, but this means you lose the fact that Freud is repudiating something in the tradition in the act of invoking that tradition's main term. Now that kind of translator's question requires one to consider the options. But one of the mistakes in talking about those kinds of issues of Freud in English – becoming too technical, too medicalised and turned into a scientific language – is to cut off the relationship of Freud to the traditions of literature, philosophy or medicine. In a sense the tendency to look at the closed world of the Freud oeuvre can lead to similar kinds of problems.

LAPLANCHE: I completely agree with you. That is, first, I don't argue about English translation. I am not in a position to argue, especially as what you say about the ego is convincing. It would be less convincing about cathexis or something like that. When I described Freud's text as an isolated island I pushed my ideas perhaps too far. But in French, and in our translation, we have been taking *le moi* and not *le je* and the explicit reason we give is because of the French tradition for using *le moi*. *Le moi* is also the first person because I say '*moi je*', and you never say 'ego I'. Also *moi* has to do with something reified, and actually *das Ich*, the ego is reified in Freud. We took it over for the exact reason you said, that is, Freud has not cut off the philosophical tradition and he took this word which was in the tradition. Now in some places we cut him off from the tradition, for instance in translating *Zwang*; but there the tradition comes not before Freud but after him. Afterwards, in France, people have said *Zwangsneurose* is *névrose obsessionelle*, and so this is how it was translated. But that is in another tradition which Freud knew but did not want to situate himself in. He invented *Zwangsneurose* as a concept, as an entity. The other reason is that we don't go to the technical but to the everyday use, and *Zwang* is a much wider concept than *névrose obsessionnelle*. For instance, Freud talks of the hysterical *Zwang*, so that if you translated it as the hysteric obsession it would be completely crazy, because psychoanalysis distinguishes between hysteria and obsessional neurosis. It should in fact be hysteric *contrainte*. This *contrainte* is in the first letters, and he uses *Zwang* not only for the obsessional neurosis, but for hysteria, for psychosis and for perversion, and so on. He talks of a perverse *Zwang*, and he uses *Zwang* in so many other uses which are completely lost with the term *obsession*.

So there he uses certain possibilities of his palace, certain rooms with connections, and he makes something with the *Zwang* which cannot be reduced either to obsession or to compulsion. So I completely agree with you about the tradition and about some contexts, but sometimes it is a human context and what we don't like is medicalising afterwards. Now let's take another word. In the English translation I talk about cathexis, but we also could talk about *Anlehnung*, which is translated by Strachey as anaclisis. *Anlehnen*, *lehnen-an* is a common German term which maybe the taxi driver would use. It means 'to lean on'. There is a tree – I am going to show you what is leaning on, exactly. You always see roadworkers leaning on their broom when you are in your car; whereas anaclisis is an invention which is a false equivalent. I wouldn't say it is a medicalisation, but just a false scientisation of Freud. It prevents the translator from seeing that the word is used in many other instances which cannot be translated by anaclisis. This restricts anaclisis to the most narrow conceptual use and doesn't allow the continuity with ordinary uses. Ego is an example which keeps the Latin, and anaclisis could be a very bad example of why not to keep the Greek.

IVAN WARD: I am thinking of the palace as Bluebeard's castle. There is a prohibition in the castle against entering certain rooms. Is that like language? The passages and rooms that you inhabit… is there an active prohibition against the other parts? If so, would that mean that the conceptual framework is actually influenced by the effect of prohibition on the other parts of the language? Is there an unconscious at work in the way you inhabit your palace?

LAPLANCHE: There are two points at least in what you say. I sometimes think of my own life in terms of the global map of the world, and if I take a red pencil I can trace my travels (three times to Mexico, never to South Africa), and that is the way I inhabit my globe. So the other places are not prohibited, but that is just my way of inhabiting the globe.

IW: Why not South Africa? You are talking to one of two non-white people here. Surely there is a prohibition there?

LAPLANCHE: But there are many places I would like to go but haven't. I will answer your question further. I think what you mean is that all the places you didn't go to are important. Even in Freud's palace – the rooms are not words but particular meanings of words – the meanings of words are selected. I will take the word *Aufhebung*, which has at least three meanings: suppressing, keeping its contrary and lifting up. Hegel said this was the same word: the language is very clever, because although people are not so dialectical at least we have some dialectical words; happily the language is more dialectical than we are. That is the way Hegel inhabits his language. In a way it is very fruitful to say that in Hegel the same word in dialectics means suppressing and keeping. In many passages of Freud, he never uses *Aufhebung* in the sense of keeping – never, never, never – it is always suppressing. I can show you. So Hegel makes another use of the same palace; he took three rooms of the same palace and knocked the partitions down to make one studio of three rooms. Freud keeps separate the meanings and uses only one of two of them. You may say that is the unconscious, that even if Freud did not use it, that is the unconscious of the language – but I don't believe in the unconscious of the language. I am not Lacanian in that. I don't think the unconscious is the latent possibilities of the language. I think everyone has his own unconscious; there is no interpersonal unconscious that would be the latent possibilities of the language.

IW: I was saying that to inhabit certain parts of the language does not just come by chance, but might be constructed through something like prohibitions.

LAPLANCHE: It may be prohibition. It may be he prohibits himself to use this word in that sense. I can take another example, that's *Lust*. *Lust* in German has two meanings: pleasure and desire. You have two comments of Freud about that. The first comment says that unhappily, in German *Lust* has two meanings and so it is an ambiguous concept; this is the reason why you have to use the foreign term libido. So Freud uses a Latin term for desire because although *Lust* would be wonderful it also means pleasure. Libido is not pleasure because pleasure is the extinction of desire. Therefore *Lust* one is the extinction of *Lust* two. Unlike Hegel, who says it is happy to have dialectical language, he says unhappily it is ambiguous. So I must clarify and use *Lust* for pleasure and libido for desire. In another place, he says the contrary. He asks why the German term *Lust* has two meanings, and at least four pregenital activities. In this case it is interesting to use it because there desire and pleasure are not completely separate and the augmentation of tension and the diminution of tension sometimes mix together. So sometimes he says: let's make one room of two; and other times: lets keep the meanings separate and make another room.

But I would not argue with the possibility that maybe it is self-prohibition, interdictions, why not? You find many, many passages where he says that you must not use this word in this way. Although, for example, *Angst* in the common language means fear, this is a false use. Let's prevent it. It means anxiety. If we want to say fear, we must say *Furcht* and not *Angst*. But a taxi-driver in Vienna uses *Angst* as fear. So this is a prohibition. He takes the word from the everyday language and forces it into conceptual differences, but there are always resonances of the old meaning. The difference from the poet is that the poet keeps as much of the resonance as possible whereas Freud tried to keep less and less of the resonance. For his own language Freud is not a psychoanalyst. Whereas Lacan tries to convey the unconscious ambiguities through his own conceptual language. This is a difference: I would not try to translate Lacan. I would not dare.

MS: Could we move to broader concepts and look at the *New Foundations for Psychoanalysis* or *Life and Death in Psychoanalysis*?

JACQUELINE ROSE: It seems as if your book *New Foundations* is a very big change from 'Fantasy and the Origins of Sexuality', the essay that was republished recently and which has become a cult text among people working on fantasy and culture.[4] In *New Foundations* you seem to take your distance from that earlier work in your new ideas about the indecipherable signifier and the advent of the self-theorisation of the child. I wondered if you could use this context to say a bit about those changes in your own thinking?

LAPLANCHE: I would say I change and am the same. I could talk also about the spiral as a mode of thinking. For this particular text I don't think I have changed so much from *The Language of Psychoanalysis*, but I have developed certain things much more. Sure, I have pointed out more and more differences, but all is present from the beginning. On this particular point, what I should stress is that this text is foremost a text about Freud, a text which firstly has unearthed the concept of primal fantasy about which no one had spoken. You will never find a text about primal fantasies before this text. Unearthing a concept in Freud doesn't mean that you agree with that concept, and yet the discovery was so important that people tend to say that Laplanche is primal fantasy. Even in this text we keep a distance from Freud's primal fantasies, and now I am taking more and more distance and explaining more and more my differences. I wouldn't say that I don't believe in primal fantasy. For Freud, primal fantasies are the core of the unconscious, as Pontalis and I try to explain it, like the Oedipus is the core of the unconscious. For me its not true; I say the contrary: maybe there are primal fantasies; if so, they are primal but secondarily primal, that is, they are secondary ways of binding something that is unbound in your unconscious. I wouldn't place the primal fantasy either at the core of the unconscious or in phylogenesis in which I don't at all believe – I don't believe in inherited psychical contents at all. I believe in inheritance but not in that way; I don't believe in inherited fantasies; I believe in inherited behaviours – for instance, walking maybe partly preformed. But Freud said there may be scenarios that are inherited because they were a reality in prehistory. Even at that time with Pontalis I challenged it. Maybe having to explain it gave us a double task at that time: unearthing something and then criticising it. First, we have unearthed a Venus, washed it and put it on a pedestal. Maybe it is a piece of art we don't agree with, a piece of thought we don't agree with, and we explain this in a recent preface a little more, and I have explained it in *New Foundations* more and more. The primal fantasy article is wonderful because Freud's idea was wonderful, in the good and bad sense of wonderful.

IW: Didn't you say in that article that there wasn't a distinction between conscious and unconscious fantasy?

LAPLANCHE: No, we said that there must be some continuity between conscious and unconscious fantasy. I come back to my previous point: if Freud writes about *Phantasieren*, in both senses of conscious and unconscious there might be some continuity. Otherwise he might have used two words. Now you see the Kleinians writing one with "f" and the other one with "ph", so that there are two concepts, exactly as we said for all the terms. If there are two egos, one ego and one I, there is no dialectic. If there is one fantasy with 'f' and one phantasy with 'ph', the one conscious and the other unconscious, then no more problem. We don't say there is no difference, but we think there must be something continuous between the two.

JR: Can I try my question again, because you didn't really answer it. It is wonderful that you thought I was asking you to talk about that article, whereas in fact I was saying that I know that article has become the article through which you are always represented, and I felt that you were, even then, pulling away from it towards concepts that are much clearer in the book that has just been translated. I wanted you to talk about that book, specifically about a concept like the indecipherable signifier and those ideas which seem to have become more central.

LAPLANCHE: I am going to say what I have said two or three times. I must repeat myself. I put it this way: a little far from the enigmatic signifier, but coming back to it. What we call in technical terms mechanisms in psychoanalysis: introjection, projection, introversion, repression, denial, foreclosure, projective identification (whether they are Freud's, Lacan's,

Klein's), for all these terms the verb has a subject, the person. That is not to say they are all mechanisms in the first person, because it could be the third person. It could be "I project", "I deny", "I foreclose", or "Sigmund does introject", "Sigmund does deny", and so on. I call these auto-centrist or better still ipsocentrist mechanisms, and psychoanalysis has dealt only with ipsocentrist mechanisms. Now I don't now plead in favour of interaction: I don't say you should take into account that, not only do you project, but... I say the primal mechanisms are "The other implants", or "The other intromits into the small human individual". That is, I de-centre the primal mechanisms as coming from the other, and the subject is no more "I" nor Sigmund, but "the other". That is a way to put it in a cut and square manner. I distinguish between two others, not the big and the small like Lacan, but I follow a few of Freud's terms: he speaks of *der Andere* and *das Andere*; German has the neutral and sometimes with the capital 'A'. There are two expressions: *der Andere*, the other person (*l'autre personne*) and *das Andere*, the other thing (*l'autre chose*). I say there are two others active towards the infant: *der Andere*, the other person, the adult, and then at a certain time after the first implantations and after the first separations *das Andere* which is the infant unconscious. Where do I put the enigmatic signifiers? That is the first messages from the adult to the child, the messages being taken not in the sense of word messages, but all types of messages an adult can send to a child (gestures, comportments, expressions and so on). And not only from one adult but from two parents; for instance, if two parents kiss in a room and the child is there, you cannot think that there is not a message sent, you cannot think the child can ignore it; it is a kind of message, an enigmatic signifier. I have taken the breast as the most common example, but we could think of societies where the breast won't exist any more as a way of nursing the child; it is possible, it might happen.

Why do I call it enigmatic? I make distinctions between puzzle, enigma, problem, mystery. As I see it, enigma is defined by the fact that it is an enigma even for the one who sends the enigma. That is, for me, the importance of the enigma. I don't know if its true in the legend, but if the Sphinx was the master of the riddle she had no reason to throw herself down and commit suicide; it was something that was uncovered for her when the riddle, the enigma was solved. The term enigmatic signifier was once used by Lacan in the *Ecrits* somewhere.[5] As Pascal said, you are never the author of anything. What would be different is that, for Lacan and for many people, all signifiers are enigmatic, because any signifier has more significations than you can grasp. But what I mean is much more precise; that is, the fact that the one who sends the enigmatic message is unconscious of the whole meaning; that is, part of the meaning comes from his unconscious sexual wishes. The adult has an unconscious and performs many gestures, unadapted but also symptomatic gestures as Freud explains in *The Psychopathology of Everyday Life* (1901). I see no other way of conceiving the unconscious: I see the infant as having no unconscious, unless you think of the unconscious as being inherited, I don't know from where; so I see the infant as having no unconscious, and not even the exact difference between conscious and unconscious as a separate splitting. This is a big difference between the adult and the infant.

NICOLA DIAMOND: I wanted to raise something about your small paper on temporality, in which you relate temporality very specifically to human existence. You say something about the animal belonging to a presence, a moment and not a movement of temporality proper. I was interested to know how that might relate to the differentiation between the instincts and the drives. I have a problem around the instincts, which traditionally has been aligned to the animal, to a kind of atemporality, prior to symbolisation and to failures of symbolisation. I am interested in thinking about that because it seems to me that the lived body that perhaps Merleau-Ponty was concerned with – where he talks about metabolism as *ekstasis* – is sometimes eluded, and we get into dual camps, where the instincts are located as atemporal animality, and symbolization and its failures comes up with the emergence of sexuality proper. Could you comment a little about that.

LAPLANCHE: I see you have read this paper which I read again on Monday, changing a few things in the translation. I was trying to situate the question of time at four levels: cosmological time; perceptual and living being time; human being time; history. I am concentrating on levels two and three, especially on level three. In Freud you have levels two and three. Level two – which people often don't think as level two – is the perceptual time and Freud's hypothesis in 'The Mystic Writing Pad' (1924), which is on perception. For me, this speculation on perception is very interesting but is not specific to the human being as human being. I would say roughly that Husserl and Augustine talk of the same perceptual, living being time. That is the way we are, just now, between the near-present and the near-future. And there is no reason to think there is no such time for the living being even in the most elementary, but also the more complicated, living being. It is a little dogmatic, but I would put Husserl on this side, on level two, and Heidegger on level three. What I am concentrating on is level three, the time of the human being. I was talking about Freud, but in Freud you have no explicit theory of time three, but you have many hints (the cure, *Nachträglichkeit*, mourning). Mourning is on level three, on the level of the human being and human existence, it is time on a wide scale. I don't see any useful connection between the sketch of Freud about perception and the time of mourning. So I am placing myself on the level of this question of temporality.

ND: That is a development of some of the issues in *Life and Death in Psychoanalysis* where the instinct is related to the presence of the object that could satisfy, and then sexuality came around with the detachment of the real object and symbolization through loss. The later development in *New Foundations* seems to involve a relationship: you are differentiating between an instinctual relationship (with a world, the mother, an other) from the sexuality relationship, which specifically involves the autoerotic or the auto-affective moment. There seems to me to be a problem, in so far as for a relationship there has to be a space between people, and for me the space between people seems to come about with some possibility of symbolisation. I am a bit unsure about the kind of relationship that is possible, prior to an auto-affective turn.

LAPLANCHE: *In Life and Death* I was stressing the auto-affective autoerotism, but now I am stressing much more the allo-affective, that is the seduction, which was already in *Life and Death*. I think you are completely right: I would grossly put instinctual life on the level of time two, and unconscious drive life (if we keep the word drive) on the level of time three. But your question is much more complicated, because you ask whether there can be symbolization at the first level. I think so, why not?

ND: It is a problem of how is differentiation – of how are differences – possible. If there was a presence of an object which was simply there without any notion of a substitution of that object, then it seems that we could be in a situation of undifferentiated presence. It is the way that the object can be there, rather than fully present, that seems to involve the need for an auto-affective turn, because separation and then a relation is possible following the separation.

LAPLANCHE: That is a question of the description of instinctual life, and I think that there is instinctual life in man too. There is a ground of instinctual life. However, what many have stressed, including Freud and Lacan, is that this instinct is much more lacunary and incomplete in humans than in the animal. You are right to say that, even in the animal, if the adhesion to the world were full, if it were the so-called Parmenidean world, there wouldn't be any perception.

ND: This is the difficulty I had in *Life and Death*, where instincts have their aim, object etc., fully worked out, as a way of clarifying the issue.

LAPLANCHE: Yes, it clarifies, but it is a little too clear-cut. You referred to Merleau-Ponty, and really he is working between times. It is a long time since I read Merleau – I was his student for a long time – so I can't say now whether to situate him between levels two and three types of time. He tries to make the junction. Although you did not refer to the concept of *Anlehnung*, or 'leaning on', for me it is now an intermediate concept. This is one difference between *Life and Death* and *New Foundations*. *Anlehnung* is still an ipsocentrist concept, and, as I tried to say in *New Foundations*, the truth of 'leaning on' is seduction. What peels the onion of self-preservation, and what peels off the leaf of sexuality, is seduction. *Anlehnung* was not an explicit but an implicit Freudian concept. It is a little like the primal fantasies: we helped unearth this concept in Freud, but it doesn't mean that it is a completely satisfactory concept. And this is because it describes the evolution as being only from the inside, that is, the sexual drive coming from the inside and leaning on or attaching to self-preservation. It is still a concept from the inside, an ipsocentrist concept.

IW: In Freud you also have the sense in which a biological organ becomes an erotogenic zone, through the outside.

LAPLANCHE: Sure, but all development is described from the point of view of the individual. There is almost no intervention as such by the other, such as sending messages.

JR: Can I ask a question about seduction because, as you are talking, it is bringing back memories of what happened when you spoke at the Institute of Psychoanalysis about five years ago. I am remembering that you caused quite a scandal because you talked about the sexuality of the mother, and about her desire, and the very few analysts in the audience said, "But no, it is the child who has these desires, you can see an erection from week six". Juliet Mitchell got up and said that it was a confusion of tongues, because what you were talking about was the constitution of the unconscious, whereas for the English analysts this wasn't an issue because the unconscious comes from the drives of the child. I can see that the theory of seduction you are introducing is an attempt to get away from ipsocentrism but without falling into the comfortable moralism of a certain object relations or interactionism. But isn't there a slight danger that you are just going over to the other side of an alternation which is the inside/outside boundary? So that the child receives everything from outside, and what it especially receives from outside, what puts an end to a fantasied world without differentiation, is what the mother doesn't know of her own sexuality. Isn't there therefore a slight risk of making the mother's sexuality a kind of culprit in the entrance of difference and trouble into the world of the child?

LAPLANCHE: It is wonderful, it is necessary. I won't say this trouble has to be cured. I'd say it's a happy fall. Happy Fall! This trouble hasn't to be cured! I am not saying the same thing as Maude Mannoni said. The pathologies that it introduces are what I would call the normal pathologies, of which Freud talks about in the *Three Essays* – human sexuality is by itself perverse, he says. To come back to this: I tried to make scandal, but you never make half the scandal you want to make. People who don't want to understand go back to their office or dining room and say, 'Well we know that' and so on. For instance, talking of erection in the small infant – you can go back to the *Three Essays* – Freud never talks about erection because it would be genitality; when he talks of infantile sexuality, he talks about oral and anal sexuality, not genital sexuality, up till four years. All the analysts forget this now, they talk of an oral relationship but not oral sexuality or anal sexuality. Sexuality, in the Freudian sense not of genitality but of the whole of sexuality, is completely wiped out of Kernberg and Klein. Its all wiped out! Out! Out! Out sexuality! So about the sexuality of the mother; one of my students, Jacqueline Lanouzière, has in publication a thesis about the breast. One of the main chapters is the sexual breasts which all analysts forget. You could read all of Klein, and will see the breast as an object, but will not find the idea of the breast as a place of sexual pleasure. This thesis reminds you that there is sexual orgasm coming from the breast, and so on. So that is a kind of denial by analysts now, but this denial comes also from Freud. Now it is extending to the whole of sexuality.

MS: I don't want to defend Klein in this context, but I think that you are unfair, because she says that this is where the splitting occurs. Where she talks about the paranoid-schizoid is precisely because the breast functions differently in different contexts.

LAPLANCHE: On the side of the mother is the pleasure-seeking breast, it is the excitation of the breast, which I don't find in Klein. Anyway Jacqueline Lanouzière is publishing two books: *The Hidden History of Seduction*, in Freud, in Deutsch, in Klein and in Bonaparte.[6] In all of them you find a hidden history of seduction and especially on the side of the breast. It is hidden because Freud had hidden, had repressed the theory. So all those women who had something to say about it did not say it exactly; maybe the one who said most is Deutsch.

Notes

1. See entry under 'deferred action' in Jean Laplanche and Jean-Bertrand Pontalis, *The Language of Psychoanalysis* (1967), trans. Donald Nicholson-Smith, The Hogarth Press, London 1973; Jean Laplanche, *Life and Death in Psychoanalysis* (1970), trans. Jeffrey Mehlman, John Hopkins University Press, 1976, chap. 2; 'Notes on Afterwardness', p.217 below.
2. 'Oeuvres complètes de Freud', *L'Ane*, July 1988 and October–December 1988.
3. See entry under 'Ego' in *The Language of Psychoanalysis*, op.cit.
4. Jean Laplanche and Jean-Bertrand Pontalis, 'Fantasy and the Origins of Sexuality' (1964), trans. and reprinted in *Formations of Fantasy*, eds. Victor Burgin, James Donald and Cora Kaplan, Methuen, London 1986.
5. Jacques Lacan, 'The Agency of the Letter in the Unconscious, or Reason since Freud' (1957), in *Ecrits*, trans. Alan Sheridan, Tavistock Publications, London 1977, p.166.
6. Jacqueline Lanouzière, *Histoire Secrète de la Séduction*, Presses Universitaires de France, 1991.

The ICA Seminar: New Foundations for Psychoanalysis?

5 May 1990

Martin Stanton (University of Kent), Stephen Melville (University of Syracuse), Peter Dews (University of Essex), Elizabeth Cowie (University of Kent), John Fletcher (University of Warwick) and Professor Jean Laplanche (University of Paris VII).

MARTIN STANTON: The first series of questions will be on the nature of foundations, opening with Stephen Melville.

STEPHEN MELVILLE: I have one question that comes up in two different forms. One striking feature of Professor Laplanche's work, both in the present book *New Foundations in Psychoanalysis* (1987) and in the earlier *Life and Death in Psychoanalysis* (1970) is an extraordinarily trenchant concreteness in the way questions of foundation are posed. It seems to me altogether salutary in a time when questions of foundation are thought to be either simply "yes" or "no". Over and against this Professor Laplanche has reached out and grasped figures for foundation that refuse that easy division between "there is a foundation" and "there is no foundation". In *Life and Death* this is above all the figure of 'leaning on' or 'propping' – as it appears in the American translation. [Laplanche: I prefer 'leaning on'.] In this book it seems to be a 'shoring up'. My question is about the movement of the first figure 'leaning on' to the second figure 'shoring up'. Part of the power of 'leaning on' as a figure was that it seems to cover both the original act of foundation, presumably the Freudian one, and the prolongation of that act in a complex history. Both were equally describable as 'leaning on' or 'propping up'. It is, I think, less clear to me that the figure of 'shoring up' does the same work, covering both the act of foundation and its prolongation. So I am asking for more elaboration of this figure of 'shoring up' and the work it does in the text, and I suppose particularly of the way in which, over and against a tendency in psychoanalysis to describe itself almost exclusively in terms of 'a return to', this figure emerges under the auspices of a book that can call itself *New Foundations*.

PROFESSOR LAPLANCHE: I don't know whether I am going to answer exactly your question. It has given me an occasion to talk about my relationship to Freud. I mean that 'leaning on' is and is not a Freudian concept. It was translated in such a way that nothing comes out of it; for example, 'anaclitic object choice' doesn't mean anything to anyone, and in France it was the same because it was translated *anaclitique*. Now there is a reason for that: 'leaning on' is what we could call a latent concept in Freud, not a concept on which he has placed emphasis; if he had, he would have paid more attention to the translation and to the way that this concept is to be found not only in a very small part of the text 'On Narcissism' (1914) about the types of object choice, and he would have traced it back to the many places where you find it (in the form of *Anlehnung* and its derivatives). That is a concept that Pontalis and myself, and my own text *Life and Death in Psychoanalysis*, have dug out and unearthed. This indicates an important distinction, which is the difference between self-preservation and sexuality and the fact that the emergence of sexuality leans upon the activities of self-preservation. This is the unearthing of something that is latent in Freud's thought, important in his thought, but that is not all. As I tried to emphasise in later texts, the truth of 'leaning on' is seduction. That is, with the concept of 'leaning on' you still remain on the ground of a spontaneous or internal emergence of sexuality in the individual. Whereas in the image that I have used, the onion of self-preservation is peeled from outside. I am taking the concept of seduction from Freud but enlarging it very much: I say 'leaning on' is still a halfway concept and it remains on the ground of internal development. That is ipsocentrism, centred on *ipse* which is not necessarily centred on 'I' – it might be centred on 'Sigmund', but is centred on the person we are talking about. Whereas the mechanism I am trying to describe is the mechanism coming from the other. Primal seduction comes from the other, not from inside, and 'leaning on' is just an internal reflection, in the physical sense of the term, of the mechanism which psychoanalysts did not grasp as coming from outside, from the other.

MELVILLE: One of the things that is powerful about 'leaning on' is the very strong way it seems to bring *Nachträglichkeit* into the centre. 'Shoring up' seems to loosen that relationship. The idea being a sense of coming from the outside, injecting the foundation when the foundation has eroded, and that seems closer to the Jungian notion of taking *Nachträglichkeit* as *Zurück-phantasien* (retrospective fantasies) than was the case with 'leaning on'.

LAPLANCHE: The phenomenon of *Nachträglichkeit* (afterwardsness) is actually an ipsocentrist mechanism. If we go back to the question of time: I said that the mechanism of the process of temporalisation is ipsocentred, but the model of time comes from the other; equally the model of the drive comes from the other – that is seduction. In my most recent, very small paper, I emphasised this again. If you take all the mechanisms psychoanalysis has described up to now, that would be introjection, projection, internalisation, repression, projective identification, denial and even Lacanian foreclosure; in all these the verb is 'I introject, internalise, project' or 'Sigmund *does* introject, *does* internalise and even *does* foreclose". That is, even foreclosure is an action of someone, the subject, even if it is something you don't want to see, it is always Sigmund – or Jacques – who does foreclose, but the mechanisms I say are primal are the ones where the other implants or intromits something into the subject. That is the primal passivity of the subject towards something that is implanted into him. Afterwards there is a transformation into an active temporalisation and that is the mechanism of afterwardsness, but the primal mechanisms are to be understood as coming from the other. I should say there are two others, latent in Freud. Freud speaks of *der Andere*, that is the other person, and *das Andere*, which we could not translate except as the other thing (in French we do not have a neuter and so there cannot be an exact translation of the *der/das* contrast in German). There are two others, and the primal other is *der Andere*, the other person, and the model of temporalisation is primarily *der Andere* and then secondarily *das Andere*, that is the unconscious which is the remainders of the other's messages.

PETER DEWS: A point which Professor Laplanche stresses repeatedly throughout *New Foundations* is what he calls a fundamental ontological proposition. He says that the human subject is a self-interpreting, self-theorising and self-symbolising subject. It seems to me that in itself the ontological proposition is not new, in the sense that it could be traced back at least as far as Heidegger's account of human being and *Dasein* as the being which poses the question of its own being. So I want to follow two lines of enquiry which follow from that. The first line is to do with the connection between this self-interpreting, self-theorising activity of the subject and the status of psychoanalytic theory itself. This self-interpreting and self-theorising is clearly not the interpreting of a pre-given entity or object, but self-theorising is also the process of self-constitution (the self constitutes itself through self-interpretation). If that is the case, a question is raised about the very status of psychoanalytic theory, because doesn't it follow that psychoanalytic theory enters into the process of self-constitution? If that is the case, how can we ask questions about the relative validity of different approaches to psychoanalytic theory, different forms of psychoanalytic theory, given that we don't have a pre-given object and that all we have is the internalisation or the use of that theory in the process of the subject's own self-theorising. As long as the theory works as a self-interpretation how can we find any more fundamental criterion to assess the relative status of different theories?

LAPLANCHE: This is a very important opportunity this week for me to make my ideas even clearer. For instance, the terms self-interpretation, self-theorisation and so on are very elusive in my thought, since they could refer to a self which could be, but in my view is not, *Dasein*. Even auto-interpreting wouldn't be exact, because what is that 'to interpret oneself'? What is that 'oneself'? That 'to be interpreted' is the most outside part of the self; it is the unconscious, or even the other's message. So I agree completely that my terms are false, and it has nothing to do with Heidegger. It is not the interpreting of oneself as always being in advance of oneself; the model of this interpretation or this translation or this metabolisation is something coming from outside, and so it is not 'self', and even 'auto' is not quite correct, except if you think of the unconscious as some core or some thing that is being put inside at one time. I put myself on the same level as Heidegger at a certain point, which is the way the human individual temporalises himself; but I am completely the opposite, in the sense that temporalising oneself is going back to something coming from an external model (the model of the message of the other, of the adult – which is what I call the enigmatic signifier); and secondly, when interpreting the remainders of this enigmatic signifier, that is the unconscious. Another point which has been stressed in the discussion is when I say that the 'to be translated' is the unconscious, it is not exact either, I should change my formulation because the unconscious is not the 'to be translated' – it is a few remainders of what had been 'to be translated'. It is the 'has not been translated' in the prior messages that had to be reintegrated. It is not exactly the 'to be translated'; it is something that comes from first attempts to give an interpretation of the message from outside. So I see something very different in my way of thinking from any Heideggerian or hermeneutic point of view. As I stressed in my paper on time, the first movement of psychoanalysis is the movement of going back to the past. This past is not something established as a text, but it's something enigmatic. In the unconscious there are remainders even more enigmatic than the other's message. Even the message of the other is not just a message that could be completely translated because this message is, for the one who sent the message, unconscious. Because the adult has an unconscious and its relation to the child is pervaded by unconscious meanings and signifiers

The next point is the status of theory. We cannot enter the question of theory without distinguishing levels of theory. Let's take different assertions: for instance, "the infant has no unconscious or no distinction between conscious and unconscious; the adult has an unconscious and is pervaded by unconscious messages"; or another statement, from Freud, that "the personality is divided between ego, id and superego". Another point of theory is that "the child should go through the Oedipus complex, that is, have positive and negative feelings towards the father, and positive and negative towards the mother"; or, "every boy should go through the castration complex". That is one type of assertion. There are other types of assertion: for instance, "Leonardo became homosexual because he was too attached to his mother and became identified with her". Now you can have more precise types of assertion: someone in analysis who says, "This happened because I hated my brother", or "At that time I thought I was menaced by castration", and so on. If you don't make a distinction between all those levels, you will say that any theory is a fantasy. For instance, the theory of castration: in Freud it is a fantasy, but asserting that everyone will go through the castration fantasy is a theory. So for me there is a complete difference of levels between the general theory of human beings that gives a framework to analysis but doesn't give any instructions for you to interpret, and the theorisation that arises in the analysis itself.

I should say in a certain manner that the reason why there will never be "Laplancheian analysts", in the way there are Kleinian analysts and so on (that is people imposing in the session itself a general theory), is because my theory is rather, "Hands off the theorisation of the patient! Hands off! Don't enter it!" (and that's from a theoretical point of view). That's the theory that allows me to say that theorisation is the theorisation of the patient, not of the analyst, which doesn't mean the analyst has no role. It is a theorisation against intervening in the theorisation of the patient. So you see, there are two levels, at least, even three; there is one general level of analytic theory, then there is the personal theorisation or interpretation of his destiny by the patient; and between them there are all the theorisations brought by the cultural environment (even the castration complex is for a large part conveyed by the cultural environment). If you don't make a distinction between levels of theory then you can say that any theory is just fantasy, which I don't accept. Many so-called clinicians would say, "Theory? Well that's your fantasy!"

JOHN FLETCHER: I wanted to start off by asking a relatively simple question about Professor Laplanche's re-use of some Freudian terms, as a way of inviting him to restate some of the basic premises of his theory of the drives. His early work is partly directed towards retrieving the specificity of the Freudian concept of the drive, of the *Trieb* as distinct from the *Instinkt*, and making us aware that this represents the beginning of a break from the biological register. His own elaboration of a new theory of the drives in *New Foundations* seems in some ways to consummate that break from the biological in a crucial way. Indeed he says himself that, if the drives are the result of messages from the other, then there is no primary or founding distinction between the instinctual and the intersubjective, or the instinctual and the cultural, which is a radical conclusion within the sphere of drive theory. He keeps the Freudian terms (aim, source, object, force), but gives them completely different meanings. He reworks those Freudian terms, terms which in Freud's accounts of the drives were already breaking from the simple biological register. In particular, one of the changes of usage is that *New Foundations* speaks of the 'source-object', in which the two terms are brought together as a portmanteau term. Obviously that means that the notion of the object of the drive has been quite radically changed, and I wonder if Professor Laplanche could comment on why he talks about the 'source-object' and brings together those two categories that have been crucial in Freud's theory of the drive, and makes them one combined term.

LAPLANCHE: Your text on this had an impact on my thought too and I was thinking about it, and would say that if I were to formulate this term I would not formulate it exactly the same way as I did. I would keep 'source' anyway because I really think that the unconscious is the source of the drive; but when I referred to an object, I think it was a reference to Klein and the internal object, more than to the outside object. But it is also a reference to the internal foreign body; so I could call it the source-body, rather than source-object, because I do not refer to object relations. It could also be source-thing, but 'thing' is already *besetzt* (occupied) too by Lacan with *das Ding* and so on. Maybe 'source-body' would be best. This means that in Freud's terminology I keep the idea of source; maybe the idea could be seen from a realistic point of view, that is, maybe the fantasy is implanted in such and such part of the body. Why not think of the lips zone as the place where the oral fantasy is implanted? Why should it be implanted in the brain, after all? I hold very much to the idea of source, but I agree with you that there is a problem about this with object.

FLETCHER: The second question follows on from that. What happens to the notion of quantity or of there being a pressure or force to the drive in *New Foundations*? The economic hypothesis in Freudian metapsychology undergoes a restructuring, or a reworking. *New Foundations* says, "The drive is in fact the force behind representatives which have acquired a separate status of their own: the status of the repressed and of the primordial unconscious" (p.143). The pressure of the drive is representing in Freud's famous phrase "a demand for work" which "does not emanate directly from somatic sources but from unconscious prototypes. It emanates from the difference between those elements in the primal enigmatic signifiers which can be symbolised and those elements which can not be symbolised" (p.143). So the force comes from the difference between signifying elements, between those that can be symbolised and those that resist or evade symbolisation. So *New Foundations* suggests that the economic factor is relative; the symbolising activity in the analytic process weakens the compulsive power of the drive, just as the repetition of seduction can give new stimulus to the drive. I want to ask a question which will invite Professor Laplanche to go over the implications of those formulations, by wondering whether these formulations aren't taking the notion of the drive, and of drive energy, in the direction of what has traditionally been labelled pathology, away from the notion of a pre-given or good bodily energy, to something which is the effect of "a compulsive power", an effect of repression. Is the drive in other words like a symptom? And while in principle it doesn't or oughtn't, might it not imply a final therapeutic elimination of the drive like the elimination of the symptom with the progressive interpretation of the enigmatic signifiers, or the differences between them?

LAPLANCHE: Just a small point first. When I read this quotation I wondered whether I had written that "the drive is the force behind representatives", since for me the drive is a force of the representatives themselves and not "behind" them,which would go back to some abstract force which doesn't exist for me. So maybe a false translation. For instance, in my book on sublimation I argue that the economic point of view of Freud should be amended, that is the idea that there is once and forever an energy that goes into this or goes into that. With sublimation it's evident that there is no mathematical balance between sexual activities and sublimated activities. We know many artists have a very important sexual life. There is something in this that doesn't make sense; or it makes sense at some times but not at others. So my point is that at a certain moment you could say there is a balance, that when he invests in one activity he has to leave the other. But as a general idea there is no such thing as conservation of psychic energy, and one main reason for that is that seduction occurs again and again. There are some neo-formations of energy by new seductions. For me, the situation of analysis is a situation which creates energy by its situation of enigma. Also the relationship to art would not only be a place that draws all the existing energy into it but also a place for creating new energy. I don't think at all of pathology; I think also that the enigmas in human beings will never be solved and that although we are trying again and again new elaborations, new metabolisations or new translations of the enigmas, there should be no fear that it will ever be solved. That was Freud's illusion in the beginning, to think that the unconscious would ever be completely solved. I would say that there are always new places where the enigma takes place and new places where psychic energy is created.

FLETCHER: My third question on your reworking of drive theory is about the notion of primal repression and the way that it is related to the temporal logic of *Nachträglichkeit*, that is deferred action or as you would translate it: afterwardsness. You write in *New Foundations*: "Primal repression is governed by the logic of *Nachträglichkeit* ... which comes into play between the two stages of primal repression, [and] also intervenes in primal repression itself (p.136). So the very activity of expelling and fixing the signifiers and in some sense constituting a nucleus for the unconscious is governed by the logic of afterwardsness. I wonder if you could go over that for us, to see how your concept of primal repression and deferred action are interconnected?

LAPLANCHE: That is a huge question. The point I made was the relation between primary and secondary repression. Actually I talked about secondary repression as the Oedipal repression and I think that is a question of afterwardsness because primal repression is not solid as long as there is no secondary repression. This is why I was talking about Oedipus and castration complexes which I make intervene later, having sown the seeds during primal repression. I think of the primal repression as much more elementary, as the first attempt to bind something that isn't bound. The first drive is unbound and the first attempt by the child is to bind it in in any way. You have different levels of binding, and I would not agree that the most important level of binding is still the Oedipal level.

STANTON: A number of questions are asked about the difference between Laplanche's and Lacan's view of the signifier. First, a question from Peter Dews.

DEWS: This is a question indirectly related to Lacan. I was very struck by Professor Laplanche's vigorous defence of what he calls the realism of the unconscious in *New Foundations*, which I assume is in some sense a criticism of the Lacanian tradition, of the linguistic interpretation of the unconscious. But I detected what I felt was a discrepancy, or incompatibility, between a strong insistence on the realism of the unconscious and what Professor Laplanche says about the primal scene. I am quoting here from *New Foundations*: "If analytic investigation interprets one scene by means of another, and if there are no meanings to be found other than that revealed by the first apophantic scene ('apophantic' in the sense of the word that is applied to the Mysteries), then it is quite obvious that we will never find a hidden scene that reveals all, which is self-explanatory and which does not refer to anything else. Indeed the search for the first scene which reveals the meaning of the whole sequence will be never-ending and will result in disappointment" (p.115). I was puzzled by the relation between the infinite regress you seem to evoke there, the impossibility of a final determinate meaning, and your defence of a realistic conception of the unconscious. I have always taken a realistic view of the unconscious to imply that there are determinate contents of the unconscious which ultimately can be tracked down. Is there any incompatibility between those two lines of argument?

LAPLANCHE: That is a very interesting question, and I am going to put it in relation to Andrew Benjamin's earlier question about what an event is. Reality means many things, and when I talk of realism of the unconscious I talk of something very different from material reality. I am very much in favour of Freud's naive, material realism and there is no argument about that, naive realism in the sense of the material world. The triad of Lacan – the Symbolic, the Imaginary and the Real – involves the Real, which he takes in a somewhat personal way and I would not be able to say exactly what it is because it is arcane in Lacan. I may well have three terms of my own, equivalent to real, imaginary and symbolic but they would be very different. I would not agree with Lacan's definition of the Real. As for the Imaginary I think it is too involved with the mirror stage, and so I would rather say the fantasy world; the third one involves the question of what an event is for a person. Is an event just a material event? Lacan took the image of the hieroglyphs found in the desert. You go into the desert and you find a stone with written hieroglyphs... So I would change the example: I go into the desert and find a road sign. Is that material reality or is that fantasy? It is not material reality because if you take a picture of this with a camera you can bring it home; you don't take the piece of iron and stone home, so you don't take the material reality home. So its something of a third reality, and that is the cause of what Freud called psychic reality, the reality of the message. Now this is the reality in the unconscious. The realism of the unconscious involves remainders of messages, signifiers, that is the reality of the signifier, which is completely different from Lacan's symbolic. Lacan's symbolic is organised signifiers, it is a language. If you find this sign in the desert it is not organised; you just know that there is a message left. You know it is a message but you don't know what it means at the level of unconscious reality.

DEWS: The point I was trying to make is that you have your road sign which you then have to interpret. Is the interpretation of the sign, then, the end-point of the process? Can we then say, that is the reality of the unconscious, or is the process of interpretation itself endless as you sometimes seems to suggest? Does the interpretation in turn become a sign which requires further interpretation or is there an end-point? Because in the book you suggest that there isn't a terminus, which for me creates an uncomfortable feeling, incompatible with this realism.

LAPLANCHE: I think this raises the question of what interpretation is. There are several meanings of interpretation, even in analysis. If you take Freud at the end of his work, he thought of interpretation not as an organised set of sentences, but just pointing out the relationship between two elements, tracing back to something deeper, element by element. That is one meaning of interpretation and I think that is where analysts now have forgotten the analytic method. This is why in this sense I am very much a Freudian because Freud said analysis was first of all a method for getting access to phenomena which we would not have access to in another way. Now all analysts think if they give an interpretation (of a Kleinian or whatever kind) that is analysis: that is not analysis. Analysis is just a way of helping people to go deeper and deeper in their associations and to go back to more primitive signifiers. There is another meaning of interpretation which is putting connections between elements; that is what I call theorising or constructing, which I assign much more to the analysand than to the analyst. It is the analysand's work to make connections; the analyst has to de-connect, not to connect.

MELVILLE: My question is about the difference between Lacan's formulations around the signifier and yours. Lacan wrote of the encounter of the child's desire with the Law of the Father in terms of a pseudo-arithmetical operation, and the writing would put signifier S1 over signifier to the subject (s) times signifier S2 over signifier S1.

$$\frac{S^1}{s} \quad x \quad \frac{S^2}{S^1} = \frac{\dfrac{S^2}{S^1}}{\dfrac{S^1}{x}}$$

And Lacan claimed that the result of this encounter was signifier S2 on top of the stack of signifiers S1, S1 and then at the bottom a tiny x, which is what was left of the subject's signifieds. Professor Laplanche, accepting the first part of the formulation writes the result differently: S2 on top, a little s in the middle and then S1 over S1 at the bottom.

$$\frac{\dfrac{S^2}{s}}{\dfrac{S^1}{S^1}}$$

I am just giving that to you as a picture without a long-winded explanation because I think what we really need is the picture. It seems to me that one way of presenting these two stacks is to observe that Lacan's stack bottoms out with this ineffable, unreachable something for the subject, this x which is at the bottom of everything. His stuff for the subject has been through this operation submitted to a sheer flow of the signifiers and language; they slide unceasingly over that x. So it is a very strong account of the subject's radical submission to language. Professor Laplanche's stack finds a very different bottom; at the bottom there is this signifier fastened to itself (S1/S1). Presumably you would call this a thing presentation (Freud's *Sachvorstellung*), that is, not language in the Lacanian sense. This also results in your referring to Lacan's schema as having a merely symbolic order, that is, the Symbolic as a dimension drops out, it no longer figures in your account. I take it also that where Lacan will read his account as a story of radical ontological failure your account comes out as one of epistemological difficulty – an unreadable sign rather than an impossible person.

LAPLANCHE: I think it may be difficult for us to discuss this without a blackboard, but this formula I made on my own, I mean I took it from Lacan and changed it. At first he didn't say anything and then he was angry – I don't mind him being angry. I think this formula helped him to introduce the phallus. In his formula there is also the *phi* (ϕ); it is not just an endless shift of significations because there is a sticking point (the phallus) which doesn't intervene in my schema. I would say the phallus is one way of stopping the process of symbolisation, an artificial way of stopping the process. This is the introduction of binary logic, which is very important for human thought (either or not, phallus or not) but I don't think it is the only way of metabolisation. It's very good in one sense because it introduces the computer society but it may be a very big restriction of human beings, to stop things with having the phallus or not having the phallus, and that's all. Also, we know the difficulty it introduces in sexual life and relationships between the sexes. As I told you before, the category of the Symbolic doesn't intervene in my elaboration now. If you go back to the text on primal fantasies I still give some place to it, at least as a question mark – would this be the Symbolic order as in Lacan? – but I now think of the Symbolic order as a way of secondary symbolisation, but not in a primal way.

MELVILLE: This is the same point we were at a while ago, where one of the things you break with strongly in Lacan's thought is this idea of binarism. All his sense of how a certain ontological question emerges shifts away for you towards a kind of epistemological problem with the enigmatic signifier. I think that also gets you free of the Derridian objection around the doctrine of the transcendental signifier in Lacan – this is what you were just saying about the phallus and your differences with Lacan. Two questions arise for me. Are you moving too close to that other end where Sartre will say, "All of this is not really unconscious but just bad faith", in so far as it is a question of knowledge? The other question is whether you have lost in any sense the confidence necessary to call a signifier a signifier in this schema. Lacan calls these things signifiers because of the very strong contrast with the x pushed down to the bottom, and I wonder if you lose that sense of signifier over and against another signifier? I think this comes back to the sign in the desert.

LAPLANCHE: I have some difficulty understanding your question exactly. One difference between Lacan and me would be that the language I refer to is not necessarily verbal language. That is important because there are all types of language, from the most organised to the less organised. Even the verbal language is not completely organised, as maybe Saussure and Jackobson thought – there are always lacks in language. The languages in which messages are sent to the child are not primarily verbal languages; for instance the primal scene is a language, is a message. As soon as you have a primal scene and you let the child listen to something of it, it becomes a message and a signifier. The other point: when I made this formula with, at the bottom, S1 over S1, it means that at this level the signifier is the signified. I see no reason not to use this. I think that at a certain point signifiers have no other signifieds than themselves. That is a point I make also in a personal way, by saying that the primacy of the signifier is a secondary one. When the signifier becomes the signified it acquires some kind of primacy, but that is a secondary primacy.

STANTON: Can we move on to look at genitality, sexual difference and the drive?

ELIZABETH COWIE: In the light of your intervention in Freud's theory of the drives, how can we understand the career of the drives in the little girl as a result of her encounter with castration?

LAPLANCHE: As I told you, I will not elaborate today the theory of feminine sexuality. I want just to try to explain that Freud's theory is very unsatisfactory, in as much as he has no proper conception of what activity and passivity are. I think there is no possibility of elaborating either male or female sexuality if you don't have an idea of that. My point is that, from a behavioural point of view, there is no way of defining activity and passivity. The best example of that is how Freud gets mixed up about lactation: when you have an infant being nursed by a woman he doesn't know who is active and who is passive from the self-preservation and behavioural point of view. For instance, Freud says in his study of Leonardo that Leonardo had a passive fantasy, with the bird coming into his mouth and so on. How can this come from the activity which is sucking the nipple, when you also say that sucking the nipple is more active than passive? You must think of being both active and passive in any kind of relationship at the biological level. Is being masochistic more passive than active? We know that masochists work in order to get satisfaction, they are very active in getting their masochistic satisfaction. I think that Freud misses completely the point of activity and passivity. He says that maybe the drives have active and passive aims, which I don't understand. Is penetration more active than receiving the penis? Why? After all it is a very superficial point of view to think the male is active and female is passive in coitus. He says that every drive, in itself, is active; it is a part of activity which wants to change the world. I would say yes, every drive is active, but is also the result of passivity, that is, our passivity towards the unconscious representations that push the drive into action. That is my point. As long as you don't have a clear idea of activity and passivity you get into ideology and say, "Well, it's too bad women are passive or women are co-active". Freud was completely taken in by this ideology. He said it is very difficult to find masculinity and femininity, but he thought he had an idea of activity and passivity which I think he didn't have. I am trying to define activity and passivity on a philosophical level, and my only point was to go back to the Cartesians, to philosophy, to define activity and passivity.

FLETCHER: This relates to and would follow on from Elizabeth's question. It is a question about how genitality is to be conceived within your theory of the drives. In *New Foundations* you say, "The human sexual drive is not initially biological, even if it does become biological at the later stage of genitality" (p.141). I want to ask what this becoming biological means. I also want to comment that it is not easy to see how the concept of *Anlehnung* could be extended from the oral or anal stages to the phallic stage in the Freudian account, because infantile masturbation and genital pleasure precede by many years the biological function of procreation which the genitals are meant to serve. On what self-preservative activity would the fantasy (or in Lacan's terms the signifier) of the phallus lean or be propped, or from what would it deviate? If there is no spontaneous autogenesis of the sexual as *New Foundations* now suggests, if primal seduction intervenes and provokes the drives, and there is no spontaneous autogenesis of the phallus as a fantasy or a signifier, how are we to understand the phallus in the phallic stage as Freud formulates it, and which he claims is undergone by both sexes? Is it the result of the mother's desire – the paternal phallus as a signifier that comes in from the mother or from the outside? If one were to move in that direction as certain moments in your work might suggest, how does this help to constitute the sexually differentiated genitality of the girl as distinct from the boy? In what sense would these be said to "become biological"? This becoming biological, after your insistence on signifiers and fantasy, is puzzling in relation to the question of the phallus and genitality.

LAPLANCHE: My answer is the same: there is no possibility for me to re-construct the whole theory of sexuality. But I think I was speaking there more of the final stage of genitality, which is not the phallic stage. I was talking much more of adolescent sexuality, where effectively the fantasy life has to merge in some way with biological excitation. As for the phallic stage, I won't say that there is a biological impact, for me the phallic stage is really 90 per cent on the fantasy level; especially it is a way of organising the world around the principle of contradiction, the way in which for human beings the principle of contradiction is imposed upon the subject. The first way of going into the logic of computers, or Boule, or Aristotle is the castration complex. When I was talking of becoming or merging with the biological I was not speaking especially of the first genital organisation, not the infantile genital organisation but the adult genital organisation.

FLETCHER: Could you say something of what it means to talk of the "becoming biological" of the adult?

LAPLANCHE: It has to merge with the excitation; I cannot give much more explanation.

STANTON: Can we go on to primal fantasy?

COWIE: My question relates to fantasy and the relation between fantasy and disavowal. In the formulation of fantasy which you and Pontalis present, a central theme is the *mise en scène* of desire and the suggestion of multiple entries for the subject. This idea of the *mise en scène* has been widely adopted, particularly in my own own field in work on representation and narrative. It seems to me that the mobility, indeed lability, of the fantasy, with its diverse and interchangeable places, is opposed to the fixity of fetishism and its array of objects, characteristically related to disavowal. However, this may only be the case if we privilege the fetishes themselves (raincoats, shoes, corsets etc.) without considering the role of disavowal. In disavowal we have the structure: "I know very well, but all the same...", that is, Freud says, two contradictory realities or knowledges which exist alongside each other without directly influencing each other. The main example of disavowal discussed by Freud is fetishism itself, that is, disavowal of the woman's lack of the penis or of her castration. However, Freud also emphasises that this same function, which he describes as a splitting of the ego, also occurs in other situations. He gives the cases of two young male patients, both of whom had failed to take cognizance of their father's death and neither of whom became psychotic. But Freud notes, just as with the fetishist, these two patients had not simply erased this knowledge wholly, but only in relation to certain areas of thinking and activity, while in other areas it was clearly acknowledged. So that one patient complained that his father was still alive and was hindering his activities, while at the same time he was carrying on as if entitled to regard himself as his father's successor. This is the example of disavowal. Here reality has been remodelled in a way more satisfying and acceptable for the subject in a process very similar to that which Freud sees in fantasy, in his paper 'The Loss of Reality in Neurosis and Psychosis' (1924). In fantasy too there is a disavowal in so far as the positions set out in this *mise en scène* of desire are both interchangeable and in a sense mutually exclusive. That is, fantasy allows us to be in more than one position at the same time, to be the father and the mother for the child in the same scenario. How far, therefore, might one be justified in seeing fantasy and disavowal as the same process, or as aspects of the same process?

LAPLANCHE: I would say there is a big difference between being able to enter the fantasy from the many entrances that are possible, which is after all the flexibility of fantasy, and the disavowal of splitting where maybe two entrances are privileged but are completely distinct from each other. I think that in perversions what is more striking is the fact that not all entrances are possible, but just one or two are privileged. I wouldn't think of them both as the same: they are two very different ways of acting with fantasy.

FLETCHER: My question is about primal fantasy in your 1964 essay, translated into English as 'Fantasy and the Origins of Sexuality', and which has had quite a bit of currency in Britain. I want to ask first about the interpretation of Freud's primal fantasies in that essay, and then a second question about your own position as outlined in *New Foundations*. In the 1964 essay, the trio of primal fantasies as described by Freud is positioned partly in relation to his 1908 paper 'On the Sexual Theories of Children', and the speculations in fantasy by children around two leading questions – "Where do babies come from?" and "What is the difference between the sexes?" In your 1964 paper you use that reference back to Freud's paper in order to offer an overall conceptualisation of the primal fantasies as answers to questions, as subjective myths of origin. I will quote from that paper: "Like myths, the primal fantasies claim to provide a representation of and a solution to the major enigmas that confront the child. Whatever appears to the subject as something needing an explanation or theory is dramatised as a moment of emergence, the beginning of a history. Fantasies of origins: the primal scene pictures the origin of the individual; fantasies of seduction, the origin and upsurge of sexuality; fantasies of castration, the origin of the difference between the sexes" (p.19). The three scenes are distinguished in terms of a particular enigma to which they are the imaginary elaboration of a solution. What I would like to observe about the primal fantasies is the centrality of the paternal figure in all three scenes as described by Freud, so that the primal fantasies would seem to entail, not just the general theme of seduction or the general theme of castration but prototypically *the father's* castration of the son, *the father's* seduction of the daughter. These Oedipal fantasies that position the subject as son or daughter form a triptych on either side of "the primal scene", which is the fantasy of sadistic parental coupling. It seems to me that all three scenes are haunted by the fantasy of castration and they are dominated by the fantasy of the phallic, castrating father. What I want to pose is this question. In interpreting or understanding these notions in Freud's own texts, don't the three scenes represent less three separate enigmas, than different ways of relating to this fantasy of the phallic or castrating father; different modalities in fantasy, different ways in which the fantasising subject is positioned by entering into these fantasies, taking up a position as son or daughter in relation to this fantasm of the phallic father? As the 1964 essay observes, Freud never explicitly theorised a relationship between these three scenes and the Oedipus, they just lie side by side. I am wondering if there isn't a latent but very strong connection between Freud's conception of the Oedipus and his account of the primal fantasies, such that the primal fantasies as not just the *mise en scène* of desire in general but specifically the *mise en scène* of the Oedipus, and the symbolic father is, as it were, the protagonist of the primal fantasies. So that there is a very strong phallocentric and patrocentric drama being played out in these three scenes.

LAPLANCHE: What you say is true. I think this moment of the primal fantasies in Freud is the moment when Freud is the most Freudian or Lacanian as possible, and also the most structuralist as possible. We gave expression to that in our article: we didn't say we agreed but we gave expression to that. My personal position is completely different. I don't think of seduction as primarily a fantasy, nor as a material reality. It may be there are fantasies of seduction, there are real scenes of seduction, abusers and so on, but the fundamental of seduction is neither of these, it is an actual situation of children in relation to the adult world they are entering. I put a complete dissymmetry between seduction and the other fantasies and I would rather think of the two other fantasies as modes of seduction, ways to convey enigmas to the child. As for the father, I would not put the father at the centre of everything, like Freud or Lacan. I am not Freudian or Lacanian in that I would completely agree that on this point Lacan was a good interpreter of Freud, he just pushed Freud to his maximum of phallocentric explanation. On this point, I am not Freudian.

STANTON: There are many more questions, however I will open questions to the floor at this point.

NICOLA DIAMOND: I just wanted to go back to my obsession, which is the instincts. There are two common movements of thought. One movement says that there is this biological foundation which provides the basis for self-preservation, and acts as a model or prop for representation which is to come with sexuality which in turn elaborates it: you have ingestion and this develops into incorporation, and so on. There is another movement, which is that the organic always already requires supplementation; because it is immature, it lacks, it is incomplete. With the first model in which biology is already there, inbuilt, there is the idea of an inbuilt homeostatic system. My problem with this model is, how does the other enter into this identity given to the biological structure? It seems to me that the second model is much more preferable because with the supplementation by the other, with the seduction if you like, comes an establishment of the function. So that the functions are forged through relationships – to mother who stimulates the child, who feeds and helps the child shit, and not only to mother but also to the environment. If we take the second model, we have a notion of homeostasis which isn't simply fixed by biology but can alter according to the forms of stimulation that the mother provides. I am concerned about this because of the way that bodies, the organic, can go mad; that not only are there dysfunctions of a hysterical form, but there can be an undecided moment between the organic and the hysterical conversion where the body goes mad and this can't be attributed simply to an organic causality. I am interested in this because in some ways we have to challenge the distinction between actual neurosis and psychical neurosis, in so far as we have to allow for a compulsion to repeat (as referred to by Joyce McDougall) with the issue of organic dysfunction. It is the problem of thinking about the instincts as having a preordained identity, and the instincts as always already immature and lacking and therefore offering an entry for a relation to others.

LAPLANCHE: I would agree with what you say; I don't think I have much to add except that it is a phylogenetic speculation to think of the instincts in human beings as being immature and incomplete. We have to suppose this but it has to be balanced by an alternative consideration, because we cannot say there are no instincts in human beings: there are instincts. We know that civilization enters at a point where the instinct is not sufficient.

NICOLA DIAMOND: Sometimes there can be a confusion between the two models and that can lead to only understanding somatic dysfunction in terms of a discharge of tension (the Freudian model) which has been taken up by the psychosomaticians in Paris, and has been taken up by Joyce McDougall, because they can't think symbolisation or the failure of symbolisation in relation to the organic.

LAPLANCHE: I would agree. Between actual neurosis and psychical neurosis there must not be a complete separation. There is always a part of both in any neurosis. The French school was wrong, in that they thought of psychosomatic as pure psychosomatic, as a domain completely outside of symbolisation.

NICOLA DIAMOND: That relates to the psychotic elements that you were perhaps talking about in relation to the unconscious, that which is not symbolised, which is a different notion of "outside symbolisation" to one which is a pure physicality in a traditional sense.

MICHAEL PARSONS: This will be rather an abrupt change of key after such an abstract, theoretical discussion, but I can't help being interested to know, as a practising psychoanalyst in the British tradition (where we are not so accustomed to thinking like this), what difference this makes to what you do in your consulting room? As you have developed your ideas, I would be very interested to know what change you found yourself making in your practice? How has it influenced the way you handled the clinical situation with a patient?

LAPLANCHE: There will not be, I hope, anything like "a Laplancheian analyst". [M.P.: There's one!] No, I am not a Laplancheian analyst. The difference is that I pay much more attention to helping the patient analyse than to help him construct. I am careful not to give my constructions as the patient's constructions. Also I pay great attention in the transference to what is the transference of the main enigmas of the patient, more than to positive psychic contents. Not just to say, "You have the same relationship to me as to your father, or to your mother", but to leave place in the relationship for the question, "What does he [the analyst] really think about me?". That has to be the centre of analysis, of transference, in my opinion.

MICHAEL PARSONS: That is familiar to me, that sort of thinking about the clinical situation. If I try to tie it to some of the concepts you have been talking about theoretically I might think, for example, that you would think it is particularly important not inadvertently to seduce the patient. If you think seduction is a very pervasive phenomenon, more so than people have realised in the past, then there are traps of being seductive towards the patient which it becomes particularly important not to fall into.

LAPLANCHE: Well, there are several ways of seducing. I think of the analytic situation, as such, as seducing. From the very beginning analysis is seduction in the way I think of primal seduction, that is as a relationship to the enigma. There is no patient who is coming into analysis who doesn't have behind himself or even explicit this question, "What does he think of what I am?" This enigma has to remain, not be filled; but be the centre of the elaboration. Now as for positive seduction, not just seduction in gestures and so on, but even seductions through imposing particular views, it is wrong, and I agree with you. That is filling the situation with contents of your own.

QUESTION: My difficulty is the opposition between seduction and freeing, which I have always understood to be the purpose of analysis. Of the little I know of the work of Christopher Bollas, there are similarities: the fact that the analysand does the work, is freed to do work. So that I would have thought that one of the main problems in analysis is for both partners to be equally aware of the problem and possibility of seduction, and for that also to enter into discourse.

LAPLANCHE: There are several roles for the analyst. I put very much emphasis on holding, as I think of analysis as *Lösung*, that is, destruction. I work with the method of Freud which is a method of destruction, debinding, of undoing the bindings. You cannot have an unbinding without something holding some boundary, because it could be just a psychotic way of acting. The binding and holding are, I think, an important contribution of Winnicott and many others. Another point is an emphasis on method, because I think there is no analysis without coming back and back again to Freud's method. Not just interpreting, giving what I would call a pre-Freudian interpretation. Interpretation in Freud's sense goes step by step: you have a patient go step by step from one representation to the other, and reminding him of those steps, which is an important rule in the analytic situation. I place very much stress on the method.

QUESTION: I am interested in the relation between the enigmatic and destructive elements in analysis. You talked about analysis as destructive or dissolving. In *New Foundations* you put forward the Sphinx as the enigmatic figure, but also a violent figure. What is the connection between something being enigmatic and being violent?

LAPLANCHE: The Sphinx in the end is a figure of self-violence, it is an image that cannot be completed in the analytic situation. I just gave this as an instance of an enigma, which is always an enigma for the one who puts the enigma. An enigma is not just to ask a question of which you have the answer; it is a question for which even you are not to have an answer. This is why I gave this example, because so much did she not have the answer that when she received it she committed suicide. But that is not an image for the analyst!

STANTON: I would like to thank the panel and Professor Laplanche, who made an inspired attempt to answer the questions put to him.

After Events

The Letter in the Unconscious: The enigmatic signifier in the work of Jean Laplanche

John Fletcher

The thought of Jean Laplanche has shown a striking consistency across its various shifts and changes, a consistency that Laplanche himself represents as a spiral, a movement of return that changes and moves on what it returns to, generating further possible shifts and movements rather than the closed circle of pure repetition. To the English language reader what is noticeable, from the joint paper written with Serge Leclaire on 'The Unconscious' (1960) through the archæological excavations of the primal fantasies with J-B. Pontalis (1964) to *Life and Death in Psychoanalysis* (1970) and the more recent five volumes of the *Problématiques* (1980–7) summarised in *New Foundations for Psychoanalysis* (1987), is the persistent concern with the systematicity of the Unconscious, the status of the elements that compose it and its articulation with the differentiated dimensions of the 'vital order' and its biological functions, the ego and its homeostases, and the processes of language and symbolisation.[1]

In 1960 Laplanche began his defence of the Freudian metapsychology of the Unconscious by posing the question, 'Is the unconscious a meaning or a letter?' Against Politzer's phenomenological reduction of the Unconscious to a meaning immanent within manifest phenomena, as in the relation of a theme to the play that embodies it or the rules of tennis to a particular match, Laplanche insists on Freud's realism of the Unconscious as a separate mental system, a second structure. He defends and seeks to elaborate those features of the Freudian conception, its impersonality or 'abstraction' and its realism, that are least acceptable to a psychology of consciousness. Where Politzer demands that, 'what is expressed in the manifest content as the act of an I, should not be reduced at the latent level to an interaction of psychical things' ('The Unconscious', p.119), protesting against the Freudian metapsychology of agencies and forces, Laplanche insists on an alternative to either mechanism or the first person. He points out that Freud's account of the dream-thoughts demonstrates 'that an utterance may take place "in person" – without, however, being in the first person, but in the alienated form of the second or third person.' When 'it talks' (*ça parle*), it does not necessarily do so in the I-voice; which leads Laplanche to speculate, 'We may wonder whether the defining characteristic of unconscious structures is not that they include voices other than that of the "first person"' (ibid, p.120). In this condensed but suggestive proposition we may hear anticipations of the theme of the primitive, pre-subjectivised forms of the primal fantasies as scenarios with multiple entries, as well as the concern with the other of personal pre-history and his/her residues, so central to *New Foundations*.

As Laplanche indicates, it is lacunary phenomena that are posited at the origin of the hypothesis of the Unconscious. The attention to the defective and lacunary nature of consciousness that Freud recommends leads to the inference of another system of mental contents that is distinguished from the manifest, and whose interpolation allows an intelligible and coherent sequence to be established. Rather than the implicit or occluded meaning of the manifest, what we have, Laplanche argues, is a fragment of discourse, an absent letter or inscription that must find its place in the chain of conscious representations and with which it enters into a dynamic relationship. What is entailed is a topography of psychic sites or places – the Unconscious as 'an other scene' – between which relations of force obtain.

The initial concern of this early piece is with the question of 'the double inscription' in Freud's 1915 paper, 'The Unconscious'. This poses a particular solution to the problem of the relation between the conscious and unconscious forms of a given idea or mental representation. Freud canvasses alternative explanations: an economic hypothesis that sees a particular representation subjected to cathexis, first by one system then another, such that its appearance in consciousness abolishes its presence in the Unconscious. The alternative hypothesis of the double inscription would entail not the passage of a representation from one system to another, but a second, further registration within the preconscious-conscious system co-existing with and not automatically effacing the unconscious inscription. While the second hypothesis has the support of the common clinical experience that an analytic interpretation, while producing a conscious representation of a repressed content, does not in itself necessarily abolish its unconscious effects, Freud does not thereby decide in its favour. Laplanche intervenes within this Freudian debate firmly on the side of the hypothesis of the double inscription and he does so in what one can see in retrospect is an uneasy alliance with Lacan's then recently formulated dictum that the Unconscious is 'structured like a language'.

The Unconscious Structured as a Language

The ensuing debate in which Lacan differentiates his position from Laplanche's can be summed up in the two opposed formulations: Laplanche's proposition that 'the unconscious is the precondition of language' and Lacan's angry reversal, 'Now, what I say is that language is the condition for the unconscious' and further that 'the unconscious [is] the logical implication of language: in effect, no unconscious without language'.[2] What is at stake here is the Lacanian dictum hovering ambiguously between homology and identification – (Fr. 'structuré comme un langage', Eng. 'structured like/as a language'). One can read the 1960 paper as the process by which Laplanche modifies and then comes to reject Lacan's formula: more or less explicitly in the Postscript of 1965, while attempting to sustain it amidst its difficulties in the main body of the text. Section IV of the essay ('The Unconscious is the Precondition of Language') begins with the Lacanian identification of the primary process – 'the free flow of libidinal energy along the paths of displacement and condensation' – with the fundamental laws of linguistics (Saussure's syntagmatic and paradigmatic operations, the rhetorical tropes of metonymy and metaphor). However, it immediately goes on to consider the Freudian obstacle to Lacan's assimilation of linguistic and primary processes, i.e. Freud's explicit location of language in the preconscious system and the secondary process that characterises it: the binding of energy and representations into relatively stable forms in the sphere of the ego and in language through the logical operations of negation, judgement, the law of non-contradiction and the rules of syntax that govern the formation of sentences and propositions (rather than the level of phonemes and morphemes). These secondary process characteristics – negation, non-contradiction, the articulatory devices of logic and syntax – Freud insists are not to be found in in the Unconscious and its processes such as the dream-work. As Laplanche points out, the 'language' that Freud describes as functioning according to the primary processes is that of psychosis: 'In schizophrenia, words are subject to the same process as that which makes dream-images out of latent thoughts, and which we have called the *primary mental process*. They undergo condensation and... displacement... On occasion the dream-work treats words as things and then creates very similar "schizophrenic" utterances or neologisms.'[3]

Having set up the problem Laplanche asks, 'How can we get out of this contradiction?' The contradiction in question is that between Freud's metapsychological placing of language in the preconscious as the site of the secondary processes, and Lacan's 'unconscious structured as a language'. As Laplanche observes, a certain regulation has to be introduced into the primary process for ordinary communicative language to exist. He does not look for this regulation, however, in the sphere of the secondary processes and those aspects of language that Saussure explicitly brackets out of his synchronic model (*langue* as distinct from *parole*), specifically syntax, sentence formation, the realm of discourse as described by Benveniste.[4] As if in loyalty to Lacan's linguistic reading of the Unconscious, Laplanche turns to the Freudian thesis of primary repression and uses Lacan's linguistic mapping of metaphorical substitution to supply what he calls the ballast, the necessary fixity and regulation to contain the ceaseless circulation of the primary processes.

The Lacanian identification/homology of language and the Unconscious is based on a particular interested reading or rewriting of Saussure and Jakobson that destabilises the Saussurian correlation of signifier and signified in the sign by absolutising the diacritical relations between signifiers. Not only is the signifier constituted only by the play of its differences from other signifiers ('... in language there are only differences *without positive terms*'[5]), but the signified is reduced from its status as a distinct order that is articulated with the order of signifiers through a process of what Saussure calls a 'reciprocal delimitation of units' (ibid p.112). In asserting the primacy of the signifier, Lacan places the signified as simply the effect of the play of differences between signifiers in the movement through the signifying chain. As the signifier acts only through its relation to other signifiers, the signified 'insists' in the chain of signifiers but cannot 'consist' in a one-to-one correlation with any one element in the chain. This produces, in Lacan's much-cited phrase, 'an incessant sliding of the signified under the signifier' and a striking metaphorical analogy with Freud's description of the primary process that is the ground of his identification of them. Indeed he explicitly identifies this diacritical instability or 'sliding' of language with the Freudian *enstellung* (the distortion and transposition of terms found in the unconscious dreamwork).[6]

The inadequacy of the Saussurian model of language, its exclusion of the processes of syntax and predication from the language system, means that it cannot give an account of discourse as such. Lacan's maximisation of its diacritical elements is even less able to account for the relative stabilities of ordinary discourse. There is then a double problem: 'the unconscious structured as a language' not only runs into the Freudian obstacle (Freud's metapsychological placing of language as preconscious, its characterisation by secondary process features), but produces in a grotesque reversal of Lacan's dictum, either as its pretext or its consequence, a schizophrenic account of discourse as 'an incessant sliding' – language structured like the Unconscious. Laplanche clearly recognises this problem when he acknowledges that, despite the resistance to any crossing over from a signifier to a signified in a stable signification that is implied by the bar in the Lacanian reading of the algorithm S/s (signifier/signified), an account must be given of 'the openness of language to the world of meanings' (p 153).

To do this Laplanche mobilises the Freudian thesis of a necessary, if mythical, moment of primary repression that institutes the primal repressed as a nucleus of representations at the kernel of the Unconscious as a second structure. Freud's account of secondary or after-repression, repression proper, describes a double process whereby a given representation is excluded from consciousness by the withdrawal of cathexis by the preconscious system and its redeployment in a substitute representation (anti-cathexis), while simultaneously the excluded representation is drawn into the unconscious system through associative pathways that connect it with the already repressed. This double process necessarily implies an originary primal repression whose sole mechanism Freud argues is anti-cathexis and 'which consists in the psychical (ideational) representative of the instinct being denied entrance into the conscious. With this a *fixation* is established; the representative in question persists unaltered from then onwards and the instinct remains attached to it.'[7] Freud in effect outlines something like a binding process whereby the formation of a substitute at once excludes and fixates. The excluded representation is preserved as the permanent site of the drive (*trieb*, Strachey's instinct). The primal repressed consists of the representatives of the drives fixed, stabilized in a provisional structure.

Laplanche maps this stabilizing action of primal repression in terms of Lacan's formula for metaphor as a substitution of signifiers 'one of which has taken the place of the other in the signifying chain, the occulted signifier remaining present through its (metonymic) connexion with the rest of the chain', ('The Agency of the Letter', p.157). In doing so he borrows from Lacan two notions: the *points de capiton*, (literally the buttons that hold down upholstery), a highly metaphorical designation of certain privileged capping points where the chain of signifiers is said to be fixed to a signified. This is sometimes exemplified in the effect of the final signifier in the signifying chain, such as the end of a sentence, where the meaning of each word is in suspension until the final word retroactively precipitates the meaning of the whole. However, without any specification of syntactical or propositional structures this remains a minimal if not vacuous gesture towards the solution of the problem of the perpetual sliding of meaning in Lacan's account of language. Laplanche maps primal repression as a fixing or capping (*capitonnage*) of the primary process through a metaphor-like substitution in a schema taken from Lacan's account of the paternal metaphor.

$$\frac{S'}{S} \times \frac{S}{s} \rightarrow S' \times \frac{1}{s}$$

Here the new signifier S′ implanted into the signifying relation S/s displaces the original signifier which results in a change of name whereby S′ now comes to signify s. To this extent the disappearance of S is 'like' the mathematical operation whereby a particular signifier is 'simplified out'. Lacan's version of the formula in his paper on psychosis from where Laplanche takes it, seems to indicate this.

$$\frac{S}{\$'} \cdot \frac{\$'}{x} \rightarrow S\left(\frac{1}{s}\right)$$

Lacan comments, 'The elision of S′, represented here by the bar through it, is the condition of the success of the metaphor'.[8] However, as Lacan's general definition of metaphor indicates, the original signifier has not been abolished but 'falls to the rank of signified, and, as latent signifier, perpetuates the interval onto which another chain of signifiers can be grafted' (Laplanche and Leclaire, p.160). Playing with mathematical conventions Laplanche attempts to represent this ambiguity of the displaced element in a second formula.

$$\frac{S'}{S} \times \frac{S}{s} \rightarrow \frac{\;\frac{S'}{s}\;}{\;\frac{S}{S}\;}$$

This, he argues, is the diagram for repression, 'in which what had been "simplified out" in preconscious speech has been preserved on another line' (p.157). By a certain legerdemain, Laplanche has treated a linguistic formalisation as a mathematical one, in the words of Lacan's criticism, taking the line separating signifier and signified in (Lacan's version of) Saussure's algorithm as the bar indicating Euclidean proportion within the mathematical fraction (a possibility that does seem to be suggested in the layout of Lacan's original formula) (Lemaire, p.xiii).

Laplanche points out the surprising identity of the two terms in the unconscious chain S/S which appear simultaneously as signifier and signified, numerator and denominator. This, he claims, illustrates Freud's solution to the problem of the double inscription. From a consideration of the peculiarities of schizophrenic word usage (language structured as the Unconscious) in the 1915 essay, Freud concludes, 'We now seem to know all at once what the difference is between a conscious and an unconscious presentation' ('The Unconscious', p.207). They are not just different registrations of the same content in different sites, nor different functional states of cathexis, but rather the conscious presentation consists of the presentation of the thing (sensory traces, primarily visual) together with the word presentation (acoustic traces of the word), while the unconscious presentation consists only of the thing presentation. What repression denies to the unconscious presentation is 'translation into words' (p.207). Laplanche connects this to Freud's *conditions of representability* that entail a topographical regression in the dreamwork to the 'language' of images (which was the moment of Freud's primary theoretical recognition that logic, syntax and the stabilizing articulations of conscious discourse are not to be found in the Unconscious). Laplanche concludes that, while the distinction between signifier and signified characterises the preconscious chain, in the unconscious chain there are only thing presentations, images. Here the distinction between signifier and signified collapses as the thing presentations, Laplanche argues, function as both: 'the signifying image refers to nothing but itself as signified' (p.163) – hence S/S.

The sense of strain and the moments of obscurity in this controversial Section IV from the 1960 paper come from what reads like an attempt to articulate two rather different metapsychologies of language, Freud's and Lacan's; to deploy Freud's 'solution' to the question of the double inscription and his account of primary repression to address the problems of the

Unconscious structured as a language (which are not Freud's problems). The incessant sliding of the signified produced by Lacan's assimilation of linguistic and primary processes is hived off by Laplanche to a mythic stage prior to primary repression in his 'Fiction of Language in a Reduced State' (the oscillation of phonemes in the *fort/da* game). In Laplanche's account, the action of primary repression inscribes 'certain "*key-signifiers*" placed in a metaphorising position, and to which is assigned, because of their special weight, the property of ordering the whole system of human language.' (p.160) They are conceived as giving an anchorage or ballast 'which removes languages from the exclusive domination of the primary process' (p.152), its incessant sliding.

Lacan's rejection of Laplanche's argument centres in part on the question of determination: it is language that is the precondition of the Unconscious and not the reverse. He rejects the metaphor of ballast or anchoring, for although it 'may provide an image, it may give a reflection of what experience confronts us with ... it is quite incapable of accounting for the dissociative, if not explosive, effect of the return of the repressed.' (Lemaire, p.126). According to Lemaire, Lacan also rejects the Freudian notion of a fixing of an instinct to a representative in primary repression that is the ground for Laplanche's postulation of an anchoring correlation or function, as this would compromise, he argues, the radical separation of the two systems. Lacan's defence of the double inscription thesis argues that, while a formally identical 'signifier' may be reduplicated in both systems, nevertheless 'each of the two inscriptions, supported, then, by the same signifier, has a different import because of the site of its support' (Lemaire, p.250).

What remains contested is the status of unconscious representations and their relation, determining or determined, to conscious representations. Laplanche's claim here, that certain privileged unconscious representations have the power to stabilise the whole system of language, is clearly misconceived. It is the product of an attempt to meet the absences and limitations of the Saussurian heritage and of its Lacanian rescension, which need a properly linguistic redress from an understanding of language as a hierarchy of levels of articulation, governed by successively more various and complex rules of combination, from the contrastive features of the phoneme up to the predicative and performative operations of sentences and their combination in the various genres of discourse. What the Lacanian formulæ for metaphor do allow, however, is the analysis of specific formations of the Unconscious within which the primal repressed can be inferred in their effects, the skewings, intensities and lacunae of the field of conscious discourse.

The 1965 Postscript returns to Lacan's provocative claim that the Unconscious is structured like a language, in order to retain from it the proposition that the reality of the Unconscious is 'of the *same type* as that of the letter of a text' (p.176), in which Laplanche argues the two Freudian discoveries overlap of the meaningfulness, the signifying force of phenomena hitherto considered as meaningless – dreams, amnesias, slips of the tongue and pen etc. – the formations of the Unconscious, and of their conflictual nature, marked by substitution and compromise. However, he goes on to insist that 'the Freudian Unconscious and the language of the linguists are in ...radical opposition to each other' (p.177). The dangers of the Lacanian formulation, he warns, are of a reduction of the specificity of the Freudian Unconscious and of the differences between unconscious and conscious representations and their modes of interrelation, on the one hand, and on the other 'a subversion of linguistic concepts ... furnishing custom-made a certain notion of language, in order subsequently to show easily enough that the Unconscious functions no differently' (p.177). In particular, he rejects Lacan's equation of the rhetorical figures of metaphor and metonymy with the primary processes of displacement and condensation, retaining the linguistic model of metaphor as a signifying substitution 'to illustrate the mechanism of repression as it functions *between* Unconscious and Preconscious, *between* primary and secondary processes' (p.177), a mechanism that is inter-systemic rather than intra-systemic.

What Laplanche remains faithful to in his later development is the notion of certain key representations that in binding the drives have an organising power to outline a preliminary constitution of the Unconscious as a separate domain. The system of such representations, distinct from verbal language, is the minimal or residual version of Lacan's dictum that the main text retains. It proposes the obsolete term 'imago' for these elementary units of unconscious discourse, Freud's thing representations drawn from the predominantly visual register, and 'promoted to the dignity of signifiers' (p.162). The problem remains of what the term 'signifier' could mean in a context where, according to Laplanche, its distinction from the signified collapses, and where the nature of the signifying chain or combinatory within which it acquires its signifying capacity – the network of the other 'key signifiers', the primal repressed – remains largely unspecified. All these issues and problems are returned to by Laplanche to be reworked in different contexts. The key-signifiers and their relation to primal repression reappear as the enigmatic signifier, the centre piece of a reworked theory of the drives, of primal seduction and the relation to the other. The issues of inscription, fixation and mobility, the different levels of organisation of unconscious fantasies and complexes taken up at the close of Section IV, point forward to the crucial archæological work that he was to begin with Pontalis on the primal fantasies. It is through a brief consideration of these that the more recent work on the enigmatic signifier can be situated.

The Temporality of Seduction

The 1964 essay with Pontalis, 'Fantasy and the Origins of Sexuality', addresses the Freudian postulate of an unconscious nucleus that would act as a template for the psychical productions – symptoms and their underlying fantasies – which Freud encountered in analysis, and that would explain both the apparently universal repetition of the same fantasmatic scenes – castration, paternal seduction and parental coitus – and the variety of their embodiments, by reference to some grounding event or reality. Laplanche and Pontalis indicate the different paradigms in Freud's thought that gain dominance at different periods without ever entirely banishing their rivals. The earliest, the seduction theory, traced the sexual fantasies underlying hysterical and obsessional symptoms to actual events of sexual seduction in childhood, that remained unintegrated and inactive until the traumatic activation of their memory traces by later events after puberty. Despite the apparent supersession of the seduction theory by the theory of an endogenous infantile sexuality with its libidinal stages of development, where an innate sexual constitution replaces the determining power of the external event (and where the object of explanation shifts from neurosis to sexual development in general), Freud does not cease to grant a determining force to actual parental threats of castration or witnessed scenes of parental intercourse (as in the case studies of Little Hans and the Wolf Man). It is in the Wolf Man case (1914) that Freud shifts from a painstaking attempt to reconstruct the primal originating event of an actual trauma to the suggestion that the primal scenes are primal fantasies, the inherited memory traces of events that took place, not in the subject's childhood, but in the pre-history of the human race. They are the traces of actual events from the period of the Darwinian primal horde, the savage dramas of the *Urvater* or primal father and his rebellious sons as elaborated in the notorious final chapter of *Totem and Taboo* (1913). An inaccessible biography is replaced by an imaginary anthropology as the bedrock of the real event.

Freud's speculative and untenable doctrine of phylogenesis whereby individual development, ontogeny, repeats the development of the species, phylogeny, through the reactivation of inherited memory traces, is interpreted by Laplanche and Pontalis as something like a theoretical symptom, a false synthesis, produced by the attempt to escape a conceptual impasse, the imprisoning either/or of the external event and the innate constitution. What Freudian phylogenesis represents, they suggest, is an intuition of structure, the postulation of a reality that has 'an autonomous and structural status with regard to the subject who is totally dependent upon it' ('Fantasy and the Origins of Sexuality' p.17). It is 'an organisation made of signifiers anteceding the effect of the event... a pre-structure inaccessible to the subject, evading his grasp, his initiatives...' (p.17–18). What we have here is a concern with an unconscious and heterogeneous nucleus, not reducible to either the biological instincts or repressed memories of the subject, that acts as the conditions of possibility for unconscious meaning, whether conceived as a specific signifying chain, network or combinatory. What is opened up is the space of a symbolic order and a relation to an other that is, if not primordial, then at least already given in advance, and not reducible to either a real event or an imaginary scene.

This is clear in Laplanche and Pontalis's return to the officially superseded but in fact never entirely abandoned seduction theory and its strange temporal logic of *Nachträglichkeit* (Strachey's 'deferred action' which Laplanche now suggests translating as 'afterwardsness'). Here the trauma of seduction takes place, not as the breaking in or flooding of the ego's defences by painful and unmasterable excitations whose discharge is either instantaneous or delayed (as in the obsolete theory of abreaction), but in the interval between two events. The first is an event sexual for the adult but non-sexual for the child (Freud's phrase is 'pre-sexually sexual') and the second, the occasion for the traumatic outbreak, a non-sexual and 'innocent' event to which the subject's response seems excessive and unintelligible. In the instantiation of this schema in the case of Emma in the *Project for a Scientific Psychology* (1895), Freud traces back the associative pathways between the two events and the role of certain symbolic elements (the shop as *mise en scène*, the shop-keeper or assistants as agents, the repeated signifier of the subject's clothes), by means of which the second event retroactively evokes the first such that its sexual meaning is now precipitated. What Laplanche and Pontalis retrieve from this temporal dialectic of the premature and the belated are two emphases. Firstly, 'sexuality literally breaks in from the outside... reaches the subject from *the other*', where its traces remain unintegrated and 'encysted'; secondly, after the events of puberty, the traumatic unpleasure 'is traced to the recollection of the first event, an external event which has become an inner event, an inner 'foreign body', which now breaks out from within the subject' (p.10). This is what Freud described as the *proton pseudos*, a primal deceit or fallacy, which is, as Laplanche puts it in a fuller discussion in *Life and Death in Psychoanalysis*, 'as though there existed in the facts themselves a fundamental duplicity' (p.34). In the interplay between two scenes, a moment of inscription and a moment of re-inscription or translation (a term that is to become central to Laplanche's later work), there arises a sexual and traumatic representation of a scene that was for the subject neither sexual nor traumatic in its happening as an event.

It is within the temporal matrix of *Nachträglichkeit*, with its problematic of the other and the other's signifying residues, the internal foreign body,[9] that we can see emerging the elements that will transform Freud's 'special case' theory of infantile seduction and trauma into a general theory of primal seduction and the enigmatic signifier. This account of an internalized exteriority, 'a kind of *internal-external instance*... a "*spine in the flesh*"... *a veritable spine in the protective wall of the ego*' (ibid. p.42), displaces the dualism of constitution and event, and has an analogy with that coincidence of the intimate and the alien that Lacan was to go on to call *extimité*. 'The extimate is simultaneously the intimate kernel and the foreign body; in a word, it is *unheimlich* ... beyond the division into "psychic" and "real" that deserves to be called the Real in the Lacanian sense.'[10] Despite their different metapsychological sitings – where Lacan's *extimité* has affiliations with the order of the Real, the enigmatic signifier is Laplanche's displacement of the Lacanian Symbolic – the similarity of their conceptual configuration is striking.

The 1964 essay suggests a structural interpretation of the Freudian thesis of phylogenesis, which it surrounds, however, with a certain caution. 'It is tempting to accept', they write, Freud's postulation of a phylogenetic pre-structure of primal fantasies that determine the subject's imaginary activity 'as a pre-figuration of the 'symbolic order' defined by Levi-Strauss and Lacan in the ethnological and psychoanalytic fields respectively' ('Fantasy...' p.17). Freudian phylogenesis would then figure as a premature structuralism *avant la lettre*. It is in the space vacated by this rejected hypothesis of a phylogenetic heritage of scenes and memories that act as a nucleus for the Unconscious, a nucleus given from the outside, from the archaic or primal other, that *New Foundations* installs the thesis of primal seduction and the enigmatic signifier. At least some of the work of Freud's conception of the primal fantasies as an organising nucleus is taken over by these later concepts which are the result of a radically innovative theoretical labour of recasting Freud's problematic of *structure*, *transmission* and *enigma*, while purging it of its pseudo-biology. The temporal schema of phylogenesis we can now read as a displacement of the temporal logic of *Nachträglichkeit*, the 'motor' of primal seduction, reduced to the provision of a ground or ballast in a mythic pre-history.

Structure and Transmission

Freud himself had suggested an analogy between the primal fantasies and the Kantian transcendental categories as conditions of possibility for experience. Laplanche and Pontalis caution against this because, as *fantasies*, they possess traits, contingent and imaginary elements, that resist assimilation to a transcendental schema. Laplanche eschews the term 'structure', from a similar wariness of its 'structuralist' implications, and returns to the older Freudian term 'primal' to designate the universal foundations of the events of childhood experience. He postulates not a structure, but what he calls a primal situation, '...one in which a new-born child, an infant in the etymological sense of the word (*infans*: speechless), is confronted with the adult world' (*New Foundations*, p.90). In relation to this universal situation, both the Oedipal situation and the mother-child relation have a certain cultural contingency. 'I am using the term primal seduction to describe a fundamental situation in which an adult proffers to a child, verbal, non-verbal and even behavioural signifiers which are pregnant with unconscious sexual significations' (p.126). It is this unconscious transmission that constitutes the primal situation as a situation of seduction for Laplanche. It was just this emphasis in the 1964 essay that was the reason for the refusal of the structuralist 'temptation' – i.e. an interpretation of phylogenesis and the Oedipus within the Levi-Straussian framework of a universal law of symbolic and cultural exchange: 'By adopting this solution the analyst would feel that he had lost an essential dimension of his experience: the subject is, admittedly, located in a structure of interrelationship, but the latter is *transmitted by the parental unconscious* [my italics]. It is therefore less easy to assimilate it [i.e. the Oedipus] to a language system than to the complexities of a particular speech' ('Fantasy...', n.34, p.31). In Saussurian terms this is an emphasis, not on *la langue* (the language system or structure), but on *la parole* (the individual speech act). In *New Foundations*, however, what is thereby transmitted is what Laplanche now calls the enigmatic signifier.

The concept of the enigmatic signifier is set up in terms of the Lacanian distinction between the signifier as a signifier *of* – of a specific meaning or signified, and as a signifier *to* – as addressed to and interpellating a specific subject, a subject who may know that it is addressed to them but may not have a signified to attribute to it. The enigmatic signifier is based on 'the possibility that the signifier may be *designified*, or lose what it signifies, without thereby losing its power to signify *to*' (*New Foundations*, p.45). An important difference from the primal fantasies is that this 'signifier to' with its lost or absent signified is situated at the level of the drives, as part of a reworking of drive theory that began with the retrieval of the Freudian notion of *Anlehnung* from the *Three Essays on Sexuality* (1905), sketched in the 1964 essay and elaborated further in *Life and Death*. Initially the enigmatic signifier is implanted in the periphery of the primitive body image or skin ego and primarily anchored or inscribed in the erogenous zones. In a second stage, with the development of the ego as agency, it is subject to a primal repression and its repressed residue acts as an internal foreign element attacking the ego as agency from within. This is the import of the previously cited metaphor of the 'spine in the flesh' or in the wall of the ego (the internally projected body surface). The idea central to Freud's notion of primal repression, of a fixing of an instinct/drive to a representation, is being reworked here, only the fixing or inscription relates a bodily zone to a non-verbal signifying element that comes from without, from the other. Anticipating this conception of the 'object-source' of the drive, Laplanche writes in *Life and Death*:

> Thus preserved from all attrition by the process of repression, the fantasy [the memory traces or 'reminiscences' of seduction] becomes a permanent source of free excitation. In this detour through the introjected, fantasised scene, we rediscover the notion of the *source* of the drive... (p.42)

Laplanche completes the break begun by Freud from the register of the biological, where a non-psychical body is both the motor-power and the source of the unfolding pattern of psychological development. *New Foundations* rewrites the schema of *Anlehnung* where the specifically sexual drive emerges propped or 'leaning on' the satisfaction of particular biological needs or functions, from which it deviates through a metonymic displacement of object (from the absent object of need – e.g. the mother's milk – to its contiguous signifier, the breast) and a metaphorical extension of aim (from digestion to imaginary incorporation). The *Anlehnung* schema is now submitted to the category of primal seduction. It retains its validity, Laplanche suggests, not as an account of origins, as the spontaneous auto-genesis of the sexual from the biological, but rather as a description of their mode of articulation. This is stated very vividly in the image of the onion:

> We have here something resembling an onion with one layer of its skin peeled off, or a flower that has lost its petal. And, to make the point succinctly, onions do not peel themselves. Seduction peels what might be called a sexual layer from self-preservation. Seduction peels the onion of self-preservation; self-preservation does not split as the result of some indefinable endogenous movement. (*New Foundations*, p.145)

If, as Laplanche insists, the drives originate in parental or adult messages, then a quite radical conclusion results: 'There is no initial or natural opposition between the instinctual and the intersubjective, or between the instinctual and the cultural' (p.137). One might suggest that what appears as 'instinctual' in the field of sexuality, as pre-given, constitutional, the 'already there' that insists from within, is a *proton pseudos*, a primal deceit or fallacy, like the traumatic memory in the old seduction theory, only now masking or disguising the residues of the seductive excitations and transmissions from the other.

Enigma

One important aspect of Laplanche's earlier interpretation of the primal fantasies that survives in the new conception of primal seduction is the notion of an enigma with its trope of a question posed and a set of attempted answers. This had derived from setting the primal fantasies in the context of the sexual theories of children and their leading questions as to the origins of babies and the meaning of heterosexual difference, by reference to Freud's 1908 paper, 'On the Sexual Theories of Children' The enigma is a signification that both excites and mystifies and can only belatedly be symbolised. It is enigmatic, not just because the adult world poses questions that are beyond the child's power to grasp or answer, but because of the role of the adult and parental unconscious. Laplanche writes that, 'The *enigma* is in itself a *seduction* and its mechanisms are unconscious... The 'attentions of a mother' or the 'aggression of a father' are seductive only because they are not transparent. They are seductive because they are opaque, because they convey something enigmatic' (p.128).

Laplanche dramatises this most memorably in his account of the role of the maternal breast in the formation of the oral drive:

> Can analytic theory afford to go on ignoring the extent women unconsciously and sexually cathect the breast, which appears to be a natural organ for lactation? It is inconceivable that the infant does not notice this sexual cathexis, which might be said to be perverse in the same sense in which that term is defined in the *Three Essays*. It is impossible to imagine that the infant does not suspect that this cathexis is the source of a nagging question: what does the breast want from me, apart from wanting to suckle me, and come to that, why does it want to suckle me? (p.126)

The maternal breast, apart from satisfying needs and stimulating pleasure is an agent of maternal fantasy, transmitting a sexual excitation with a hidden or unconscious meaning, a lost signified, and so posing a question for the infant which it is constitutionally ill-equipped to answer. This has the scandalous effect of building a structurally inescapable perversity into the adult-child relation:

> In the primal situation we have, then, a child whose ability to adapt is real but limited, weak and waiting to be perverted, and a deviant adult (deviant with regard to sexual norms ... deviant or split with regard to himself) ... given that the child lives on in the adult, an adult faced with a child is particularly likely to be deviant and inclined to perform bungled or symbolic actions because he is involved in a relationship with his other self, with

> the other he once was. The child in front of him brings out the child within him ... we have a 'Traviata', someone who has been led astray and 'seduced'. (p.103)

The return to the seduction theory (and Laplanche points out *vis à vis* Masson that what is at stake is an original, theoretically articulated problematic, not just the clinical observation of abuse and its suppression), the archaeological reconstruction of the temporal schema of afterwardsness (*Nachträglichkeit*) and the relation to the other, produce a series of theoretical transformations. The seduction theory, as a theory of *primal* seduction, has become an account of the structural formation of the Unconscious and the drives through primal repression. The very term 'enigmatic signifier' is itself a trace of the theoretical spiral by which Laplanche, in returning to Freud, is also reworking the point of his original differentiation from Lacan. The phrase comes from Lacan's *écrit*, 'The Agency of the Letter in the Unconscious' (1957), where Lacan identifies the mechanism for metaphor with the formation of the symptom:

> Between the enigmatic signifier of the sexual trauma and the term that is substituted for it in an actual signifying chain there passes the spark that fixes in a symptom the signification inaccessible to the conscious subject in which that symptom may be resolved – a symptom being a metaphor in which flesh or function is taken as a signifying element. (p.166)

Here Laplanche returns to that signifier in the Unconscious, fixed by virtue of its submission to the signifying substitution of repression, and characterized by its double status as both signifier and signified. It remains a latent signifier through its relation to the sexual trauma, but it now also functions as the signified of the term that has replaced it, and their relation constitutes the inaccessible signification and potential resolution of whatever derangement of the body or its functions acts as its support. In Lacan's text its double status is a function of its occluded position as 'fallen to the rank of signified' within the structure of secondary repression (his 'flesh or function' points towards hysterical and obsessional symptoms). Laplanche's concern, however, is with primal repression and its effects within a situation or structure of seduction. Here the enigma for the subject is located in the other, the other's already constituted Unconscious, and the seductive excitations of the other's desire as it bears on the subject. It is this that will remain permanently enigmatic in the very fixity of its traces and deposits and will constitute the residue of primal repression as, in a recent formulation of Laplanche's, the 'à traduire', the (always yet?) to be translated. It is this absented signified that keeps the double status of the primal thing presentation from collapsing in on itself as a merely self-referential imago, as in the 1960 paper. The relation to the other and his/her encrypted desire and its possible meanings is inscribed in the very constitution of human subjectivity.

It is the ramifications of this double status of the enigmatic signifiers that might suggest possible answers to recent questions posed to Laplanche's work. In the Conference at the ICA included in this volume, Peter Dews asks whether there isn't a contradiction between Laplanche's strongly defended thesis of the realism of the Unconscious and his rejection of what he calls 'the apophantic illusion', the belief in 'the hidden scene that reveals all, which is self-explanatory and which does not refer to anything else' (*New Foundations*, p.115). If the latter leads to an infinite regress, as Laplanche suggests, (and the Freudian concern with the bedrock of the real event and with phylogenesis would be a case in point), would not the same thing apply to a realism of the Unconscious that implies 'determinate contents ... which ultimately can be tracked down'? (Dews, above p.75).

If we recall Laplanche's question with which we began, 'Is the Unconscious a letter or a meaning?', then it is clear that the form this 'realism' takes is that of a realism of the letter not of the meaning. It is a realism of psychic inscriptions or signifiers and their enchainment in the determinate sequences of *unconscious* fantasy (the always unconscious second stage of the beating fantasy Freud analyses), not of the situational or narrative signifieds or derivatives that emerge into consciousness as memories, screen-memories or fantasies (the fragmentary memories of the first stage or the conscious fantasies of the third stage of the beating fantasy).[11]

Laplanche invokes the distinction made by Freud between material reality or the reality of the event, the psychological field, and what he called 'unconscious wishes reduced to their most fundamental and truest shape ... psychical reality',[12] identifying 'psychical reality' with the reality of the signifier whose signified is absented from the signifying exchange by the already constituted Unconscious of the other. 'Psychical reality' is not, however, simply given, whether endogenously or from the other, but produced by the signifying work of primary repression. Laplanche reinvokes the formula for repression as metaphor and in the ICA discussion it is by reference to its paradoxical S/S that he proposes what he calls a primacy of the signifier that is acquired or secondary: '... at a certain point signifiers have no other signifieds than themselves ... when the signifier becomes the signified it acquires some kind of primacy, but that is a secondary primacy' (p.79). However, there is a problem with this return to the 1960 gloss on the formula. It threatens to rehearse, in this self-evidence and transparency of the signifier as its own signified without any mediation or relation to a signifying chain or combinatory, the 'apophantic illusion' of a bedrock element or scene 'which is self-explanatory and which does not refer to anything else' (p.115). Laplanche's thesis of primal seduction with its introduction of the dimension of the other and the enigma would prevent any such coincidence of a signifier with its own signified. The double status of the S/S, in Lacan's terms both a latent signifier and 'fallen' to the signified, is a function of its relation as signified to the binding substitutions and translations of the subject and its continuing relation as signifier to the desire of the other.

$$\frac{S1}{s} \quad x \quad \frac{S2}{S1} \quad \rightarrow \quad \frac{\;\frac{S2}{s}\;}{\;\frac{S1}{S1}\;}$$

(*New Foundations*, pp.131–2)

In this reprise of the formula for primal repression from the earlier text,

Laplanche distinguishes two formal possibilities. First, the substituted for signifier is 'simplified out' without remainder, which he calls an 'amnesiac' substitution that abolishes the original signifier. Alternatively the displaced signifier depends from the new translation, S2/s, in an algebraic contrivance S1/S1, that represents both its double status and the formation of the drive's 'object source'. The formula S1/S1, I would suggest, can also be taken conveniently as a mnemonic of that 'splitting' of the enigmatic elements performed by the first translations and substitutions, for as Laplanche indicates, 'part – but only part – of S1 is wrested out of its obscurity, and part of it is repressed' (p.133). We can borrow Freud's formulation of psychical reality as 'unconscious wishes *reduced* [my italics] to their most fundamental and truest shape', using the 'reduced' to indicate the active production of an irreducible remainder, the always residual '*à traduire*', which as the object source of the drive fixed and preserved around an absent signified is the impetus to the subject's constantly renewed translations and reinscriptions. The primacy of the signifier is established then, not in a mythical moment of self-coincidence and self-identity (of ballast or bedrock), but as a point of dislocation, resistance, enigma (in its double status caught in different signifying chains) in a staggered intersubjective relay or stand-off between subject and other.

At this point the interpretation by Stephen Melville in the ICA Conference of the differences between Laplanche and Lacan evident in their different formalisations of repression is relevant. He suggests that what in Lacan is an ontological question shifts in Laplanche to an epistemological question. The schema for primal repression for Lacan results in a stack of signifiers – S2/S1/S1/s – that in Melville's words 'bottoms out with this ineffable, unreachable, something for the subject, this 'x' which is at the bottom of everything' (p.77, above). If Lacan's 's' or 'x' is a mysterious ontological fragment, irreducible to the order of signifiers, approached perhaps through his concepts of the *objet a* and the Real, then Laplanche's 'signifier fastened to itself', the S1/S1, the enigmatic signifier, is the object of an epistemological quest. It is clear that both thinkers are deploying the mathematical conventions so that the positions in the stack function differently, with Laplanche's most obscure element, the other's sexual signified, actually figuring in the upper chain along with the term S2 that claims to bind and 'translate' it, while Lacan's fragment of lost being is represented metaphorically at the bottom. Nevertheless, Melville's distinction seems initially plausible if we think of Laplanche's humorous anecdote of the infant interrogating the breast, or his gloss on the S1/s relation in *New Foundations*, 'in the case of the first parental signifiers, s, is simply replaced by a question mark ("What does he/she/it want with me?")' (p.131). In the Kent seminar, Laplanche comments on this point that primal repression consists of the child's attempts to understand and to bind what is coming to him, to produce a meaning and an answer to the question of the other's desire. 'It is the attempt to elaborate that excludes ... any mental organisation has an effect of repressing, anti-cathecting what doesn't fit into it.' The translation is always partial – there can be no question of a direct or transparent transmission from the parental Unconscious – 'so the part that is not translated comes down under the bar' (p.29 above).

I have argued above that the enigmatic remainder of the parental inscriptions and their translations, S/S, caught in different signifying chains and between moments separated by a distinctive temporal logic (*Nachträglichkeit*), cannot be understood as a founding or 'apophantic' self-identity of signifier and signified. Further, we should recall the echo in the infantile question described by Laplanche of the '*Che vuoi?*' ('What do you want?') and the subject's question to the Other ('What does he want of me?) from the Lacanian graphs of desire,[13] on the one hand, and Laplanche's account of the enigmatic signifier as an internal foreign body, an antecedent 'spine in the flesh' attacking the ego from within in the very process of its formation (as among other things a possible epistemological subject), on the other. These might suggest that the substantial differences between them are not so readily to be aligned with Melville's counterposition of 'ontological failure' as against 'epistemological difficulty', of 'an unreadable sign' as against 'an impossible person'. A consideration of Laplanche's separation of the Lacanian intrication of primal repression and the paternal metaphor and its displacing of the Oedipal Symbolic order might be a more productive point of interrogation for the clarification of the differences between the two thinkers.

If the Unconscious is organised around the fall-out from a process of primal inscription and translation, then the work of analysis is not, Laplanche suggests, a translation of a translation, e.g. in the pursuit of 'determinate contents ... which ultimately can be tracked down', in the words of Peter Dews, ie. stable representations as the mimesis of causal events, the final moment of total recall beloved of the flashback melodrama (Hitchcock's *Spellbound* or *Marnie*). Laplanche describes instead a work of de-translation, a work of dismantling and unbinding of existing translations. He invokes two parallel distinctions from the work of Walter Benjamin and Freud. He takes Freud's recasting of the notion of interpretation in the late essay 'Constructions in Analysis' (1937), where Freud distinguishes interpretation as a work on signifying connections, 'something one does to some single element of the material, such as an association or a parapraxis' (p.261), from constructions which present 'a piece of [his] early history that he has forgotten'. Freud's account of constructions leads to various problems and paradoxes (the frequent absence of a confirming memory from the analysand who produces instead vivid memories of 'adjacent objects of minor significance', or the 'seductive analogy' between the illusions of psychotic patients and the constructions of analysis) (pp.266, 268).[14] Laplanche makes a connection with Benjamin's argument, in his essay 'The Task of the Translator', that words and not sentences are 'the primary element of the translator' who must aim beyond the transmission of content or subject matter at a 'nucleus', 'the element that does not lend itself to translation'. Access to this does not come at the level of the sentence or proposition but through what Benjamin calls *Wörtlichkeit*, translated by Laplanche as the 'word to word' (in preference to Zohn's translation of it as 'literalness'). Hence Benjamin's metaphor from which Laplanche's essay takes its title: 'For the proposition [sentence] is the wall in front of the language of the original; the word for word the arcade.' (Laplanche's translation, 'The Wall and the Arcade', p.197, below). The analogy is between Freud's reformulation of 'interpretation' and Benjamin's *Wörtlichkeit*, the arcade that gives access and circulation rather than blocks out (it is not clear if Laplanche would consign Freud's 'construction' and its problems to the limbo of the proposition).[15]

Laplanche develops his de-translation model of analysis by comparison with the translation strategies of André Chouraqui, the French translator of the Bible. While there are both Greek and Hebrew versions of the Old Testament, the New Testament exists only in the Greek version. Chouraqui translates it, not on the supposition of a missing Hebrew ur-text, but on the hypothesis that the authors of the New Testament were immersed in the language worlds of Hebrew and Aramaic. As Laplanche puts it, 'he re-translates the Greek while aiming the translation through the Hebrew' (p.208), picking up homonyms, rhymes, resonances from the Greek word to Hebrew or Aramaic words behind them. What is lost is not, then, a fully formed ur-text that could function as a ground or indisputable origin, but what Laplanche calls 'certain points, words and specific inscriptions', that cluster as a *sub-text*, haunting and structuring the signifying chain as an absence. The aim for Chouraqui (and Laplanche) is then to work on or de-translate the given Greek word to word so as to release the connections to the Hebrew or Aramaic not-said and to incorporate the non-translated, the *à traduire*, to include in the new translation what has been discarded or repressed in the 'original'.

The fascinations of the comparison find an echo within Freudian practice in the patient of the 'Fetishism' article (1927), whose sexual satisfaction required a shine on the nose (*Glanz auf der Nase*), a fetishistic precondition whose hidden signification revealed, in the English language of his childhood, a forbidden *glance* at the nose, behind which Freud reconstructs the desire to see the maternal phallus. However, if the translingual rhyme *Glanz/* glance enchains the gaze to the glow, the full signifying formula for the situation Freud constructs remains incomplete unless we hear also, through the other language of his childhood, the Latin *glans* that makes of the nose a penis, in which the subject's gaze (glance) finally coincides homophonically with the *jouissance* (*Glanz*) of the other's body (*glans*). The other in question is more likely the father, directing his shine, the *Glanz auf der glans*, to the Wolf Man's sister, if Abraham and Torok's identification of Freud's fetishist patient with the little multi-lingual Russian is correct. Abraham and Torok reconstruct the Wolf Man's trauma or primal scene rather differently from Freud, following trans-lingual signifying paths between German, English and

Russian words, to reveal his witness of a scene of sexual rubbing, *tieret* (Russian) – the Wolf Man's magic word – between the father and the sister to whom he was bound by ties of identification and envy, and the significance of whose sexual precocity with her little brother seems to have gone unexplored. Without venturing into the field of cryptonymy and the authors' claim to reconstruct an actual event, we can nevertheless hear within the orgasmically invested translation (*Glanz*/shine), the occulted homophone, (glance/*glans*), the enigmatic phonemic fragment that condenses the twin points of the staggered inter-subjective circuit: the other's body (*glans*) with its enigmatic desire directed elsewhere and its inscription in the subject (glance) as the shine of *jouissance* oscillates between them. Here the enigmatic signifier is a Freudian switchword or *knottenpunkt*. As the support of his potency it preserves the subject's *jouissance* (thus differentiating the perverse or fetishist object choice from the neurotic symptom), while encrypting the moment of perverse implantation in its passage from the other.[16]

This analogy with translation returns us once again to Laplanche's abiding concern with the elements of the Unconscious and their specification through the binding substitutions of primal repression. *New Foundations* as a text is centred on the reconceptualised drives and the moments of their inscription and translation as the privileged site of parental transmission and the effects of primal seduction. The 'secondary' matter of the Oedipus and castration complexes get relatively little elaboration. Indeed, Freud's primal fantasies, the *mise en scène* of the Oedipus, are demoted or 'de-primalised', at least in their Oedipal functions. The Oedipus is no longer primal in the sense of first, but topographically located as secondary, even though it may involve the re-elaboration of earlier inscriptions and translations, and it is no longer primal in the sense of universal but culturally contingent. Laplanche insists: '...*castration* is primarily an answer not an instinctive question ... a secondary idea if ever there was one ... a secondary logical pattern which is inherent in verbal communication' (*New Foundations*, p.36). This separation of the Oedipus from primal repression and the constitution of the Unconscious consummates his break with Lacan's notion of the paternal metaphor, which was an implication he had yet to draw in the 1960 essay, where in the Postscript he still associates the 'binding of meanings' in primal repression with 'the law of castration, "of the father"' (p.178) and contrasts it with the binding by the ego. This has the effect of leaving open other possibilities than psychosis, the failure of primal repression, for those psychic trajectories that swerve from or attempt to rework the normalising function of the paternal Law and its Oedipal polarities (e.g. the various female and male homosexualities). However, it was precisely through the symbolic apparatus of the Oedipus and the primal fantasies that the constitution of a normalising 'Law' of sexual difference and its psychic costs have been thought.[17] What Laplanche's reworking of the drives in the context of primal seduction now leaves unclear or untheorised, is how the psychic constitution and inscription of a sexually and genitally differentiated body image, (the repression and symbolisation of what enigmatic signifiers?), the ground or at least terrain for the formation of gendered identities, is now to be rethought.

Notes

1. Jean Laplanche and Serge Leclaire, 'The Unconscious: A Psychoanalytic Study' (1960), trans. Patrick Coleman, *Yale French Studies* no. 48, 1972; Jean Laplanche and Jean-Bertrand Pontalis, 'Fantasy and the Origins of Sexuality'(1964), trans. and reprinted in *Formations of Fantasy*, Victor Burgin, James Donald, Cora Kaplan (eds.) Methuen 1986; *Life and Death in Psychoanalysis* (1970), trans. Jeffrey Mehlman, John Hopkins University Press, 1976; *Problématiques* I–V, (1980–7), Presses Universitaires de France; *New Foundations for Psychoanalysis* (1987), trans. David Macey, Basil Blackwell 1989.
2. Jacques Lacan, 'Preface', Anika Lemaire, *Jacques Lacan* (1970), trans. David Macey, Routledge and Kegan Paul, London 1977, p.xiii.
3. Sigmund Freud, 'The Unconscious' (1915), trans. James Strachey (1957), reprinted in *On Metapsychology*, The Pelican Freud Library, vol. 11, p.206.
4. Emile Benveniste, *Problems in General Linguistics*, trans. Elizabeth Meek, Miami University Press, 1971.
5. Ferdinand de Saussure, *Course in General Linguistics* (1916), trans. Wade Baskin, Fontana, UK 1974, p.120.
6. Jacques Lacan, 'The Agency of the Letter in the Unconscious' (1957), *Écrits*, trans. Alan Sheridan, Tavistock Publications, 1977, p.154, 160
7. Sigmund Freud, 'Repression' (1915), trans. James Strachey (1957), reprinted in *On Metapsychology*, The Pelican Freud Library, vol. 11, p.147
8. Jacques Lacan, 'On a Question Preliminary to any Possible Treatment of Psychosis' (1957/8), *Écrits*, trans. Alan Sheridan, Tavistock Publications, 1977, p.200.

9. For a detailed discussion of this concept, see *Life and Death in Psychoanalysis*, op.cit. chap.2; also 'Fantasy and the Origins of Sexuality' op.cit. and the entry under 'Deferred Action' in Laplanche and Pontalis, *The Language of Psychoanalysis* (1967), trans. Donald Nicholson-Smith, The Hogarth Press, London 1983; for some of Laplanche's more recent reflections, see 'Notes on Afterwardsness' in the present volume.

10. Mladen Dolar, 'I Shall Be with You on Your Wedding-Night: Lacan and the Uncanny', in *Rendering the Real*, Parveen Adams (ed.), *October* no. 58. Fall 1991, p.6.

11. Sigmund Freud, 'A Child is Being Beaten' (1919), trans. Alix and James Strachey (1955), in *On Psychopathology*, The Pelican Freud Library, vol 10. Laplanche comments on Freud's analysis of beating fantasies in relation to the theory of the enigmatic signifier in 'Interpretation between Determinism and Hermeneutics: A Restatement of the Problem' (1991), *International Review of Psycho-Analysis* (forthcoming).

12. Sigmund Freud, *The Interpretation of Dreams* (1900), cited in 'Fantasy and the Origins of Sexuality', op.cit. p.8.

13. Jacques Lacan, 'The Subversion of the Subject and the Dialectic of Desire in the Freudian Unconscious' (1960) in *Écrits*, op.cit., p.312 et.seq.

14. Sigmund Freud, 'Constructions in Analysis' (1937), trans. James Strachey (1950), The Standard Edition of the *Complete Psychological Works of Sigmund Freud*, vol. xxiii, p.257–269.

15. Walter Benjamin, 'The Task of the Translator' (1923), trans. Harry Zohn, in *Illuminations*, Hannah Arendt (ed.), Collins/Fontana 1973, pp.75, 79.

16. Nicholas Abraham and Maria Torok, *The Wolf Man's Magic Word* (1976), trans. Nicholas Rand, Foreword by Jacques Derrida, University of Minnesota Press, 1986.

17. For an attempt to use the problematic of the primal fantasies to account for the processes of Oedipal normalisation and its difficulties, see John Fletcher, 'Freud and his Uses: Psychoanalysis and Gay Theory', in *Coming on Strong: Gay Politics and Culture*, Simon Shepherd and Mick Wallis (ed.), Unwin Hyman 1989.

The Seductive Theories of Jean Laplanche: the drive, passivity and femininity

Elizabeth Cowie

> The mechanism of the turn from the active to the passive, moreover, pervades woman's entire instinctual life.
>
> (*Helene Deutsch*)[1]

The equation active=masculine/passive=feminine is one of the most disputed but also resilient premisses within psychoanalytic theory. If it is simply true, then as feminist theorists we will have to pack up our books and go home, for how can psychoanalytic theory be used to argue against this set of equivalences which it has instituted for itself? A way out of this impasse has been opened up, however, through the path-breaking work of Jean Laplanche on the theory of the drives and the transformation of our understanding of passivity in his new conceptualisation of the role of seduction for the child, which he outlines in his *New Foundations for Psychoanalysis*.[2]

Freud, in his own writings on the drive, does not offer a fully realised theory of the sexual drive, its essential nature or its genesis in the infant. Moreover, Freud's view of the relation of the sexual drive to other psychical structures underwent substantial transformations. Initially it is seen as a disruptive force which produced an unbinding in contrast to the self-preservative instincts or ego-instincts which defended the ego against sexuality. With the development of the theory of the Death Drive, sexuality was subsequently identified with Eros and seen as a principle of cohesion in opposition to the death drive. On the one hand the absence of a fully-developed theory of the drive seems like an extraordinary omission, on the other hand it has not at all hindered psychoanalysis insofar as Freud's most important discovery, that of infantile sexuality, is used and affirmed in clinical practice. It is the riddle in Freud's writings concerning the emergence of the sexual drive and its relation to self-preservation which Jean Laplanche addressed in his study *Life and Death in Psychoanalysis*.[3] Central to his project in that book, which also involves a reconsideration of the emergence of the ego and narcissism, is his recovery of the concept of *anaclisis*, or 'leaning on' (Freud's *Anlehnung*, translated by Mehlman as 'propping').

Freud had introduced this concept in his earliest discussion of the sexual instinct in *Three Essays on Sexuality*[4] in order to describe the way in which the sexual drive leans on the self-preservative instinct.[5] He also uses the term to describe and distinguish an anaclitic type of object choice (*Anlehnungstypus*), based on the model of the mother, that is, on the object of the function of self-preservation, in contrast to the narcissistic form of object choice.[6] The earlier use of the term disappears with the later topology of id, ego, and super-ego introduced in 1923,[7] (though not the concept of an anaclitic object choice), in which Freud assigns self-preservation to the agency of the ego, but this is clearly a later structure for the subject. Laplanche argues that there are in fact two forms of self-preservation are in play here: a 'primary' self-preservation prior to the emergence of any psychical agency; a 'secondary' self-preservation, emerging with the ego, as 'self-love' (narcissism). This 'primary' – in the sense of being first, and not in the sense of being determining – self-preservation, namely the functioning of the 'vital order', is non-sexual but nevertheless involves *activities*, feeding, digestion, defæcation etc. It is from these excitations or functional pleasures that *organ* pleasure arises.[8]

Freud does not develop the concept of anaclisis in relation to the emergence of the drive, but it is this concept of 'leaning on' which Laplanche takes up precisely for its explanatory value in relation to the emergence of sexuality. He proposes that the term instinct (*Instinkt*) be used to refer to the vital order, the functions of the body in its sustaining of the living being's existence, as opposed to the sexual register (p.16). In contrast, Freud's term *Trieb* must be translated as drive, as a form of 'pushing' or pressure exerted on the mind. This drive is always a sexual drive:

> ... it is sexuality which represents the model of every drive and probably constitutes the only drive in the strict sense of the term.
> (*Life and Death*, p.8)

This drive leans on the vital order of self-preservation, that is on the bodily functions; but this does not involve the body as such, that is, as a body-image, since the bodily functions are not yet organised into a body-image, nor can they be until the emergence of the ego in the mirror stage. Biological function is involved, but not as a topography, not as an organised space or image.[9]

The primacy of the self-preservative instinct as defined by Laplanche is not thereby determining. There is no linear progression from an originary point which remains both intact in its original mode, and implicit in every subsequent stage which it has given rise to. Thus, 'Whilst self-preservation does have a role to play, it must be quite categorically stated that it is not a protagonist in psychical conflict' (p.141, *New Foundations*). Once the sexual drive emerges, self-preservation as an instinct will be wholly displaced, and its role played instead by the sexual drive as represented in the narcissism or self-love of the ego.

This move and the emergence of the sexual drive as such derive from the moment when the self-preservative instinct *loses* its object and a *representation* arises in its place – the breast replaces milk in a metonymic displacement which is also at the same time a metaphoric condensation, for when the baby cries out of hunger it anticipates milk which will satiate its need, milk which is identified with the breast which thereby becomes the signifier of its desire to be satisfied. As soon as need becomes desire it is adrift from mere function, of feeding in order to live.

While the source of the drive is, Laplanche says, 'the instinct in its entirety', that is, the 'vital order', it is so as the 'source of a process which mimics, displaces, and denatures it' (*Life and Death*, p.22). As a result the erotogenic or somatic zone is not a source for the drive in the way it may be for the self-preservative instinct, and Laplanche emphasises Freud's notion of sexual excitation as a concomitant effect, marginal or by the way, so that 'any function, any vital process, can "secrete" sexuality; any agitation may participate in it' (p.22). The importance of this lies not primarily in the affirmation of the polymorphous character of sexuality but rather in the way that it shows again that the drive, sexuality, is not determined by its source in the body. Moreover Laplanche suggests, in an anticipation of his later development of a theory of seduction, that these erotogenic zones 'focalise parental fantasies and above all maternal fantasies' and that through these is 'introduced into the child that alien internal entity which is, properly speaking, the sexual excitation' (p.24). Seduction produces a split in self-preservation, it 'peels away' a layer and this then constitutes the sexual drive. Once instituted in the subject, the source of this drive is no longer the vital order as such, but a psychical representative, a residue of primal repression, but this is 'anchored in the erotogenic zones as a result of the phenomenon of seduction' (*New Foundations*, p.143). This does not, Laplanche emphasises, make the sexual drive originally biological, though it does subsequently become biological in the later stage of genitality (p.141). A corollary of this is that the two forms of the drive which Freud subsequently posited, namely the life and death drives, both 'exist within the field of the sexual drive' (p.145–6).

From this two further points can be established: first, the drive is always the sexual drive. Second, it is not characterised by and in any one organ or several particular organs or even by the erotogenic zones as such – the oral, anal and genital drives are not determining of sexuality as a result of their bodily origin but as a result of the specific organisation of sexuality. While the drive can only be known or analysed through its emergence as a *partial drive*, these do not thereby together produce a unity or unification of the sexual drive; the partial drives simply name particular pathways for the organisation of the sexual drive and tell us little more about the processes of the drives.

The drives are not fixed or determined in any originary way. Once in play, they are extremely vulnerable to being transformed. The concept of the drive, however, is a composite: it involves not only the force which is exerted on the mind, and perhaps body, in relation to a 'demand for work' (Freud, 1915, p.122), but also an aim and an object for that 'pressure'. Freud is subsequently concerned not with the drives as such but with the forms and consequences of the vicissitudes encountered by the drives, most obviously repression, which bear primarily upon the aim and the object of the drive. (It is of course through repression that the unconscious is constituted, so that the pressure of the drive following repression will nevertheless continue in relation to unconscious representatives.) The vicissitudes to which the drive is liable are not simply external constraints or imposed limitations from a coercive society. On the contrary, the most important vicissitude for the drive is external reality itself and the very fact of its externality.

In his discussion in 'Instincts and Their Vicissitudes' (1915), Freud argues that these transformations are not arbitrary but involve four distinct processes: 'Reversal [of the drive] into its opposite. Turning around upon the subject's own self. Repression. Sublimation.'[10] Freud's concern in the remainder of this essay is with just two of these processes: reversal into its opposite, and turning around upon the subject's own self. And it is these which will be the main focus of this discussion, for it is here that Freud presents the mechanism for the emergence of the drives as either active or passive on which he then bases his theory of sadism and masochism. It is this account which Laplanche re-reads in order to resolve the ambiguities surrounding the emergence of aggressivity and its role in the death drive. At the same time this offers, I suggest, a new perspective on the issue of feminine passivity.

In the two vicissitudes Freud described as 'reversal into its opposite' and 'turning around upon the subject's own self' the drive is manifested, but subject to a structural change in regard to its object or aim or both. The reversal into the opposite is the change of the drive from active to passive, a change in the aim from a wish to do something to a wish to have something done to one. Freud's example is the drive to mastery which thus appears as a pair of opposites – sadism/masochism:[11] 'The reversal affects only the *aims* of the instincts. The active aim (to torture) is replaced by the passive aim (to be tortured)' (ibid, p.127). The choice of example is important, for in fact Freud is primarily concerned to understand the move from active to passive, and the correlative sadistic or masochistic positions produced. It is this which is also of central interest here, in relation to the subsequent twinning of passivity/masochism with femininity. The turning around of the drive, however, involves a change in the *object* of the drive, and can be a change from an external to an internal object: the ego itself. But for both the examples he considers here – sadism and scopophilia – Freud notes that the 'turning around upon the subject's self and the transformation of activity and passivity converge or coincide' (ibid, p.127). This appears to produce a simple binary opposition and, as Laplanche points out, it suggests a complementarity between the two positions and a reversibility comparable to the grammatical move from an active to a passive proposition (ibid, p.88), so that sadism/masochism and voyeurism/exhibitionism are seen as pairs of opposites. A rather different structure, however, is proposed in the schema Freud outlines for scopophilia:

(α) Oneself looking at a sexual organ	=	A sexual organ being looked at by oneself
|		|
(β) Oneself looking at an extraneous Object (active scopophilia)		(γ) An object which is oneself, or part of oneself, being looked at by an extraneous person (exhibitionism)

Freud now points to a preliminary stage, represented in the schema as (α), which he defines as autoeroticism. It is this which he argues is 'the source of *both* the situations represented in the resulting pair of opposites, the one or the other according to which element in the original situation is changed' (p.130). Freud initially doubted that such a preliminary stage existed in sadism, but later revised this view, arguing that sadism too followed from an earlier moment, an 'original, erotogenic masochism'.[12]

Using this concept of a 'reflexive' stage, Laplanche reformulates Freud's schema of the drives and in effect proposes two stages. The first involves a turning around of the initial drive for mastery, which Laplanche sees as simply a hetero-aggression propped on the vital order and with no necessary sadism, that is, it is not linked to sexuality. Freud implies this when he states that:

> Psychoanalysis would appear to show that the infliction of pain plays no part among the original purposive actions of the instinct. A sadistic child takes no account of whether or not he inflicts pains, nor does he intend to do so. (ibid., p.28)

This hetero-aggression is turned around to produce self-aggression or a primary masochism and only now does it emerge as sexual inasmuch as pain, a perturbation like any other, can 'produce a pleasurable condition' (p.128). This stage for Laplanche is the primary form of the sexual drive and he designates it as reflexive masochism: 'sexuality emerges only with the turning round upon the self, thus with masochism, so that, within *the field of sexuality*, masochism is already considered as primary' (p.89).

This primary masochism or self-aggression is not yet passive, however, since no reversal of aim has occurred. It is, Laplanche argues, an intermediate stage in which, as Freud says, 'The active voice is changed, not into a passive, but into the reflexive, middle voice' (p.128). It is in this reflexive, auto-erotic phase that sexuality emerges, propped on the vital functions but in which there is no object as such. This primary masochism is the basis for the second stage, so that it is only with a second turning around that the active drive, and sadism proper arises. In this second turning-around an external object is again the object of the drive. Sadism is then the active position producing a search in the external world for an object capable of being substituted for the original object while the passive position of masochism requires that another subject be substituted for the subject's own self.

The passive drive and masochism as such only arises with the reversal of the drive, when the active *aim* is replaced by a passive aim, which implies the search for another person as 'object', that is, object of the drive but who will be the subject of the action (*Life and Death*, p.92). It is through the object of the drive that the aim, satisfaction, can be achieved. Where this primary or reflexive masochism is reversed in its aim, from active to passive, the subject itself is now the 'object' of the action giving rise to a satisfaction occurring on the subject's own body – an action by an external object which is thus also the aim of the drive. There are therefore not one but two objects of the drive here and, one must suppose, two forms of satisfaction, the first in relation to having the other do something to oneself – the pleasure, one might say, of bringing the other to undertake the action in relation to oneself. The second is the pleasure the action as such brings about on the body of the subject itself. In the passive position, then, the object of the drive is also the subject itself, but acted upon from the place of another. Here, unlike the position of reflexive masochism, in which there is no object as such differentiated, the subject is its own object.[13] This 'self-as-object' is constituted through the action of the other upon the subject, whereby the agent of the action stands in for the subject itself, so that this is thus also an identification. Identification is also involved in that particular turning around of the active drive which Freud describes as regressive identification – the drive turns away from the external object, but now the internal object to which it is directed is not simply the subject's ego, but the external object introduced as an internal object.[14]

Sadism and masochism, voyeurism and exhibitionism, are not, therefore, simple opposites, and the complement of the masochist is not a sadist but a person who can be brought to or put in the position of the subject itself. Similarly the exhibitionist is not the complement of the voyeur.[15] Moreover Freud himself commented that the transformation of the drive is never exhaustive and that the different stages, the auto-erotic as well as passive and active forms, co-exist alongside one another ('Instincts and their Vicissitudes', p.130).

Laplanche's re-reading of Freud not only resolves many of the ambiguities in Freud's theory of the drive. It also implies a radically new view of the relation of active and passive in the emergence of the drive, namely that the drive is first constituted in relation to passive aims. This new understanding is closely allied to Laplanche's development of a theory of primal seduction. This both draws upon Freud's rejected supposition of infantile seduction and transforms it by relating it to the emergence of the drive and the unconscious. Primal seduction, for Laplanche, describes 'a fundamental situation in which an adult proffers to a child verbal, non-verbal and even behavioural signifiers which are pregnant with unconscious sexual significations' (1987, 1989, p.126). These signifiers are however enigmatic to the child, and hence are not fully symbolisable, instead Laplanche argues, there is a residue of signification which is yet 'to be translated' and as a result is repressed by the infant and this forms the core of the unconscious. The intrusion of these enigmatic signifiers upon the child – and this has no necessary relation to the adult's conscious intentions, but may figure unconscious desires – is experienced both as an excitation and as a pressure, a demand upon the child which produces a concomitant drive for meaning in the child. As a result the very origin of the drive lies in this coming into the child of these signifiers which are experienced as irresolvably enigmatic. The corollary is that this origin is constituted as passivity.

Laplanche's revised theory of the drive has important implications for our understanding of *feminine* passivity, for it offers a solution to the problem in Freud's theory of femininity which requires the little girl's to replace her original active aims with passive aims.

Freudian Femininity

Freud's views on femininity and the 'fact' of feminine passivity contain a series of discontinuities, and even downright contradictions, so that he appears to give with the right hand what he takes away with the left. In 'Femininity' Freud rejects the equation active/masculine and feminine/ passive, saying, 'I advise you against it. It seems to me to serve no useful purpose and adds nothing to our knowledge'.[16] However, while he goes on to say that 'we must beware in this of underestimating the influence of social customs, which similarly force women into passive situations', he nevertheless suggests that femininity may be characterised psychologically as:

giving preference to passive aims. This is not, of course, the same thing as passivity; to achieve a passive aim may call for a large amount of activity. It is perhaps the case that in a woman, on the basis of her share in the sexual function, a preference for passive behaviour and passive aims is carried over into her life to a greater or lesser extent, in proportion to the limits, restricted or far-reaching, within which her sexual life thus serves as a model. (p.116)

He continues:

All this is still far from being cleared up. There is one particularly constant relation between femininity and instinctual life which we do not want to overlook. The suppression of women's aggressiveness which is prescribed for them constitutionally and imposed on them socially favours the development of powerfully masochistic impulses, which succeed, as we know, in binding erotically the destructive trends which have been diverted inwards. but if, as happens so often, you meet with masochism in men, what is left to you but to say that these men exhibit very plain feminine traits. (p.116)

While affirming that passivity is always a question of the aim of the drive, Freud has introduced a constitutional element in relation to the passivity of femininity, and allied this with social convention, producing 'masochistic impulses'. Masochism is then identified with femininity, for the display of masochism in men is described as a 'feminine trait', although the argument here is quite distinct from any thesis of bisexuality.[17] Freud had introduced this correlation in his discussion of 'A Child is Being Beaten' in 1919, and retains it in 'The Economic Problem of Masochism' in 1924. However this constitutional prescription arises not at birth for the little girl, but in consequence of 'castration', which is not the case – or not in the same way – for the male masochist. Femininity is not a simple biological inscription but a psychical construction arising as a result of the little girl's perception of her lack of a penis as 'castration'. Freud's thesis is that up to a certain point the girl has 'lived in a masculine way', with active wishes towards the mother and genital pleasure through clitoral masturbation. But, as a result of her sense of lack in the face of 'the boy's far superior equipment', she loses her enjoyment in her phallic sexuality, and thus 'renounces her masturbatory satisfaction from her clitoris, repudiates her love for her mother and at the same time not infrequently repressed a good part of her sexual trends in general' (p.126).

The little girl's original active aims must be replaced by passive aims, then, in order for her to achieve femininity. This, Freud says, is brought about by her penis-envy which causes the girl to give up her active aims, and thus leads to a 'wave of passivity'. Freud's argument slides together repression with the reversal and turning around of the drive, in order to produce a 'wave of development' whereby 'passivity now has the upper hand', which will 'smooth the ground' for femininity. Freud, however, discusses the reversal and turning around of the drive only in relation to scopophilia and sadism/masochism, so that it is difficult to understand their role for femininity in producing the 'wave' of passivity.[18] Moreover, Freud's reference to the role of repression seems to assume the existence of an original reservoir of instinctual drives in the little girl which have both an active *and* a passive aim with only the active aims being repressed.[19]

By contrast, Laplanche's account of the drives has shown that the active and passive are not inversely related in this way, but rather are two *distinct* forms of the drive. Both forms emerge from a primary masochism, involving auto-eroticism, which is structurally prior to the emergence of the active and the passive aim. As a result there can be no 'pool' of active and passive drives or aims. In addition, in Laplanche's account the passive aim emerges through the turning around not of the active aim, but of the auto-erotic or primary masochism – the subject moves from being its own object to being an object for someone else. Masochism, as self-aggression, is primary for the subject, and represents the tendency towards zero or the death drive. It is not, then, a question of moving from active to passive.

The role of repression in producing passivity as femininity is also problematic in Freud's account.[20] Freud says that the repression of the active in the little girl arises because of the abandonment of a satisfaction as a result of penis-envy, but why is envy able to transform a pleasure into an unpleasure? If it is on the basis of the analogy that bigger is best, as Freud suggests, this can only be as a result of a sense of lack in being in the child which exists prior to castration. In this case the little girl's pursuit of sexual pleasure in her clitoral masturbation brings her up against the knowledge of her lack and hence produces unpleasure (the body is not a sufficient condition for desire), so that the repression of the wish for genital satisfaction removes the risk of that unpleasure. However this will apply to both the active and the passive aim, to the wish to take pleasure in her genitals and to be pleasured in her genitals. Of course the boy, too, experiences an inadequacy in relation to the much larger penis of his father, and gives up masturbation as a result of the castration complex, but this is not described by Freud as a renunciation of activity.

Repression, moreover, acts not on the drive as such or in general, but on an idea, a wish, whose satisfaction would be pleasurable in itself but at the same time would risk incurring unpleasure as a result of other requirements.[21] Repression itself does not produce a passive aim, but an inhibition of the drive, whether active or passive. More likely for women in the sexual domain, repression will produce frigidity, which of course has so often been confused with passive sexuality. Indeed Freud seems to acknowledge this for while he asserts that where activity remains, femininity is not fully achieved, at the same time he notes that not too much must be lost through repression for a normal pathway to femininity to be achieved (p.128).

In fact the girl's passivity is posited by Freud not in relation to the repression of masturbation, but in relation to a new wish, and one which is not repressed, namely the wish for a penis (this is also a form of turning around of the drive, from the clitoris insofar as it is an internal object, to an external object, the penis). The aim of this wish may be active, the wish to take the penis from the mother or the father. However Freud sees the aim of the wish for a penis as passive insofar as it is a demand to – in the first instance – the mother, the phallic mother – from whom the little girl expects to receive a penis. It is only with the mother's refusal of the demand, or as Freud puts it 'the discovery that her mother is castrated' (p.126–7) that she turns to her father. The final transformation, Freud says, will then be the substitution of a wish for a penis by a wish for a baby.[22] In order to distinguish this as a passive aim – whether for a penis or a baby – Freud very clearly rejects confusing the little girl's post-castration wish for a baby with her earlier games with her dolls, for these, just as they do for the boy, 'served as an identification with her mother with the intention of substituting activity for passivity. *She* was playing the part of her mother and the doll was herself: now she could do with the baby everything that her mother used to do with her' (p.128). Instead, in Freud's account this is a new wish and it must involve a passive aim, since the girl has repressed her active aims and thus has given up her phallic activity. If this has not occurred – as with the masculinity complex – it is because of 'a constitutional factor, a greater amount of activity, such as is ordinarily characteristic of the male' (*Femininity* p.129–30). But there is no pool of active or passive drives; if there does arise on the part of the girl a wish for a penis, it must be shown why and whether the aim is passive rather than active. No doubt this may arise as a defensive reversal of the drive so that the little girl will be *given* the penis/baby, and hence avoids the feared retribution of her father, or mother, for her wish to take the penis. The reversal of the drive therefore enables the wish to escape repression. But this does not account for the *general* turn to passivity Freud claims for the girl. As a result what must still be explained is the specific relation to active and passive aims – if any – which is brought about by the instituting of sexual difference in the child, boy or girl.

Laplanche's re-reading of Freud's theory of the drive has emphasised the constitutive role of passivity for the subject, whether male or female. As a result, it has opened the way to radically new approaches to the issue of the construction of sexual difference. Post-Oedipal sexuality can now be understood as arising from the encounter of passive and active aims – in which passive aims are primary – with the transformations demanded by the Oedipus complex.

Notes

1. *Psychology of Women* vol.1, p.240, Grove Stratton, New York 1944.
2. Translated by David Macey, Basil Blackwell 1989. First published as *Nouveaux fondements*

pour la psychanalyse, Presses Universitaires de France 1987. The discussion which follows is drawn from a chapter in my forthcoming book *To Represent Woman?* (Macmillan) on which I had based my original question to Professor Laplanche at the ICA conference. Its revision has benefited greatly from Professor Laplanche's contributions at the conference, and from the additional material published in this volume.

3. *Life and Death in Psychoanalysis*, translated with an introduction by Jeffrey Mehlman, The John Hopkins University Press, Baltimore 1976 (*Vie et mort en psychanalyse*, Flammarion, Paris 1970).

4. *Three Essays on Sexuality*, 1905, *The Standard Edition of the Complete Psychological Works of Sigmund Freud*, vol VII, henceforth indicated as *SE*.

5. 'The satisfaction of the erotogenic zone is associated, in the first instance, with the satisfaction of the need for nourishment. To begin with, sexual activity attaches itself to functions serving the purpose of self-preservation and does not become independent of them until later' *Three Essays on Sexuality*, pp.181–2, ibid.; the second sentence added by Freud in 1915.

6. In 'On Narcissism, An Introduction, 1914, *SE* vol. XIV.

7. *The Ego and the Id*, (1923) *SE* vol. XIX.

8. 'Every activity, modification of the organism, or perturbation is capable of becoming the source of a marginal effect, which is precisely the sexual excitation at the point at which that perturbation is produced' (Laplanche, 1970, 1976, p.88).

9. Laplanche's concept of 'leaning' or 'propping' has been taken up in relation to feminism and film theory, though in different ways, by Mary Ann Doane 'Misrecognition and Identity', and by Joan Copjec '*Thriller*: An intrigue of Identification': both essays are in *Cinetracts* vol. 3 no. 3, Fall 1980. It is also discussed by Joan Copjec in '*India Songe/Son nom de Venise dans Calcutta desert*: The Compulsion to Repeat', *October* 17, 1981.

10. 1915, *SE*, vol. XIV p.126.

11. Freud makes a distinction here between a change from activity to passivity, and a reversal in content, but which is found in only a single instance, in the reversal of love into hate; the distinction raises further conceptual issues in relation to the emergence of ambivalent feeling, but this does not bear on the arguments pursued here.

12. A footnote added to 'Instincts' in 1924 acknowledges this new view: 'In later works (cf. 'The Economic Problem of Masochism', 1924) relating to problems of instinctual life, I have expressed an oppostive view' (Footnote 2, p.128, *SE* vol. XIV). In that 1924 essay, Freud posits a 'destructive instinct, the instinct for mastery'. Where this is directed outwards it is sadism proper, but 'a portion does not share in this transposition outwards', instead forming an 'original, erotogenic masochism'. If subsequently the sadistic drive outwards is once more introjected, then, Freud argues 'a secondary masochism is produced, which is added to the original masochism. This new view was developed after 1920 following the theory of the death drive in *Beyond the Pleasure Principle*. The concept of a primary masochism, however, implies a more complex relation to sadism, involving a tripartite structure in which the initial stage is no longer sadism as an activity directed outwards to an external object, but

the reflexive, masochistic moment: to make oneself suffer or to destroy oneself. This is taken up by Laplanche in his revised schema for the drives.

13. Mikkel Borch-Jacobsen has pointed to the importance of distinguishing the two senses of object invoked here, the first being the object of the drive, through which the drive reaches its goal, its *Ziel*; the second sense is used by Freud in a more specific, more classical sense, Borch-Jacobsen suggests, 'as everything that is opposed to the subject, everything that confronts it – in short, everything that it is "not-ego" – is, then, an "object". It is in this second sense that autoeroticism, for example, is said to be "deprived of an object" (even though this is not true in the first sense).' In *The Freudian Subject*, p.64, trans. Catherine Porter, Macmillan, London 1989.

14. This is outlined in 'Mourning and Melancholia', 1915 *SE* vol. XIV.

15. It is here that Deleuze drew upon Laplanche for his own discussion of masochism in *Coldness and Cruelty – Sacher-Masoch*, trans. Jean McNeil, Faber & Faber 1971, reprinted by Zone Books, New York 1989. First published in France as 'Le Froi et Le Cruel' in *Presentation de Sacher-Masoch*, Editions de Minuit 1967.

16. *New Introductory Lectures* p.15, *SE* vol. XXII.

17. Freud had introduced this correlation in his discussion of '"A Child is Being Beaten": A Contribution to the Study of the Origin of Sexual Perversions' in 1919 (*SE* vol. XVII), and retains it in 'The Economic Problem of Masochism' in 1924 (*SE* vol. XIX). This feminine masochism is a secondary masochism, added to the original masochism. Its status as feminine seems to derive from this passivity – the wish to be beaten, punished (although Freud acknowledges the infantile character of this too), its scenario of castration of the subject, and 'the situations of being copulated with and of giving birth, which are characteristics of femaleness.'

18. In 'A Child is Being Beaten', Freud does discuss the girl's fantasy as masochistic, but he terms it masculine, since she fantasises boys not girls being beaten. In contrast, the boy's fantasy is feminine.

19. This accords with what Freud elsewhere describes as the bisexuality of the drive. It is Freud's emphasis on and commitment to a notion of bisexuality which has always made Freudian psychoanalysis so interesting for feminists.

20. Laplanche has put forward a different view of repression. He sees it as arising as the result of the inability of infant wholly to transform passivity into activity, that is, to 'translate' the enigmantic signifiers penetrating it from its parental figures or carers. Activity, Laplanche says, is this effort of translation and the resulting integration. However, a part of these enigmatic signifiers remains unintegrated, and this forms the unconscious. In the Kent Seminar published in this book, Laplanche says, 'Towards this part the individual remains passive, that is the passivity towards the adult in the beginning becomes our passivity towards our unconscious. We are deeply passive in our relationships to the remainders of the adult messages' (p.25 above). The implications of this for retaining a notion of feminine passivity are not explored here.

21. 'Repression', 1915, p.147, *SE* vol. XIV.

22. It is in this final transformation, Freud says, with the substitution of a wish for a penis by a wish for a baby, that true femininity is arrived at. However, he also notes that the archaic wish for a penis always lies behind the wish for motherhood. As a result, as Rachel Bowlby shows, Freud ends up defining femininity as the wish not to be a woman, since penis-envy remains behind every substitutive wish (in 'Still crazy after all these years' in *Between Feminism and Psychoanalysis*, ed. Teresa Brennan, Routledge, London 1989).

The Unconscious: structuring as a translation

Andrew Benjamin

What *it* is, that is there at the centre of psychoanalysis, must *itself* go unnoticed. In an exact, though in the end misleadingly simple formulation of the unconscious in the *New Introductory Lectures on Psychoanalysis*, Freud describes the "oldest and best meaning" of the term as what has "effects" even though it has an existence "of which we know nothing".[1] The problem posed by this lack of direct awareness, the absence of immediate knowledge, is not that of access since the unconscious is known precisely through its effects. The problem therefore is not in any straightforward sense epistemological. It pertains, rather, to the existence of the unconscious (as opposed to how that existence is known) and is thus present within the question of what status is to be given to the unconscious. In this instance status is to be understood as referring specifically to the question of the mode of being proper to the unconscious. As such what emerges in the abeyance of the hold of epistemology – an abeyance recasting but not denying knowledge – is the question of the ontology of the unconscious. What, in other words, is the *it* that it is?[2]

Moving ontological considerations to the fore is not a narrowly delimited concern for it is at this precise point that a great deal of recent psychoanalytic thinking can be introduced. Most of such work can be read as in part exemplifying a concern with the status of the unconscious. There are however divisions, for what characterizes many of these undertakings is an approach to the unconscious that is neither structured around the presence of the effects of the unconscious, nor presented in terms of the unconscious being the originator of those effects, but in relation to what in the end amounts to no more than a posited homology between effects and the unconscious. The positing of this homology – homology here being an identity in regards to the status of each, i.e. an ontological homology – gives rise to far more than a mere reciprocity of explanation in which unconscious and effects are explained in terms of each other. Moreover it entails something in addition to the presence of a static model. There is the more emphatic consequence that the essentially linguistic understanding of these effects – their existence as signifiers – and hence their formulation (though in fact reformulation) in linguistic terms, determines and therefore also structures the presentation, the re-presentation, in theory of the unconscious. It also entails that access to the unconscious and with it the actual construal of the unconscious *itself* is constrained to take place both in and as the linguistic. The unconscious comes to be that which is at once working as, as well as at the same time being the work of language. The co-presence of time and existence articulated within and thus articulating the Same is staked out by the effective presence of the homological. Homology takes place and thus endures within that positioning of the unconscious in which it is presented as structured "like" a language.[3]

In the writings of Jean Laplanche, however, it is possible to note that a shift of emphasis is taking place. (It will be suggested however that the force of this shift, at least as it is presented in the writings under consideration, is in part diminished by the absence of a pre-given and hence repeated language posited as the medium of translation.) The change is not just a move within the presence of linguistic models attesting thereby to the diversity or plurality of such models. Indeed it can be argued that the radical nature of this shift is that it should be construed as involving a move away from the potentially static and towards a dynamic conception of the unconscious. With it a fundamentally different answer can be taken as being given to the question of the mode of being proper to the unconscious. (The proper here marks the centrality of the ontological in that it marks the posing of the ontology of the unconscious as a question). Furthermore, the position of the static, that which works within an ontology of stasis – namely the given as given within it – comes to occupy a place that is itself the result of a rethinking and thus repositioning of the given. The giving again of the given, now outside of the parameters of a certain linguistic model, means that the relationship between time and words – a relationship figuring, as shall be argued, within and as narrative – is itself recast. Recasting, understood as the movement between translation, detranslation and retranslation, is a process enjoining its own recasting of movement and with it of movement's time. While it will employ a formulation differentiating itself from Laplanche's, the movement in question can be articulated in relation to the presentation, deferral and subsequent re-presentation of narrative. It will be in relation to this formulation that it will become possible to take up Freud's description of the contents of the unconscious as being essentially "timeless".[4]

With Laplanche's work while elements of the linguistic are retained e.g. the use of models of signification to explain and account for the effects of primary repression – they are none the less refracted through, and thus mediated by, what Laplanche borrowing from Novalis describes as "la pulsion de traduction" ("*Trieb zur Übersetzung*").[5] The "pulsion", this "drive to translate/drive for translation", is from the start inextricably linked to Laplanche's formulation of the unconscious as the "*à traduire*" (to translate/to be translated). It is the dynamic quality inherent in the verbal formulation, capturing and presenting potential, that can be read as beginning to take up the nature of the existence of the unconscious. (Again it is ontology in the place of epistemology, still re-incorporating knowledge). The dynamic, perhaps the unconscious's will or even the unconscious as will, must form part of any explanation of the mode of being proper to the unconscious. Particular attention will have to be paid therefore to Laplanche's precise formulation, for it is within that formulation that the unconscious comes to be named:

> *Le "à traduire" primordial, nous le nommons: l'inconscient.* The primordial "to translate/to be translated" we name it: the unconscious.[6]

Given the precision of this formulation equal consideration will also have to be given to the function and consequence of this primordiality. However in more general terms Laplanche's continual attempt to think the unconscious, its effects, presentations and the ambit of possible responses to them, in terms of translation, can be taken as marking a fundamental reorientation of the psychoanalytic and thus of the thinking of its concepts. In sum they can be taken to comprise a refounding, hence the provision of new foundations. Laplanche's own attempt at erecting new foundations should not be seen as having a necessary insistence on the primacy of the ontological. In this instance that primacy marks the place of another project.

Here the foundations identified by Laplanche are not themselves under consideration – these present concerns are more modest – rather, what is at stake is Laplanche's presentation of the unconscious within the interplay of time and translation. This presentation will in turn be taken as an attempt by Laplanche, though perhaps in the end *pace* Laplanche, to respond to the question of the unconscious; the question of what is the *it* that it is? Laplanche's most recent attempt to formulate this interplay is in "Temporalité et Traduction: Pour une remise au travail de la philosophie du temps".[7] It is, of course, a work that must be read as an attempt to further the cause of his *New Foundations for Psychoanalysis*.[8]

Part of Laplanche's more general concerns is the re-articulation of the temporality proper to psychoanalysis in order that its reintegration rework and thus refound the psychoanalytic enterprise. The guiding thread in this undertaking is what could be described as his reconceptualisation of the process identified by Freud with the term *Nachträglichkeit*. As this process of working and reworking the Freudian legacy takes place, time and translation come to be thought together. However, with Laplanche, what comes to be introduced into the structure of translation/new translation is the necessity of a "de-translation"; the intervention of another term that breaks the passage of continuity and displaces the role of teleology by introducing the work of repetition; presented as at work.

> ...for as much as the analytic process can be understood by a process or the procedure of translation, the interpretation in

> terms of the past [*de passé*] (infantile archaic) is not a translation but a detranslation [*detraduction*] a dismantling, a retrogression [*retrogradation*] of a translation.[9]

The existence of this work on the already worked over explains why for Laplanche "analytic interpretation consists in undoing [*defaire*] an existing translation".[10] What is of central importance here is the nature of this "undoing"; in other words its particular relation to the done, to what has already been made.

The naming of the unconscious as the "*à traduire*" positions the analyst as responding to the presentation of this movement; a movement in which the content of the unconscious cannot be presented as such. Laplanche by insisting on the formulation of Freud's 'Constructions in Analysis' (1937) rather than the one found in the earlier *The Interpretation of Dreams* (1900), moves both the site of translation and that which is identified as translation. For Freud, in the earlier work, the analyst was a translator, uniquely a translator. In the later one the analyst is both constructor and translator. There Freud describes the analyst's task in the following terms.

> His task is to make out what has been forgotten from the traces that it has left behind, or more correctly to construct it.[11]

This construction is for Laplanche a reconstruction, another translation. In 'Constructions in Analysis' Freud distinguishes between "interpretation" [*Deutungen*] and construction. The specificity of construction lies in the precise nature of what the analyst gives in responding to the analysand.

> It is a construction when one lays before the subject of the analysis a piece [*ein Stück*] of his earlier history he has forgotten.[12]

This is to be distinguished from "interpretation" – Freud's interpretation – which is more concerned with an "element of the material". Examples given by Freud are "an association" and "a parapraxis". The question that must be addressed is, holding to the difference between "interpretation" and "construction", how is what is identified as "a piece" [*ein Stück*] to be understood? It will be seen that any answer to this question will depend upon the introduction of narrative. Narrative is what allows for the introduction of time into presentations. Laplanche's "undoing" – the detranslation – is linked to Freud's position presented as part of a general elucidation of the process of construction. Before returning to the question of narrative, provisionally the interplay of sequential time and presentation, it is essential to trace Laplanche's arguments concerning the relationship between what he terms the "temporality of the cure" and "human temporality". It is in this relationship that a significant structural commonality can be identified.

Inside of that which is given by the analysand in the analytic encounter, within the presentation as translation, are pieces, extracts, that in being taken from the translation allow for new translations. It will be suggested further on, that a way of construing this process will be in terms of having taken an element from that which was inherently diachronic with the result that this has the effect of turning that element into an instance of the synchronic; in sum a move from sequence to instant. Furthermore, it is at this point that it needs to be indicated that the the element's synchronicity should be understood as providing the conditions of existence for a new translation. The rule of time, coupled to a radical shift in temporal structure, is indispensable for an understanding of the movement from translation, through detranslation, to retranslation. What is at stake here is precisely not temporal sequence. It is in relation to the advent of new translations that Laplanche locates the possibility of the "cure". It resides in the potential for another translation, a new translation that will be "less partial, less repressive, less symptomatic". For Laplanche there is an analogical situation taking place in the presentation of mourning. Again it involves a state of affairs incorporating the ternary structure of time which itself stems from a reworking of *Nachträglichkeit*; its generalised repositioning.

Laplanche interprets mourning as having, in outline, the following fundamental determinations.[13] The present is comprised in part of a fundamental and constituting link to another person. This link is established as "a real [veritable] conception of existence". With the loss of that other person what then collapses is this "vision of the world" Understanding the work of mourning, Laplanche argues, depends upon correctly grasping what Freud had himself only ever inadequately formulated, namely "detachment" [*Lösung*]. Freud's own formulation was presented in terms of a rupture, a break in time, an emptying of continuity that was overcome in time. However the time in question – Freud's time – amounted to no more than the simple positing of the past, present and future. Posited time caught in the inexorable movement sanctioned by teleology marks the result of Freud's failure to develop a psychoanalytic conception of time. The attempt at such a development forms a central part of Laplanche's undertaking. This is why "detachment" will, in its re-theorisation, result in the identification of a more subtle and complex process consisting of different temporal designations.

> ...the loss obliges one to effect a disentanglement, a painful meditation. But each thread, if it is detached by me from the all... is not broken as Freud pretended. On the contrary it is overinvested [*surinvesti*], meditated on in isolation, brought to its own history [*histoire*]... and outside of this common history [*histoire*]... to a more englobing and much older history [*histoire*].[14]

Central to this construal of mourning is the conception of a new existence as more than just a simple incorporating of the old, but one where the work of mourning is the reworking of those older elements such that their reintroduction occurs as a consequence of the reworking, and that therefore their existence in the "new vision" is as the *already reworked*. The difficulty here pertains, firstly, to the temporal complex and secondly, though relatedly, to the fact that this formulation provides for the possibility that something may occur again, even though the specific occurrence, now constituted as an event, is taking place for the first time. Once more it goes without saying that central to this formulation, to the complex, is the process identified by the term *Nachträglichkeit*. It is a process which in the most minimal terms is concerned with providing a re-presentation within repetition but one that no longer has the quality of a representation. As such it establishes a critical distance from the domination of the image that is entailed by the classical conception of mimesis. The challenge that this presents lies in the possibility of thinking this – the interplay of re-presentation and repetition as well as the critical distancing – as an occurrence.

While there is an analogy between that which is at work in mourning and the "cure" – an analogy given by the temporal structure – there remain important differences. For Laplanche, the fundamental point is that the possibility of reworking what are described as "imperfect translations", a possibility mirrored in the work of "spontaneous mourning" [*le deuil spontané*], indicates that the process of "translation and detranslation-retranslation" is already present in "human existence". It is at this precise point that Laplanche introduces the unconscious. The human being is a creation, a self-creation, a translation into self. It is this translation that is self-creating and self-sustaining and as such brings with it the question of an originary translation. Here the origin is itself repositioned in terms of the dynamic "*à traduire*". What is there to be translated exists as a consequence of repressions. The unconscious as the site of the untranslatable (the already translated) continually being presented, or more accurately to use Laplanche's term "retranslated," is the work of the "drive to translate"; a dynamic that is literally essential to the unconscious itself.

Taking these considerations a step further necessitates recognising that for Laplanche the constitution of the unconscious involves recourse to primal seduction. It is at this point, with the primal seduction, with it as a founding moment recasting the origin, that a radical dissymmetry is introduced and which determines the stakes of the complex process marked out by the movements of translation. Laplanche uses the term "primal seduction"

> ...to describe a fundamental situation in which an adult proffers to a child verbal, non-verbal and even behavioural signifiers which are pregnant with unconscious sexual significations.[15]

These signifiers are "enigmatic". They are given and taken unconsciously. Primal repression is the response to them. The human being starts the process of translation, retranslation, in relation to the drives. The movement is always a moving beyond the untranslatable in terms of the "*à traduire*". The continuity, the temporal continuity of present translations is the presentation of self to self ("*auto-traduction*"), itself occurring as a translation; now as a moving through that necessitates a leaving behind. The link that is established here involves the drives. What this comprises is a presentation. That is why for example the "pressure of the drive" is described as,

> ...emanating from the difference between those elements in the primal enigmatic signifiers which can be symbolised and those elements which cannot be symbolised.[16]

Furthermore it is here that the presence of the will can be reintroduced. It has already been argued that Laplanche's use of the linguistic is mediated by the presence of a "drive to/for translation". Moreover it is the dynamic that is used by Laplanche to describe the continuity of the activities of the unconscious, the ceaseless drive for presentation operating within and as translation.

> ...the moment of self translation comes... not from the translator but from the untranslated [*intraduit*] or from the imperfectly translated which demands [*exige*] without ceasing a new (better) translation.[17]

It is precisely the structure of this "demand" (the "*exigence*"), the ontologico-temporal nature of the "without ceasing", and the link between them that will form an integral part of any understanding of the ontology of the unconscious. Offering any further clarification of these links and thereby continuing to trace the interplay of time and translation in Laplanche's work will necessitate returning to the possible reformulation of this connection within the frame provided by the structure of narrative. With narrative, time can be given a more adequate formulation and the being of the unconscious approached. The structure of narrative, here, is the site of a particular ontologico-temporal concatenation.

The analytic process as presented by Laplanche involves a "detranslation" of a given translation, one sanctioning the possibility of a new translation. (The new in this instance should not be understood as marking singularity and with it complete differentiation, but as a presentation within and as repetition.) The new brings with it the possibility of a release, and thus the creation of a state of affairs that is for the analysand less repressive and less marked by symptoms. What occasions this change is explicable in terms of that construal of the unconscious in which it is presented as the "*à traduire*"; i.e. the dynamic of a self-presencing that is always, and of necessity, incomplete.

As has already been indicated the procedure of "de-translation" involves more than a simple alteration of what has been given. There is a far more radical change, one that is determined by time; time and existence figuring here as necessarily interarticulated. The alteration takes place therefore on the level of the ontologico-temporal. In addition, it is the very nature of this change that allows for the reintegration of the elements that are the "de-translated" to be either reincorporated into a new translation or to provide the basis for such translations where, in both cases, their presence should not be construed in terms of their having been re-presented but rather as the enactment of repetition. It is, of course, a repetition in which what is happening happens again for the first time. This movement, the presencing through and via repetition is the work, the effect, of *Nachträglichkeit*. It is this possibility that is of central importance. Not only does it reiterate the structure of the unconscious, but there is in addition, though here it is no simple addition, a recasting of the given and with it the time of interpretation. Recasting and reiteration are not secondary. Indeed the secondary, and with it any posited secondariness, form part of the temporality of continuity articulated within and as teleology. Here what the suggestion of the secondary – a suggestion held open by a sequential interpretation of the "re-" – indicates is the anoriginal presence of the structure of repetition and with it of an ontology of difference.

The effective presence of time is already present in the actual construal of "de-translation" when it is taken as comprising a move from the diachronic to the synchronic. While the terms diachrony and synchrony bring with them their linguistic heritage, in this instance they are to be understood as marking out two positions in relation to the interconnection of narrative and time. The translation provided by the analysand is diachronic in the sense that it involves the sequence of narrative – the time of narrative – in which the meaning of each of the constitutive parts is provided by the sequence in which they take place and therefore which they form. This is the determination of meaning within and due to narrative. Meaning depends upon narrative time. It is articulated within it. The analyst in the process of "de-translation" works to break the translation into significant elements in order that they can be presented to the analysand. Freud in 'Constructions in Analysis' describes this process as a "laying before". The question that arises here is, what is the status of that which is given, the segments of the "de-translated"? Answering this question means recognising that a fundamental shift has taken place. It occurs both on the level of meaning – incorporating both the actual site of meaning as well as that in which meaning can be said to inhere – and in regard to the temporality proper to the segment. The reason why this can be described as a move from the diachronic to the synchronic is that "detranslation" involves not just the removal of the segment from its place within a narrative, and thus also from its articulation within narrative time, but is also a repositioning and thus a redesignation of the place of meaning. In other words a movement that has both a spatial as well as a temporal component.

In the first instance – on the level of the diachronic – the segment's meaning was provided by its place within a sequence, within narrative. Then in being removed, in the reversion to the synchronic, the segment itself became that which harboured meaning. It would no longer form a simple part in a more general bearing of meaning. The move to the synchronic is not the denial of time, but the repositioning of the temporal (and with it of the ontological) away from narrative towards what, following a lead from Laplanche, could be described as the archæological, and thus as another site of meaning; even another place. (Here alterity denotes more than the introduction of variety or diversity within a sequence. It attests to the presence of difference as differential; i.e. as involving different ontological and temporal considerations. Hence what is actually involved here, in and as this site, is the possibility of an-other place.) Explorations into the segment, into that which has been extracted, give the site a unity that sanctions an investigation that will in the end yield a new translation. That "de-translation" is fundamentally different from the presentation of a new translation or even the positioning of the analyst as only a translator, is a possibility that is itself also indicated by Freud in 'Constructions in Analysis'.

In taking up the problem of how negation and affirmation are to be understood, Freud approaches it in terms of an example of what he takes as an indirect form of confirmation occurring within the analytic encounter. What is being confirmed is the viability of what may have been said within the interchange between analyst and analysand. When the analysand responds to a suggestion by the analyst with an assertion in the form of, "I didn't ever think that", Freud adds that this response "can be translated without any hesitation".[18] The translation is of course an interpretation by the analyst. The translation is simply,

> Yes, you are right [*richtig*] this time – about my unconscious.[19]

Translation here is kept strictly to the level of interpretation, and then to an interpretation that stems from the analyst in relation to his/her understanding of what has been said by the analysand. The translation pertains to the understanding and as such is to be differentiated from the activity of construction. The giving of a translation, even in this anecdotal and perhaps therefore minimal sense, is not "a laying before".

The "de-translated" elements come to be mined for the possibilities that they may contain. In being mined, excavated, and thus in being placed into a new translation, the extracted segment repositions the "drive to translate", that which "demands without ceasing". It can now be taken as re-enacted on the level of diachrony. Again there is the presence of a fundamental move, occurring within and as repetition. It is not as though the synchronic has been reinserted or placed back into narrative, it is rather that the move to the synchronic is that which enabled there to be a further translation and thus the advent of a further narrative in which the synchronic (or aspects thereof) is/are repeated with a fundamental change. Once more it is a change that pertains to the interarticulated presence of time and meaning;

the time of synchrony and diachrony and their co-joined though differing *topoi* of meaning.

The intriguing element here is that the move from diachrony to synchrony, and then (again) to diachrony – a move that lends itself to the other description as taking place from narrative to anarrative, to narrative (again) – seems in some way to rehearse the temporal distinction between the unconscious and the conscious. Or at least in a form in which that distinction is present in Freud. Freud's claim that the unconscious is "timeless" needs to be understood, as has been suggested, as a claim concerning narrative. In other words the unconscious, or perhaps more exactly the contents of the unconscious, are anarrational. While they may be explicable in terms of signifiers – Laplanche's "enigmatic signifiers" – they are not organised or thematised as a sequential signifying unity. They are not, that is, organised into and by narrative. The coming to presence of the unconscious, the effective work of the "*à traduire*," can be interpreted, in part, as the provision of a narrative for that which had been hitherto essentially anarrational.

If the move from synchrony to diachrony – from anarrative to narrative – is a move in which the "timelessness" of the unconscious in being reasserted seems, as a consequence, to be repeated, then does this mean that it is a repetition of the unconscious outside of itself? Present beyond its own confines? Clearly the answer to such questions is in the negative. Nonetheless, what they suggest is that there is a structuring presence that works both in relation to the unconscious (the unconscious construed as the "*à traduire*") as well as in the move from the detranslated to the new translation. The structuring presence is *Nachträglichkeit*, here present as the ternary structure of time articulating repetition. It is precisely because of this extension, that what is opened up is the possibility that the reach of *Nachträglichkeit* will be greater than that established for it within the confines of the strictly psychoanalytic. With this extension what is thereby opened up is the possibility that *Nachträglichkeit* could harbour – harbour by providing – the temporality of interpretation itself.[20]

In sum, therefore, and retaining the distinction between synchrony and diachrony while articulating it within narrative, what occurs in the move from translation, to "de-translation", to new translation, can be reformulated in the following way. The synchronic (the anarrational) moves to a new translation and hence to an-other diachronic presentation. What makes it other is not its singularity in relation either to the first translation or the "de-translation". Indeed it is not singular at all. Its relation however is not that of chronology and with it of teleology. It is not therefore an addition within the putative diversity of generality. On the contrary the relation is provided by the repeated presence – though now repeated within a different temporal scheme, i.e. narrative and thus with a different criterion of meaning, namely sequence – of the detranslated. While it employs a different language of explanation, this possibility, the varying movements and repetitions stems from what Laplanche described as "human temporality". A temporality marked by the work of *Nachträglichkeit*.

The question that endures and which is posed in and by the naming of the unconscious as the "*le à traduire primordial*" ("the primordial to translate/to be translated"), concerns the actualisation of that which is primordial. Here the process of actualisation pertains to more than just a formal possibility but the means, the present means, of actualisation itself. The primordial refers to the presence of what Laplanche describes as the "inscription", the unconscious inscription of "enigmatic signifiers". The primordial designates a location, a topos, if not a time prior to translation. Its specific function, however, is as that which provides translation with its conditions of existence. The unconscious becomes, though only in this precise respect, the condition of and for language. (The condition is not straightforwardly transcendental. To think that it was, would render otiose the formulation of the unconscious in terms of an unending dynamic of presencing. In place of the transcendental, it is more appropriate to think of the move from the unconscious to the conscious as a presentation within a generalised becoming. Expressed in this way the differences between the sites is itself expressed as ontological difference, and thus with it the connection or interconnection between them – the sites – is to be construed in terms of repetition.) Returning to Laplanche's formulation, what it is that takes place in the move from the unconscious to the conscious presentation is to be understood as a translation; a translation enacted by the "to be translated". The unconscious conceived in terms of the will to translate has a content which is presented, translated, via a movement, a presencing, one of the descriptions of which is "self-translation" ["*auto-traduction*"].

While the movement of "self-translation" may come from the "to be translated", it nonetheless still necessitates the presence – and here presence must be a possibility that has already been given a theoretical description rather than a simple given – of a given language into which it is translated. In other words while presentation, the consequence of the "*à traduire*", can be described as a translation, translation as movement, as a dis-placing, because that into which this translated (translation as presencing) is itself translated is not given, there must be another level of translation. This other level establishes and thus comprises the particular or specific form taken by translation.

Even though the actualisation of the primordial may have the formal description of a translation, its specific actualisation however – and here this means its being actualised in a particular way, in one particular form rather than another – will imply that the specific presence of the actualisation is not going to be as a translation, where the latter is understood purely formally. It needs to be underlined that what is at stake here is not the description of a formal possibility but of an actual presence. And it is for this reason that a problem emerges at exactly this point. The problem is simply that that this particular type of translation – the actual presence – has not been identified as such by Laplanche. If anything it has been conflated with translation as a formal presencing.

The actualisation, itself already a translation, has to be presented. Its presentation as a translation accounts for its being actualised, it comes to presence as a translation. The form taken by the presence – its presentation – involves its translation into words. In other words it comprises a second translation resulting in specificity. This other translation, again alterity enjoining complexity, demands a different description. A task which can be begun by building on the recognition that what is at play in this instance – with the precise form taken by a presentation – is a translation that involves the repetition of language – the repetition of the given – as the presentation of translation, as that which presents it. Moreover, the only way to give an adequate account of the process identified by Freud as at work in "construction" or present in what Laplanche identifies as "de-translation" (and the ontologico-temporal potential within "de-translation"), would have to be premised upon the effective presence of the relationship, between firstly what is sedimented in the word (where the sedimentations are part of the word's history), and secondly that which is sedimented in it in terms of the analysand's own private history. Indeed, it can be argued that it is the interplay of the two – the two senses of sedimentation and word – that will occasion the form, and with it the specificity, of the new translation. Both are necessary in that the process identified as a new translation is possible. Moreover, without both of them, the process out of which the new translation arises would comprise no more than a mapping of interpretations on to extracts; a one-to-one correspondence. Finally, the opening created by "de-translation" would come to be closed off and the potential inexhaustibility of associations ended. The movement incorporating translation, "de-translation", retranslation demands that not only could the new translation never be coextensive with its primordial source, but that equally the actualisation of the word – the public word – never be taken as coextensive with all that the word can actualise. The word even when extracted, a piece even when related as an extract, will always bring with it more than the personal history that it harbours. It will bring that potential that is there inherent in the word itself. In other words it will be accompanied by its own history and range of associations which are themselves already present in the word. Again, it is the relation between them that will account for the effectuation of, and thus be that which facilitates, the new translation.

Perhaps a way towards a more precise expression of what is involved here may come from a brief consideration of both a marginal as well as a textual comment made by Freud during the analysis of one of his own dreams in *The Interpretation of Dreams*. The dream in question is "Irma's injection".[21] In this instance the detail is not of fundamental importance. It is rather the strategy and possibility of analysis that is central. In breaking down the dream Freud provides an interpretation of the constitutive elements. To each element what comes to be offered is an explanation/interpretation that seems already to have been provided by the element itself. Not, that is, by the element in terms of its place in the related narrative of the dream, but in terms of its decomposition into significant elements. The relocation of the significant is precisely that which sanctions the element's subsequent reintegration – thus repetition – into another narrative, the new translation. The force of the example is limited by Freud's reluctance to open up further possibilities within the very words, the extracts, in which the dream is related. This hesitancy, though only read as hesitant *après coup*, is in part accounted for by what can only be described as an intentionalist reading, on Freud's part, of the content. At this stage two important points – albeit interpretive points – need to made about Freud's undertaking.

They are, firstly that what can be observed here is that the locus of meaning has shifted from the diachronic to the synchronic, and secondly that the presencing of the unconscious – what Laplanche names as "the primordial "*à traduire*" – is only available, present, by the process of translation itself having taken a particular form; i.e. having itself been translated. The particularity of the form means that what is at play is the interrelation of the word's history and the private history it has come to bear. It is the force of what is at stake here that comes to be restricted, even though it is a restriction that will be opened up by the time of construction, by the marginal presence of time. The latter being a time in which the lack of completion is taken as a lack that can be overcome.

At the time of writing the text, Freud signaled that the interpretation given and thus the meanings adduced did not comprise the totality of what could have been said. The interpretation he suggests is not "without a gap". In a footnote added to the text nine years after it was first published in 1900, he adds a important qualification, namely that,

> it will be understood that I have not reported everything that occurred to me during the process of interpretation.[22]

It is of course clear that part of what was not given, and this because it was a self-analysis, was any of the relevant sexual content that the dream may have had. In both instances something remains left undone. A "gap" demands filling, "everything" remains to be said. At this stage in Freud's writings what demands and what remains figure as absences and thus as lack. (The figuring may only be a flickering and implicit possibility caught by the words that suggest it and thus as a presence which may be contradicted by formulations occurring elsewhere in texts of this period of Freud's writings.) Nonetheless, what is eventually taken on by Freud is that once the "gap" is generalised and the "everything" posited as a possibility, then these unaccomplished states are able to be taken as comprising that which marks and determines the psychoanalytic endeavour itself. It is however an endeavour – a task that takes the enduring presence of the gap and the impossibility of everything being stated as given, and thereby as the *sine qua non* of analysis itself – that is constrained to work with an unannounced, and in that context yet to be formalised, conception of the word. (The word construed here and elsewhere as both itself – literally a word – as well as a generalised site of meaning.) The word, especially the literal word, as is indicated by the plethora of examples in *Jokes and their Relation to the Unconscious* as well as the verbal slips etc. recounted in the *Psychopathology of Everyday Life*, becomes that other site in which what the word brings to its being announced is exactly that which allows for the analysis, interpretation and hence possible new translation to take place. It is in this exact sense that the word can be taken as always working beyond itself in presenting itself.[23]

The general argument here is that, to the extent that there is a recognition, both within Freud's own writings and in the more general development of psychoanalysis, that what comes to presence can never, potentially at least, exhaust the associations to which it may give rise or ever be absolutely coextensive with its interpretation (these two points are differing restatements of each other), then what has to be taken into consideration is how language – the words – facilitate precisely this possibility. In outline, it is simply that it is made possible by the nature of the unconscious and its mode of self-presencing, but also, and fundamentally, because the nature of the word is such that it can itself never be coextensive with its own actualisation. The actualisation of the word, its contextual determination, is marked by other possibilities that can always, in changing the context, come to be opened up. Sedimented into the word therefore are the same conditions of possibility that are present in the "to be translated"/translation relation. While what must be undertaken here is the task of giving a theoretical elaboration of this connection, one that would include the nature of the connection, it should not be thought that what is being suggested is that the word has, even if only formally, an unconscious. It is rather and perhaps more radically that both the word as well as the presencing of the unconscious, the translation of the "to be translated," are to be understood as articulating and thereby being articulated within the ternary structure of *Nachträglichkeit*. Furthermore in allowing for such a possibility what is moved to the fore is that conception of repetition which, while allowing for repetitions taking place within the Same, must always allow for the presence of an original repetition.

Once the general point concerning *Nachträglichkeit* is conceded, however, what comes with it is the necessity of the two levels of translation. Indeed, it is the inevitable presence of both levels and thus their ineliminable possibility, that works to introduce what was identified above as a complicating factor. The existence of such a factor means that the translation, understood as a translation into language, needs the addition of a theory of language, perhaps a theory of the word, that will allow for a theoretical understanding of the relationship between firstly, the personal history of the analysand (though this will pertain equally to the personal history of any language user) and secondly, the public history of the word; the latter ironically appearing as essential for any understanding of the synchronic, the anarrative. If there is a limit to Laplanche's project as developed thus far, it can be argued as occurring at precisely this point. It should be added, however, that this is a complication that emerges because of the reformulation of the ontology of the unconscious as a dynamic process to be thought through the temporality of *Nachträglichkeit*, i.e. the complex temporality of repetition. In fact it is the centrality of repetition that will allow for the eventual obviation of the problem, as what this will involve is a reconsideration of what has been identified above as the interplay of narrative and anarrative in terms of the repetition of words. This is, of course, merely to announce the possibility of a further project; again *Nachträglichkeit*'s extension.[24]

Notes

1. *The Complete Psychological Works of Sigmund Freud*, (SE) Vol. XXII, page 70.

2. Arguing for the centrality of ontology should not be understood as a simple furthering of the Heideggerian project of fundamental ontology. It is rather the attempt to rework the ontological in terms of the necessary presence, anoriginal presence, of specific modes of being. This position has been argued for in considerably greater detail in my *Art, Mimesis and the Avant-Garde*, Routledge, London 1991.

3. While the formulation is different, a hint of a similar type of critical distancing from the primacy of the linguistic can also be identified in S. Leclaire, "Unconscious Inscription: Another Memory" in A. Roland. (ed.) *Psychoanalysis, Creativity and Literature*, Columbia University Press, New York 1978. See in particular page 81.

4. The "timelessness" (*Zeitlösigkeit*) of the unconscious is identified, for example, by Freud in 'The Dynamics of the Transference' (1912). As will be argued the absence and presence of time needs to be understood in relation to the absence and presence of narrative. I have tried to argue for this position in *Translation and the Nature of Philosophy: A New Theory of Words*, Routledge, London 1989, pages 134–149.

5. Laplanche uses Novalis's formulation in a number of places. It is put to an important use in "Le mur et l'arcade" in *Nouvelle Revue de Psychanalyse* No 37, 1988. Translated and reprinted below, pp. 197–216.

6. page 29, "Temporalité et Traduction" (TT). See footnote 4 for full reference. All translations from this text are my own. The difficulty of translating the term "*à traduire*" must be noted from the start. This accounts for why it has on occasion be left 'untranslated'. It is essential to recognise that what it marks out is a process, a continually self-actualising process. It will be in terms of continuity and thus the continuity of a self-presenting mediated by repression that it will become possible to draw some tentative conclusions concerning the ontology of the unconscious.

7. *Psychanalyse à l'université* No 14, 1989. Translated and reprinted below, pp. 161–77.

8. *Nouveaux fondements pour la Psychanalyse*, P.U.F., Paris 1987. English translation by David Macey, *New Foundations for Psychoanalysis* (NF) Basil Blackwell, Oxford 1989. I have tried to situate Laplanche's work in a more general treatment of the relationship between psychoanalysis and translation in 'Translating Origins: Psychoanalysis and Translation' in L. Venuti (ed) *Rethinking Translation: Discourse, Ideology, Subjectivity*. Routledge, London 1992.

9. TT. page 26.

10. TT. page 25.

11. SE. Vol. XXIII. pages 258–9.

12. SE. ibid page 261.

13. This description of mourning is provided by Laplanche in TT. pages 28–9.

14. TT. page 29. The link between the "histoire" (history/story) and the presentation of narrative needs to be noted.

15. NF. page 126.

16. NF. page 143.
17. TT. page 30.
18. SE. Vol. XXIII. page 263.
19. SE. Vol. XXIII. page 263.
20. It is precisely this possibility that I have attempted to establish in *Judging Events,* Routledge (forthcoming).
21. SE. Vol. III. pages 182–199.
22. SE. Vol. III. page 195.
23. If only as a beginning what needs to be pursued in order to develop this point is that type of treatment words receive in the work of Nicolas Abraham and Maria Torok. A fundamental text here is N. Abraham *Rythmes*, Flammarion, Paris 1985.
24. This paper could not have been completed without the assistance of John Fletcher. A number of the formulations offered in the paper are the result of our lengthy discussions of Laplanche's work.

Translations

Psychoanalysis, Time and Translation

A lecture given at the University of Kent, 30 April 1990

What is philosophy's present position with respect to the question of time? Did Freud bring new elements to this discussion? Can psychoanalysis after Freud offer a positive contribution to this investigation or is it, as merely one empirical form of understanding among others, condemned to model itself on the answers proposed by philosophy?

These three questions are connected and each one is of considerable scope. They are connected, for, in order to sketch a psychoanalytic philosophy of time, it will be necessary to situate the argument in the aftermath or afterwardsness (Freud's *Nachträglichkeit*, Strachey's deferred action) of the successive waves of philosophic advance, whether they are named Kant, Hegel, Dilthey, Bergson, Husserl or Heidegger, but also in the afterwardsness of Freud's discoveries. My talk will be in three parts.

I. With the philosophers, since Kant.

II. With Freud.

III. In the afterwardsness of the philosophers, and of Freud.

I. With the philosophers, since Kant

To date the modern philosophy of time from Kant is only proper. I shall not have the temerity to attempt this history here in a few words, but I cannot fail to cite a certain number of attainments on the part of philosophy since Freud.

1.1. The philosophy of time has been disengaged from the problem of cosmological time to which it had been bound since Aristotle. This can be expressed in another way by saying that temporality becomes independent of time. This separation appears to us as well established, but it is not without risk. Cosmological time, if one dare hazard such a bold statement, has not itself remained unchanged since Kant, and has been definitively freed from the old clockwork of the spheres. A theory such as relativity, or more recently the postulation of an absolute beginning and end of the physical world, opens the door wide to a renewed philosophic *speculation*. The old so-called 'rational cosmology' has witnessed the blurring of the boundaries that separate it from that imaginary cosmology which is science fiction: a rapprochement, even a delegation of powers, at which Kant would be neither astonished nor shocked.

1.2. Freed from the physical world in the largest sense of the word 'physical', temporality could only be ascribed to a subjectivity, which term is to be taken in the largest and the most extended sense possible: as a transcendental subjectivity with Kant and Husserl; as a historic subjectivity of the Spirit with Hegel; as *Dasein* or being there in situation with Heidegger or Sartre. Among the various possible 'subjects' of time, I must pause for a moment on the term 'life', because of the ambiguity it presents as it appears in Dilthey or Bergson: the boundaries between the life of the living being and the life of the spirit tend here to become blurred in a 'vitalism' into which would be subsumed the life of the organism, as well as the life of the individual human, that of evolution, of mankind and civilisation etc. Given this caution concerning 'life', let us retain this minimal requirement: a theory of subjective time cannot neglect to distinguish the time of the living being and the time of the human subject.

1.3. A third point which we may consider as well established is the link of temporality to a movement of temporalisation, that is to the capacity which the human being has of creating, of secreting – *sit venia verbo* – his own time. The notion of an *active* temporalisation has surely received its most elaborate expression on the one hand in Hegel, and on the other in

Husserl and Heidegger. It remains, nonetheless, a fact that it was Kant who paved the way for a theory of active temporalisation with his notions of 'transcendental imagination' and of 'schematism': it is time, as movement, which activates the putting into play of the categories of Pure Reason.

1.4. Finally, in this appeal to 'temporalisation' – however significant the differences between Hegelian dialectical moments and phenomenological *ekstases* – one finds a similar attempt to theorise the movement of progression as *ternary*; a dialectical ternary corresponding to the three dimensions of past, present and future, with a priority generally accorded to the future, synthesis in Hegel or 'being for' in the existentialists. The process of temporalisation is understood as oriented by its end, even if this concept does not include an explicit and theological finality. For the sake of clarity, let me summarise what I first called attainments but what in fact opens the way to new interrogations.

1. There are three good reasons to consider the problem of time at various and well separated levels:
I. Cosmological time;
II. Time of the living being;
III. Time of the human individual: temporalisation;
IV. Time of human societies, civilisations, or of mankind as a whole: that is, history. History implies recapitulation as can be seen in the classical difference between historical (with writing, with recapitulation) and prehistorical societies. Levels II and III shall be from now on my main and even sole object.

2. Philosophers now seem to link the idea of subjective temporalisation with that of *activity*. Is this linking an absolute one? We shall be surprised, maybe, to discover the unsuspected part of passivity at the basis of the so called subjective activity.

3. In what we call the dialectical ternary, besides its positive aspects, don't we find too easy a tendency to give priority only to the *future*? Such a finalist perspective, evident in the hermeneutic or existentialist points of view, has to be challenged or at least balanced, in my opinion, with a new taking into

account of the category of cause or causality in so far as the human being as such is concerned.

II. With Freud

Turning back to Freud after the considerable advances of Kantianism and post-Kantianism, would be, to all appearances, to yield to a movement of considerable reaction and degradation from the philosophical point of view. Nevertheless, let us examine matters a bit more closely.

2.1. It is indisputable that Freud, although perhaps with some measure of bad faith, claims to be a non-philosopher. When treating philosophical questions he contents himself with a few simple and naive metaphysical assertions, such as the undisputed positing of an external world. With regard to the categories of time and space, however, he makes an explicit appeal to Kantianism, but to a debased, ready made Kantianism such as was in currency towards the end of the 19th century. This Kantianism of Freud could deservedly be termed primary; there is no place to show in detail how it permits him some truly stunning reversals. But, concerning the very question of time, it would be a mistake to limit Freud's conception to the debased so called Kantian assertion that, he says, time and space are necessary forms of our thought. Actually, Freud's contribution develops in two completely different directions: the first being properly abstract and metapsychological and the second much nearer to clinical observation; the first pertaining to our level II and being explicit, the second to our level III and being implicit.

2.2 The first, the explicit contribution, is presented as an original hypothesis long kept, he says, in reserve or in secret. Mainly developed in an article called 'A Note upon the Mystic Writing Pad' (1924), this highly interesting model bases the perception of time on the mode of functioning of our perception of the external world. This perception is seen not as continuous but as periodic, like a light ceaselessly turning off and on. The image proposed by Freud is that of an organism, a protozoan stretching out feelers towards the external world and hastily withdrawing them as soon as they have sampled the excitations coming from it. The reason for this periodicity is to be sought in two necessities: on the one hand consciousness, in order not to be overburdened by contents, must constantly empty itself of these representations to receive fresh perceptions; on the other hand, since external perceptions are too aggressive for the organism, it must diminish their intensity in order to accommodate them. Receiving a perception for one tenth of a second, then remaining closed to the perception for nine tenths of a second, is the equivalent of dividing by ten the intensity of what is perceived.

The factor of *rhythm*, which arises with external perception, is encountered again in internal perception with respect to pleasure and unpleasure, and it is curious that Freud did not make the connection between the two. Indeed, when he contemplates the significance of the principle of unpleasure-pleasure from the point of view of energy, he cannot long hold to the conception, which runs counter to experience, according to which all unpleasure corresponds to an increase of tension, and all pleasure to a decrease. We are thus obliged to postulate the existence, in the qualitative perception of pleasure or of unpleasure, of a function (in the mathematical sense) of the increase or decrease of tension, which is not purely proportional: "The factor that determines the feeling is probably the amount of increase or diminution in the quantity of excitation in a given period of time";[1] "Perhaps it is the rhythm, the temporal sequence of changes, rises and falls in the quantity of stimulus".[2]

This explicit theory of Freud concerning time has yet to receive a full investigation. A few statements of principle will suffice us here:

> In no case is there any question of a general theory of time, or of temporalisation. What is at issue is immediate perceptive time, in the flow of the present time.

> This time of perception can properly be conceived as being of the same order in man and in animals. It is the time of the living being immersed in its *Umwelt* (environment) or reacting to its *Innenwelt* (inner world), which at this level furnishes only

> sensations of pleasure and unpleasure. The image proposed by Freud of a rudimentary animalcule sending forth pseudopodia, is highly significant. It is both an elementary model and a prototype: the little protoplasmic animal is simultaneously a reality and an example of what takes place, with certain modifications, in a more complex living being. Once again in Freud the example is the thing itself.
>
> The essential element in external perception (sensoriality) or internal perception (pleasure-unpleasure) is that of a *rhythm*. This eliminates the objection that we are contending with a sort of vicious circle: time as the self-perception of a functioning which is itself temporal. What is at issue, at this level of immediate biological consciousness, is, properly speaking, the *time of the time*, that is *rhythm*. Objective, physical time must reduplicate itself (in the quasi-mathematical sense of a derivative), if it is to become self-perception of time.

In conclusion, this Freudian theory of time must be restored to its proper context, which is that of immediate time, in all probability perceived by the living being and the only one to be perceived by him. The animal has a memory-bank (in the most modern sense of these words) but no temporalisation and no history. On the other hand it has an immediate time. The model proposed by 'A Note on the Mystic Writing Pad' is very precisely that of the living being, and not that of a historical human being.

2.3. To say that Freud takes no position on the subject of both the temporalisation and the historicity of human beings (and also of human societies), would be correct from a formal point of view but unfair. Freud never explicitly thematised a conception which nevertheless surfaces at every moment in his work. Here I will only enumerate these elements of a theory of the temporality of human being.

2.3.1. Everything in his theory which belonged to a temporal ordering

Freud terms very early and very consistently phases, stages, times and epochs. As for the term 'period', reserved for the precise notion of a recurrence at regular intervals, it is abandoned at the moment when the exchange with Fliess ceases. This ordering by stages extended not only to the genesis of the libido and of the ego, but also to the succession of pathological fixations, in ontogenesis and even in phylogenesis (periodisation of epochs of prehistory, and so on). To this ordering are linked a number of complex notions such as fixation and regression.

2.3.2. Freud's theory is a theory of memory, or more precisely of memories, since memory as a faculty is very nearly non-existent in Freudianism. Memory can only be understood through the opposition of unconscious memories (not reworked, susceptible only of resurgence) and preconscious memories. The theory is best apprehended through pathological avatars: illusions or errors of memory, *fausse reconnaissance*, screen-memories etc.

2.3.3. A third aspect of this immense inventory would involve temporalisation and its strategies, as witnessed principally in the psychoanalytic cure with the contrast between 'Remembering, Repeating and Working Through' (1914), or again with the problems of 'Analysis Terminable and Interminable' (1937), but also in a much wider perspective that of the clinic: in the strategies of mourning, of deferral, fantasising or daydreaming.

2.3.4. Finally, we should consider in Freud the entire relation of this individual time to collective time. We need but recall what a large part of the Freudian corpus is devoted to the problems of history, pre-history, archaeology, and myth, and also to reflections on the present or the future of civilisation.

2.3.5. At the close of this cursory inventory of the Freudian problematics of time, let us underscore our aim: to propose a post-Freudian point of view which allows us to place in perspective all of these innumerable elements scattered not only throughout the work of Freud, but also throughout the whole of psychoanalytic reflection on the human being.

2.3.6. It should be noted that I have to this point set aside certain concepts that I consider to be essential but which were neither sufficiently elaborated by Freud, nor placed in relation to each other. It is precisely these three concepts which are at the centre of our own reflections: *Nachträglichkeit*, *l'après coup*, afterwardsness or the afterwards effect; the translation in its relation both to interpretation and to transference; and finally seduction, an essential component of the theory, which, to our way of thinking, must not be submitted to an empirical evaluation, but rather accorded its originary value as a central element in becoming human.

III. After Freud

What follows will very likely appear schematic, since it invites reference both to other publications in which certain points are discussed at greater length and to future amplification yet to come.

3.1. Our point of departure will be a privileged experience of the workings of human time, that which presents itself in the *psychoanalytic experience of the cure*. Bypassing the lengthy exposition which a discussion of the analytic situation and the notion of transference would necessitate, let us proceed directly to another central point: interpretation.

Interpretation, we are accustomed to say, consists in translating a given datum – compared in an approximate analogy to a text – into another text. The given, a manifest dream for instance, is, according to Freud, to be ascribed a latent content. But a dream is not the only manifest phenomenon which lends itself to being so 'translated': likewise a symptom, a period of life, a parapraxis etc.

Let me insist first of all on a point which will perhaps not reveal its full sense until somewhat later: psychoanalytic interpretation is inseparable from a *method*, one which bears no relation to a vague, intuitive process. It proceeds step by step, and the essence of its progress is the *destruction* of the apparently rational constructs of the manifest phenomena. The process of this interpretation is, inherently, a process of *analysis*: the reduction to elementary particles each of which puts us on the track of one or several associative trains of thought.

With this priority of the method in mind, let us consider the great debate which arose between Freud and Jung, and which reverberates to our day, in the work of Ricoeur, with the opposition: *arche-telos*. Analytic interpretation, it is said, not without some justification, is retrogressive: it dismantles *present* constructs in order to reconstitute anterior tendencies, wishes, sets of events belonging to the past. We explain, supposedly, the symptoms of an obsessional neurotic but also perhaps the activity of Leonardo by referring them to this or that lived experience, trauma, fantasy or wish, which is seen as having persisted, unaltered since childhood.

Psychoanalysis thus sees itself blamed for being a flight into the *past*, a movement which can only reinforce the natural tendency of the human being to flee the responsibilities and tasks which are proposed to him by the present. From the very beginning almost, Jungian thought opposed a progressive interpretation to the retrograde or regressive one, seeking thereby to confront the human subject with his tasks and his being-for-the-future. The anagogic interpretation of Silberer, the Jungian interpretation, the invocation of *telos* by Ricoeur, all tend in this direction.

Let us pause for a moment on this debate, first to note that here, more fundamentally, there is a confrontation between different conceptions of temporalisation with its three *ekstases*: past, present and future. The three are explicitly placed in the following order by Freud: the present reawakens a past wish which then seeks its fulfilment in the future. Thus the cure would do nothing other than follow this movement: drawing our present acts back to our most deeply buried past motivations, with the aim of...?

It is here that the objections raised become pressing: here is why you always choose this or that type of woman who automatically makes you unhappy (present); it is owing to certain avatars of your infantile object choices (past). "Very well!" the analysand will retort, and not without a fallacious appearance of justification, "But what am I to do with this translation in terms of an infantile, more archaic wish? Must I abandon this early wish? Fulfil it? Sublimate it? (future)". In Molière's *The Doctor in Spite of Himself*, a buffoon impersonating a doctor solemnly intones a long string of gibberish Latin, concluding with the diagnosis, "And that is why your daughter is mute". Beyond the inanity of such an explanation, it is the inanity of *any* explanation that is evident. This objection of the teleologists is not without plausibility. But a flight into the future, which it proposes in opposition to a flight into the past, appears to us to open the door to a utopian or mystical illusion. To invert the present, past, future triad into present, future, past; to consider the past as being no more than the putting into perspective of a history which acquires a sense only through my project, this is the modern version of one and the same illusion, whether this illusion marches under the aegis of a philosophy of values, or a philosophy of the absurd or of being-towards-death.

In considering the psychoanalytic cure, let us hold fast to the Freudian triad: present, past, future. Let us consider that the movement proper to interpretation is to be located in the first dialectical moment, that which proceeds from the present towards the past; but contrary to Freud and to the whole of classical psychoanalysis, let us not assimilate this interpretation to a *translation* of the present into the past, and, even more importantly, let us not consider the past text as having more truth than, and surely not containing *the truth* of, the present text. Let us then propose the following thesis: in so far as the analytic method can be understood by the analogy with the process of translation, interpretation in terms of the past (infantile, archaic) *is not a translation but a de-translation*, a dismantling and a reversion of the translation. As the teleologists would maintain (and quite rightly) there is translation only in a progressive movement. But *analytic* interpretation consists in undoing an existing, spontaneous and perhaps symptomatic translation, in order to rediscover, anterior to the translation, what it so ardently wished to translate and possibly to permit a 'better' translation; that is to say one that is more complete, more comprehensive and less repressive.

In opposition to an entire tradition which cites Freud's authority and which is reproached with 'reducing' the present to the past and with considering that 'the die is cast at the age of five', our task is to expose forcefully several indications in Freud's work which accord with our interpretation. First, there is the fact that in his later thought ('Constructions in Analysis,' 1937) he reserves the term 'interpretation' not for the 'construction' of an infantile scenario which would underlie the adult scenario, but only for the precise, *analytic* bringing-to-evidence of a connection between a certain *element* of the present scenario and an isolated *element* of the past. The analytic method, as I have stressed above, proceeds by individual concatenations and, as it were, word by word, from representation to representation, never from phrase to phrase. The other evidence in support of our position – this time concerning the second movement of our triad (from the past to the future) – is Freud's persistent refusal to yield to the temptations of 'psychosynthesis'. You destroy, you reduce to fragments, he is reproached, and so you leave your unfortunate patient disjointed, in pieces. To which Freud's reply was always that the individual has only too great a tendency to recompose a unity, to re-translate, to recast a synthetic vision of himself and his future.

To conclude for the moment our discussion of the cure: the cure is not in the main the translation of a present scenario into a past scenario, from which point, and one knows not how, the patient would be required to fend for himself in attempting to integrate it into a project. The temporal movement of analysis in its exemplary and prototypical form is that of the splitting up of signifying sequences, be they present or past, into elements, isolated and, in the last resort, *enigmatic* elements, in order to permit the analysand to proceed spontaneously to a new synthesis or translation, one that is less partial, less repressive, less symptomatic.

3.2. The psychoanalytic cure, as innovative as it may be in the history of interhuman relations, can have neither sense nor results unless it encounters and enters into relation with something pre-existent and fundamental in human existence and its movement of temporalisation. What I am describing here, as the temporality of the cure, must find its equivalents in human temporality, in situations which could be considered as imperfect precursors or analogues of what it carries to a certain degree of purity and efficacy.

3.2.1. *Precursors and analogues*. There must exist in spontaneous existence moments, situations that can be described as periods of detranslation-retranslation. I have further postulated that there cannot exist any sort of 'translation of a translation' which would be authentic and that any progressive movement is possible only by a preliminary scraping and scouring of the present translation. The Latin Vulgate was a splendid moment in the translation of the Bible, as is the Bible of Luther. But Luther was compelled to dismantle the Vulgate in order to forge his translation, just as a modern translator must first dismantle both Luther and the Vulgate.

A situation analogous to that of the cure can be found in the painful experience of mourning. A thorough description of this experience which would take into account the whole of psychoanalytic study and observation is beyond my present scope. Let us merely indicate its salient elements. From the start, mourning was conceived by Freud as work and reworking. What I must however criticise in his conception is the fact that it places the accent primarily on the detachment of the subject from the loved one, the 'lost object'. The work of mourning is certainly much more complex: what Freud and probably the majority of analysts have missed is what this bears on, and the temporal dialectic which corresponds to it.

The movement in three stages could be described in this way: I have woven with a person a stable bond, a conception of existence which encompasses my activities, my hopes, my dreams. This is the text of the present. Now the sudden loss of the loved one causes the brutal collapse of this entire vision of the world. But mourning does not remain at this stage of pure and simple destruction which threatens to carry me away with it, and it is here that the key notion of work comes into play: "Each single one of the memories and expectations in which libido is bound to the object is brought up and hyper-cathected, and detachment of the libido is accomplished in respect of it."[3] Everything rests here on the notion of detachment (*Lösung*) which Freud, in an entirely inadequate understanding, considers as the liberating severing of a bond with the object, and not as an *analysis*. Upon the fabric of my existence, woven with the web of the other (now lost), loss causes me to perform an unravelling, a painful meditation. But each thread, although I indeed separate it off from the whole (…there is the spring where we used to drink together), is not broken as Freud claimed. It is, on the contrary, over-invested, contemplated separately, reintegrated into its history (…do you remember the first time you met her, beside this spring?) and beyond this history in common, of the couple for instance, reintegrated into a more inclusive and much longer history (...and it was beside this same spring that you played as a child, lovingly watched over by your mother).

Without dwelling further on this point, I wish merely to point out that the loss necessitates the work of a reordering of my existence, of a new vision which will take into account the absence of the loved one, but also will encompass his or her memory. But this new version or translation is only possible if it is preceded by the painful work of *Lösung*, of detachment from the former version; a work that is nevertheless fruitful, for each element is made richer by assimilation of its entire history, before finding itself reincorporated in a new attempt at living, in a new pro-ject.

Amongst those *elements*, to which the work of mourning causes us to come back to again and again, let me underline the importance of the *words and phrases* uttered by the other person. A major part in the pain of mourning is bound to the interrogation about what the *other* really wanted to tell me and about the dialogue we were unable to carry through with him. Far be it for me to wish to blur the differences between the psychoanalytic cure and the spontaneity of mourning. The cure seeks to be more *profound*, and the past elements that it seeks are more deeply buried and, as I stressed before, inaccessible without a *method*. The fact remains that if analysis proposes to undo the imperfect translations that the patient presents in his present life, his dreams, his symptoms, then there exists already, in human existence in general, something akin to a movement of translation, and of detranslation-retranslation.

3.2.2. This leads us to the view that the human being creates himself, ceaselessly, only by proposing to himself a self-representation, a 'theory', 'version' or' translation' which is the best possible (the most comfortable – the most faithful – the only one possible at a certain moment and under certain circumstances) Is it a translation of... himself? Psychoanalysis has taught us to consider this 'self' neither as auto-nomous, nor as transparent, nor even as auto-centred.

Let us go further. The movement of auto-translation, the drive to translate (*Trieb zur Übersetzung* – to use Novalis's term) issues, springs up, not from the *translator* but from this untranslated or this imperfectly translated, which endlessly *demands* a translation. What is then the originary to-be-translated? Here we arrive at the basis of the process of temporalisation, or to put it in another way, at the point where temporalisation, *active as it may be in its process*, is fundamentally passive as far as its motor and incentive is concerned

This primordial to-be-translated, this other of the process of temporalisation, is to be discovered at two levels: the inside-other (Freud's *das Andere*), that is the other-thing in us, and the outside-other (Freud's *der Andere*), that is the other person of our personal pre-history). The inside-other is termed the unconscious, but only on condition we consider the unconscious neither as a reservoir of the irreducible biological instincts, foreign to the human world, nor, on the contrary, as a structured discourse which need only be deciphered. The unconscious, as I envision it, is the result of repression bearing on fragments of communications which it, by so doing, makes foreign to the context which is their origin. In the unconscious the representations (verbal or non-verbal signifiers) exist side by side without organising themselves and even without contradicting each other. This resembles, if you will, the Parmenidean Being, but a being fragmented and not unique, which, and this is the key, has taken on the stability of being-reposing-in-itself or of thing-in-itself only *secondarily*, that is to say precisely by the act of repression.

It is the inexhaustible stores of material that each human being in the course of his existence strives as a last resort to translate into his acts, his speech, and the manner in which he represents himself to himself – it is this untranslatable that I term the unconscious, untranslatable but endlessly retranslated (more or less successfully depending on the case) – upon which the auto-theorisation of the human being seizes but which it cannot reduce except in an unstable and asymptotic fashion.

3.3. Can we still go further? Can we find a more *fundamental* origin for this diachronic imbalance which is established between the 'to be translated' and the present imperfect translation and which ceaselessly (or at least at each turning point of existence) pushes for renewed translation?

'Fundamental', as I intend it, does not signify abstract or transcendental. Beyond the empiricity of human existence, what I am seeking is a universal, ineluctable situation, but a situation which is that of the human being and not of a subject-in-general. In this sense, my philosophy remains an anthropology and my view remains that the only possible philosophy is anthropological, a fact which does not imply relativism but prompts us to define universal categories both of being human and of becoming human.

The *universal and originary situation* that I posit at the basis of the interhuman relation is that of *seduction*. This term, understood in the generalised sense that I am defining, encompasses a considerable number of variants for the adult (amorous seduction or the seduction inherent in the analytic cure itself) as well as for the infant (infantile seduction or precocious seduction). But beyond these situations, defined, despite their generality, as being *contingent*, (even the relation to a father or a mother is contingent, as general as it may be), what I am seeking to uncover is the essence of the seductive phenomenon or originary – primal – seduction. Seduction must be defined as a passivity-activity relationship, itself understood in the Cartesian sense: the active one is the one who has at his disposal more knowledge, more experience etc, than the passive one. In addition psychoanalysis introduces an essential component into the definition of this asymmetry: this "more" is *a-more-of-unconscious-knowledge* in the seducer, rather than in the seduced. Seduction is an asymmetrical relationship, whose prototype is furnished by the infant-adult couple. An infant is confronted by an adult world which from the beginning sends him messages, suffused with sexual meanings, unconscious meanings, which are unconscious for the transmitter of the message himself; messages perceived as enigmatic, that is as a 'to be translated'.

With respect to our present concern, temporalisation, let us note that this imbalance in itself is atemporal or rather *synchronic*. It is a situation which involves not time but rather the confrontation of two individuals of unequal development: a fully developed and complex adult, with his knowledge and his partially unconscious sexual particularities; and a child in a state of helplessness, in the sense that he has only rudimentary means to translate the messages and excitations that are presented to him.

A veritable *unmoved mover* of the movement of temporalisation, this imbalance gives rise immediately to what I shall characterise as an attempt at translation, an attempt which always fails in part, leaving behind it untranslated elements which constitute the first rudiments of the unconscious. What Freud designates on occasion as 'primal repression' is nothing other than the result of what can legitimately be called the proto-historisation of the human being: his manner of auto-theorising from the start, of responding to what I designate as 'enigmatic signifiers' with a world view, and thereby entering into time by means of translation, which is at once a taking oneself forward and a leaving behind. Soon the new translations will cover up this archaic to-be-translated. The succession of developmental stages, infinitely more complex than the tenets of the manuals of psychoanalysis would have it, is finally only this movement of detranslation-retranslation of an 'originary' (an adult originary, then the originary of the individual unconscious) according to available idioms: the 'languages' of orality, anality, genitality etc.

Let us consider once more the three ekstases: the human being reaches towards a future only because he is auto-theorising and auto-translating: each important circumstance of his life (and I have given the examples of mourning and the psychoanalytic cure), is for him the occasion to call into question the *present* translation, to detranslate it by turning towards the past and to attempt a better translation of this past, a more comprehensive translation, with renewed possibilities. The fundamental moments of human temporalisation are those in which this reworking takes place through the afterwards effect (*dans l'après coup*).

4. Conclusion

More schematic and condensed than truly developed here, our theory seeks to impart new impetus to philosophical reflection on the subject of time, dormant since the advances made by the post-Kantians, by the phenomenonologists as well as by the philosophers of history. The triad of temporal *ekstases* remains at the foundation of all dialectic conceptions. It remains for us only to take a position on the manner in which this movement proceeds, that is to determine what imbalance gives rise to it.

The Hegelian dialectic appears to us to locate this *imbalance* in the opposition past (thesis), present (antithesis); the movement thus being past > present > future. Even if, by a supreme reversal, the future is itself seen to be the truth of the past, or even to coincide with it.

The dialectic of existentialism in its most general sense, privileges 'being for' and therefore the imbalance present-future, the vision of the past being shaped in accordance with the project: present > future > past.

From its very beginning psychoanalysis has privileged the movement which begins with the present and turns towards the past. It remains for us to interpret this sequence: present > past > future, in the light of the translating-detranslating theory of human existence, and to connect this movement, generative of diachrony itself, to its synchronic model which is the originary situation of seduction: a situation of fundamental passivity (and not of so-called interaction), where the main process is that of *implantation* – and sometimes intromission – of the enigmatic signifiers from the sexual and sexually unconscious adult into the infant.

Notes

1. Sigmund Freud, *Beyond the Pleasure Principle* (1920), *The Standard Edition of the Complete Psychological Works of Sigmund Freud*, ed. James Strachey, (London, Hogarth Press 1955), vol.18, p.8.
2. S. Freud, 'The Economic Problem of Masochism' (1924), *S.E.* (1961) ibid., vol.19, p.160.
3. S. Freud, 'Mourning and Melancholia' (1917), *S.E.* (1957) ibid., vol.14, p.245.

The Drive and its Object-source: its fate in the transference

Why the drive? What is the drive for?[1] For me, this is a question that I think conceals a trap, like all questions if one answers them in their own terms. It is a question that one must question. Its formulation – fortunately – is ambiguous: is it a question of the 'drive' or the 'concept of the drive' that one wants to 'do' something with? I have no doubt that, in the minds of most of us, it is a question of the concept: a scientific and theoretical concept, as one says. How to use it? What use is it to us? In posing the terms of the question this way, one rallies to the pragmatist conception which has currency everywhere in the natural sciences and probably in psychoanalysis too. Certainly, (to follow this little detour), modern science does not give its allegiance to an immediate technicist 'doing' (*faire*). 'What for?', in the end, can mean: how does that help us understand? and not in order to act directly. (I think, for example, of concepts like those of astrophysics). But unfortunately, I would say, analysts seem to wish to give advice to physicists in matters of pragmatism. Tied to a daily practice, they demand that every concept helps them daily, at least to take their bearings, if not to construct and interpret. As for the 'what for?' asked about the concept of the drive, it is not unusual for us then to move on openly to a more general 'what for?' asked about theory itself. What is theory for? Theory is on the way to becoming one of the scapegoats of psychoanalysis. The other scapegoat being so-called applied psychoanalysis, which I call extra-mural psychoanalysis (*psychanalyse hors les murs*). Also, for theory as well as for extra-mural psychoanalysis, there is a double phenomenon of repulsion which makes them one.[2] The reason for this double banishment lies in a certain conception of theory as necessarily 'applied' (that is, technicist).

In answer therefore to our initial question 'what for?', I propose to formulate a double questioning: should one do something with the drive? and, secondly, what is the status, function and distance of theory in relation to experience (our experience, that of analytical practice)? And if I have posed in this preamble two questions which only add up to one in the end, an answer to this might come from the very content of what I intend to propose to you. Analytical theory ought to help locate the place of theory. I will return to this therefore at the end of this questioning.

My second comment in this preamble is as follows: it refers to history. The problem that we are posing for ourselves as analysts in 1984 is, of course, the drive. But can we untie this from every historical approach, every problematization, and every reference to preceding work, notably to Freudian work? I have expressed myself too often on this point to make more than a brief allusion here. Between us here I do not think that there can be a question of dogmatism. But Freudianism, as much that of Freud as those following him, is an experience, and, unfortunately, in French we do not have a single word to designate both acquired experience (*experience* in English) and scientifically codified experience which is *experiment*. In German as well there are two words.[3] What I want to say by this is that the experience I speak of is that conveyed by the English word experience, be it applied to practice or theory. For theory is also an experience, and precisely not in the sense of experimentalism. There is a living experience of concepts, of their derivation, what they borrow, their diversions and misleading directions. There is a way in which the evolution of theoretical experience is wedded to the ups and downs of the evolution of the thing itself, that is, the human being; and this wedding goes right to this being's errors about itself, as if the errors of the human being about itself were doubled yet again in the theoretical errors, which, of course, are to be located and transcended.

I would like to proceed now with experience in its second part (still within this English sense of *experience*), that is, in the common compost one calls practical or 'clinical' experience. In my meaning, this particular 'what for?' must answer to our thought about the drive. I will try to enumerate these requirements of practical experience in four points.

1. The first requirement is psychic determinism. There is a general affirmation of psychic determinism that no analyst will deny. The psychic domain like all others must be able to be ordered by reason. Chance must be banned from it, etc. It is a pretty general Freudian postulate. It is a postulate for psychologists, and not just analysts. Freud sides openly with science here, in the sense that man is a part of nature. But (as there is a but), if there was only that, psychoanalysis would only be a psychology; it would be a science like all the others and must follow the movement of all sciences, that is, the passing by of confused subjective notions (notions like will, motivations, i.e. causes, and that is the point, of course); it must move away from the notion of cause, as has long been said about the natural sciences, and move towards the establishment of *laws*, that is, of constant and quantifiable relations between phenomena. As for the notion of cause, one can justly suppose that it is drawn from a certain subjective experience of psychic activity, and that it is first found projected into the external world; we suppose that the world itself is moved by something in the way that we ourselves have the impression of moving or being moved. Gradually within the sciences of the external world, this cause gives way to the establishment of regular sequences of which the ideal is the mathematical function. So if one follows this movement of science, the reflux must come into play: there must be a re-interiorisation of the law-governed determinism, that is, of mathematical (or some would say mathemic) determinism of the inner world; there must be a re-conquest of the psychic by natural science.

Now there is a 'difficulty' (os) which bars this reflux (you will excuse this slightly incoherent metaphor).[4] This 'difficulty' is not the recourse to meaning, it is not the personalist claim. It is the resistance and deepening of the notion of cause offered to us by psychoanalysis. The investigation, analysis, interpretation of the symptom, dream, lapsus, parapraxis etc., can well be called the search for meaning. But, beyond meaning, as Freud shows us, there is another content, and, because of this fact, there is a real cause that we are searching for. And within the constant evolution of Freudian thought on this theme, there is the idea of the Id; the idea that we are acted upon by that ensemble of obscure causes that he calls the Id, puts a quasi-definitive seal on the recognition of our fundamental de-centring.

2. My second point, still within these requirements we have made of every notion of the drive, would be the following: the cause, the causes that psychoanalysis researches and discovers are of the order of representation. They are memories (*souvenirs*), fantasies (*fantasmes*), or imaginings, imagos (unconscious representations) with a double peculiarity. It is a question of representations as set or fixed beyond the meaning that can inhabit them, and beyond the multiple meanings that we can give them. These fixed or set representations have the productive power of schemas at the same time as the materiality of quasi-things. It is thus that I have commented on the translation problem posed by Freud's term *Sachvorstellung*, which is of course representation of the thing as the object of intention, but which in the unconscious becomes a real representation-thing. This movement from the representation of the thing to thing-representation signifies precisely that fixation beyond all meaning, that is, beyond all reference, as linguists say. The second particularity of these representations is that they are unconscious or they dive into the unconscious, and that a part of them at least is incapable of becoming conscious again, even, as we know, through analysis. Analysis can only state that a part of the unconscious can never be re-memorized and brought again to consciousness, but only be enclosed in a network of constructions which tries to approach it but never reaches the thing itself, the thing-representation itself.

3. My third requirement is that these representations have a great deal to do with bodily processes, and organize themselves around the body, or some of its zones or functions. This is the essential recognition of the 'organizations' – or of the complexes – of the libido, which are the fantasmatic organizations well described by Freud. From this centring on organizations, it is only a

step to seeing in the erogenous zone (oral, anal, genital etc.) the source of the drive. A step that is easy to take and which Freud seems to take briskly in the *Three Essays on the Theory of Sexuality*; but this briskness is perhaps relatively easy when it is a question of the genital zone (to say that the penis or the female genital organs are the source of the drive seems to make sense), or even of the anal or oral zone (but *where* really is the somatic source of oral excitation? in the end, no one has formulated it persuasively). In any case, this metamorphosis of the source is much more difficult to maintain when it comes to something like the drive to see (is the drive to see an excitation of the eye? is there an ocular orgasm? few amongst us would agree with this); or again when it comes to the sadistic drive originating in a supposedly muscular excitation?

4. My fourth requirement, finally, is to account for the phenomena of displacement. Freud underlines from the beginning of his first writings, notably the *Studies on Hysteria*, experiences of the fact that the same affective reaction can find itself connected to a completely different representation from the real circumstances of its origin; there is something that we cannot avoid in our experience and reflection. Or the stifling of affect, the 'beautiful indifference' of hysterics as one says, and its supposed re-appearance in the somatization of the hysterical attack. Or the detachment of the affect from all representation, its disqualification, and, in place of a qualified specific affect, anguish arrives unexpectedly. Or phenomena like transference, in all the meanings of this term, be it the dream transference, that is, the transference onto the residues of the day in dreams; transference of certain affects, certain wishful movements; or even transference in the usual sense that we employ it, that is, transference in the psychoanalytic treatment. There we have the multiple experiences of analysis, which perhaps only come to radicalize a certain spontaneous way of seeing; I want to say that displacement is an experience of analysis, but that it is already a daily experience, an experience of daily language. What else do we do when we say (and we say it without Freud): 'we carry over our love for such and such a person onto another', 'we have an aggressive potential that only wants to find an object, no matter which, the first which comes to hand, the first occasion etc.'? In

short, the phenomenon of displacement, indeed of condensation too, leads very naturally towards a theory of the radical separation of affect and representation, and towards a schematization that renders the one independent of the other; the one, the affect, following the physical model, being the mover, the other, the associative track (*voie*), leading from one representation to another (incorporating all the Freudian metaphors about chains and steel tracks). There is a very powerful, and persuasive, if not convincing, experience there that leads straight to physicalist models formed in terms of quantity and neurone, energy and structure, or formed even in terms of figuration and movement, as one said in the 17th century. This model dominates Freudian thought throughout its evolution.

I will give more detail on my position on the economic hypothesis in a moment. I want only to stress that no metapsychological thought can neglect taking account of the displacement that is our daily experience. But, conversely, we must recognize that absolute displacement, that in which affect retains nothing of its representation of origin, is only a case of a figuration that has never been achieved; it is asymptotic, as would be an absolute primary process. It is obviously psychopathology (in the broadest sense, *Psychopathology of Everyday Life* included) which provides the models of the most radical displacements (or as I tend to put it: the 'most oblivious' displacements, oblivious of whence they came). But a radical displacement, an absolute primary process, ought to be able to translate itself into the sequence: 'I've forgotten – what? – I've forgotten – what? – I've forgotten'; which is precisely the absolute limit posed for analytic investigation, if it wishes effectively to search for what has been forgotten; which supposes that the primary process might not be absolute.

A causalist determinism renders us strangers to ourselves and alienates us in an Id/It (*ça*). A determinism through unconscious structures works through representations that drift about in complexes linked to the body or some of its parts and functions. The phenomenon of displacement does not allow itself either to be neglected or to be driven to the absolute. These are four results of analytic experience. I do not mean raw experience (there aren't any empirically), but an experience relatively independent of all theoretical system. It is there that the theory of the drive grafts itself, if there is a drive. It is there, with remarkable success, that Freud comes to introduce two models that are nonetheless very different: a so-called physicalist model, taking all phenomena back, as I said a moment ago, to energy + figuration or energy + representation; and a biologizing model, founded in the principle of invariance, that is, the undeniable tendency of every organism to maintain its structural difference and energy-level difference from its environment. These two Freudian models sometimes compete with each other, and most often combine with each other, but their place must be incessantly re-evaluated. To offer a word about my own personal evaluation of these two models, I would say that the principal virtue of the physicalist model is its physical falsehood, which renders the model more appropriate to account for an *alien* materiality, which is as hard as iron or harder than it, and which we designate as 'unconscious psychic reality' or as the 'alien internal body'. It is certainly there that the return – or the re-introjection, as one says – occurs, the return of false physical causality to its place of origin: the psychical unconscious. As for the homeostatic, biologising model, the most verifiable aspects throughout the Freudian elaboration concern the ego (*le moi*).

My aim is in no way to explicate the Freudian theory of the drive as constituting a sort of synthesis or compromise between physicalism and biologism. I will only enumerate: source, thrust, aim, and object, with that famous contingency of the object which brings us so many problems. And I will only remind you of the biological origin of the sexual drive, according to Freud, which, moreover, is under the same heading as the biological origin of the self-preservatory functions. You know the most synthetic formula: the drive is a 'concept-limit between the psychical and the somatic'; it is 'the amount of demand for work imposed on the soul (*âme*) as a consequence of its relation to the corporeal'.

Let us turn our sights on this massive recourse to the biological in the light of our previous four requirements. The requirement of a cause that alienates us and renders us foreign to our own acts; certainly, yes, the biological reference renders us foreign to our own acts. The intimate connection with body-zones (my third requirement above): this also seems to fit... even though the state of tension, tumescence and detumescence, might only be a very poor model to account for the notion of drive-source (I evoked the ocular drive above). What about our fourth point, displacement? Well, the biological theory of the drive takes account of Freud's theory, but at the cost of pushing it to the absolute. The contingency of the object is total. The drive is summed up in a thrust (the only thing that remains from this kind of common tool we call the drive is the *Drang*), an energy thrust that attaches itself to (and detaches itself from) anything, just as in a lure. But it is our second requirement concerning a relationship to representations (memories and fantasies), where the biological theory is weakest and most arbitrary, as it denies to these representations all their own efficacity, only to see there the site for an engagement or investment by some undifferentiated and floating energy. To my mind, the recourse to a biological drive to account for unconscious determinism is an unverifiable and disputable hypothesis which is outside analysis.

Let us go further. The hypothesis of an innate drive-equipment necessarily carries with it the idea that fantasies (*fantasmes*) are only efflorescences, psychic translations of an endogenous and finally maturational evolution. This is Freud's postulation at the most biologizing moment of his thought between 1897 and 1905, following his famous letter to Fliess of 21 September 1897. This is also proved by Melanie Klein, for whom fantasy (*fantasme*) and drive are closely linked, and, in the end, endogenous (something she has been accused of so many times), not only in their power but in their modalities of making themselves manifest. There we are on the route to biological idealism, where the lived experience (*le vécu*) is only a fastening or anchoring point. There we have a decisive objection to every psychoanalytic theory which sets itself up around a confrontation between a biological or psycho-somatic organism, and an environment which is essentially considered to be non-psychic.

Is it possible to formulate another drive theory, or must we abandon all notions of drive? Can we propose another 'take' on the Freudian approach, the return to another Freud, a third model, say, sketched by Freud but left in its card-board box? One of many directions might come from the fact that the *Trieb*, the drive, only comes to the fore in 1905 (even if the term appears once in the *Entwurf* [*Project*]).

But, of course, the notion of internal excitation at source was present previously. Internal excitation, Freud reminds us, is something we can subtract ourselves from only through motility. This is an undeniable definition, but, from the outset, the question remains *open*: is it only through the body one can remove oneself by motility? Or is the body internally alien to itself, and also therefore to reminiscence? There is another (German) word in the Freud letters to Fliess, and this is *Impuls*; this word can be found in a number of very specific contemporary texts, and is translated in the present edition of *Naissance de la Psychanalyse* (the French translation of the Freud/Fliess Correspondence) by the French term 'pulsion' ('drive' in English). There is no doubt that these are neither corporeal forces nor even investments of fantasy. From these *Impulsen*, these meaningful drives (as in physics or electronics), the very action of repressed fantasies is born and flows as if from its source. You will find this notably in the *Draft N* (Freud/Fliess Correspondence, pp.250–2). These texts with their precursory use of *Trieb* are wholly situated in what one calls the seduction theory, in other words, the Freudian model of *primal seduction and repression*, which I am trying to get to working through the origin of the drives.

The presentation which follows should only be taken as a general schema. It should not be seen in a strictly chronological way, although it is a schema of 'giving birth' (*engendrement*), and in the broadest sense a genetic one (if one takes 'genetic' in the broad sense of 'giving birth'). Whereas the classical theory of the drives proposed antecedence and a single expository stage of endogenous somatic stimuli, we think it is necessary to conceive of a dual expository stage: on the one hand, the preliminary stage of an organism that is bound to homeostasis and self-preservation, and, on the other hand, the stage of the adult cultural world in which the infant is immediately and completely immersed.

Let us go into a little detail. We oppose self-preservatory functions to sexuality. Self-preservatory functions, like all biological and bio-psychological functions, aim at maintaining the structure and constancy of the organism, and so are assimilable to a homeostatic level of energy: in the end, this was the model that physics took up again in its regulatory and feed-back systems. Self-preservation is primary for humans just as for all living things. I insist though that it implies an immediate opening to the world – a perceptive and motor opening of the organism to its environment. The idea of an organism which is first closed in on itself, then secondly opens itself to an object (or, who knows, perhaps even constructs it?), is one of the forms of biological idealism and solipsism that many psychoanalytic theoreticians have unwisely adopted.

Conversely, following Freud, and marginally also Bolk, one has rightly insisted on the partial lapse, or on the delay of adaptive mechanisms in the human being, rather than the special fulfilment (*pregnance*) of self-preservation. This dependency of the little human being on the adult, which is much more marked than in other species, favours the dislocation (*décalage*) in which humanization originates, namely the precocious sexualization of the human being. However, modern research (such as Brazelton's) has shown just how much the small infant's perceptual and adaptive openness to the object should not be underestimated. There anyway is the first expository stage around the nuances necessary to apply to the notion of self-preservation.

The second stage concerns the adult world which confronts the newly born organism. Quickly, we repeat that this is a world of signification (*signifiance*) and communication, where everything overflows the infant's capacities for apprehension and mastery. Messages are put out everywhere. By messages, I do not primarily or necessarily mean verbal messages. Every gesture, and every mimicry functions as a signifier. Let us name these primal and traumatic signifiers 'enigmatic signifiers', and state precisely what we understand by this term. These signifiers are not rendered enigmatic by the simple fact that the infant does not possess the code that he will need to acquire. We know well that the infant starts to inhabit verbal language without anyone providing it with a preliminary code, just as one can acquire a foreign language by simple daily practice. That's not the issue. The issue is rather that the adult world is entirely infiltrated with unconscious and sexual significations, of which *the adult too* does not possess the code. And, on the other hand, there is the issue that the infant possesses neither the emotional nor physiological responses which correspond to the sexualized messages that are proposed to it; in short, its means to establish a substitute or provisional code are fundamentally inadequate.

What then is seduction, both as a datum and as a theory? At this very moment, quite a meal is being made out of it, based on the Freud/Fliess Correspondence, and what Freud might either have remained silent about or repressed, that is the historical facts of seduction that he might have been confronted with (as much in his self-analysis as in his first analytical cases). Anecdotes are one thing and seduction as a structural phenomenon is another. And perhaps even the former have been harmful to the latter? I would like to say this: perhaps the partial abandonment of the seduction theory in 1897 was due to Freud's own confusion between the contingency of so-called 'perverse' adult sexual behaviour and the general nature of the seduction situation. Freud cast aside his 'neurotica', whereas perhaps he would have done better to go deeper into it, notably in the direction of fundamental and primal seduction. Later, he partially corrected his aim by underlining the general nature of seduction in connection with maternal care. But it is still necessary to take this further, and see the daily practice beyond exciting, perverse, or simply naive behaviour.

I quickly take up again my example of the breast, with all the extreme and perhaps exorbitant importance that is bestowed on it by psychoanalysis. Now amidst all this efflorescence around the breast, the good and the bad, and the given or refused breast, and with respect to its omnipresence amongst analysts, notably child analysts, I will underline the absence in psychoanalytic reflection of the erogenous and erotic breast. The breast is a major erogenous zone in a woman, which cannot fail to perform that function in relationship to the child. What does this breast which feeds and excites me want of me? What incites me to be excited? What does it want to say to me that it doesn't know itself? The example of the breast is perhaps only a fable, above all for the modern infant who has increasingly less contact with it. But it does have the merit of enabling us to grasp on which bases the constitution of the first object-sources, interiorized or rather introjected objects, are produced. In the beginning, there is a relationship centred on self preservation and the satisfaction of a major adaptive need (feeding). In the beginning also, there is the centring on the oral zone, which is an exchange zone between the exterior and the interior of the body, understanding here that this might become the rallying and fixation point of an erogeneity, without there being any need to attribute to it any specific physiological erectility whatsoever. In the beginning also, concomitant with the contribution of food (milk), there is the instrumentality of the breast which is imposed as an enigmatic signifier, and laden with a pleasure which is unknown to itself and impossible to encircle.

In passing, and without delay, I will grasp this opportunity to say a few words about the theory of 'leaning on' . This theory was given prominence, put aside, then recovered by Freud, and later by others of us. This theory of 'leaning on' affirms the surge of the sexual drive in support of (*in Anlehnung an*) the function of self-preservation. This support articulates or translates itself (*se traduit*) through the fact that both the sexual drive and self-preservation originate in the same place, in the same source, and in the same activity, then the object and the aim start to diverge in a progressive cleaving movement. The object, as you know, undergoes a diversion of a metonymic kind, through contiguity: that is, to the breast from the milk; and the aim is diverted metaphorically in relation to the aim of feeding, namely through modelling itself by analogy with incorporation. 'Leaning on' has actually become a very muddied term. It has been turned into the mind's 'propping' on the body, and one has talked of 'counter-propping' (of the body on the mind) etc. But even taken in the best sense (the Freudian sense), it is only the extreme of a physiological conception of a sexual drive which must be upset and overturned. It is inconceivable that sexuality emerges biologically from self-preservation, even if this were by a dislocation between aim and object. This is the extreme, the *ne plus ultra* of Robinson Crusoeism, by which we should understand the attempt to reconstruct the cultural world starting from the endogenous resources of the solitary baby-Robinson. My formulation will therefore be: the only truth of 'leaning on' is primal seduction. It is because the adult's gestures directed at the child's preservation carry unconscious sexual messages (i.e. unconscious for them), which in turn cannot be mastered by the child, that such gestures produce the movement of cleaving and drifting (*dérive*) that eventually ends up in autoerotic activity. But the obligatory vehicle of autoeroticism, that is, what stimulates it and makes it exist, is the intrusion of enigmatic signifiers brought by the adult, then their subsequent repression.

It is necessary therefore to talk here of primal repression, because it is from this single movement that a primordial unconscious is split from the psyche and becomes an Id (*ça*), and constitutes the first object-sources, that is, sources of the drives. In conformity with the Freudian theory of afterwardsness (*Nachträglichkeit*), we conceive this primal repression in at least two forms of time. The first form of time, which is passive, as with implantation, is the first inscription of enigmatic signifiers before they have been repressed. They have a sort of dormant status, or an external-internal one or even a sexual/pre-sexual one (following another of Freud's expressions). The second form of time is linked to a reactualization and a reactivation of these signifiers, which henceforth are internal and attacking, and which the child must try to link together. It is the attempt to link, to symbolize dangerous and traumatic signifiers, which results both in what Freud calls the child's theorization (infantile sexual theories), and in the partial failure of this symbolization or theorization, let us say in the repression of an unmasterable, unencirclable remainder. These are thing representations (*Sachvorstellungen*), which have become thing-like representations, and assume an isolated status, outside communication and signification (*signifiance*), in what one calls the Id.[7]

The drive is therefore neither a mythical entity, nor a biological force, nor a borderline concept. It is the impact on the individual and on the ego (le moi) of the constant internal stimulation exercised by the repressed thing-(re)presentations, which one can designate as object-sources of the drive. As for the relation of the drive to the body and to erogenous zones, this relation should not be conceived with the body as starting point, but rather as the action of repressed object-sources on the body; and this action takes place across the ego (*le moi*) which is first of all a body-ego (*le moi-corps*), and in which, very naturally, erogenous zones become the sites which precipitate and organize fantasies.

A brief word on *drive dualism* to recall a thesis which argues that there is *an internal dichotomy articulated within the sexual drive*. It is a function of the very nature of the object-source to distinguish between life-drives and death-drives. In the death-drive, the object is reduced to a single, unilateral, fractured, stimulating, and indeed destructive aspect. In the life-drive, the object always has unified and totalized aspects, even if it's a question of what's called a part-object, that is, a part of the body. And so the object-sources of the life- and death-drives are finally the same, but, in the latter case are reduced through desperate conflict and cut down in their level of excitation, whilst, in the former case, recover their own tendency to unify and synthesize in the very presentation of the object-source.

I would like to repeat a few things about the so-called 'economic' conception of the drives to distinguish between quantitative aspects and modes of functioning. First of all, to postulate the idea of a relatively constant drive-strength remains plausible , even if it is utopian to to wish to quantify that power. It is a question here of nothing other than the 'exigency of work' that is exacted by the 'repressed unconscious prototypes'. If I had to make a quasi-metaphysical hypothesis about the final origin of that power, I would say that it measures up to the difference or imbalance between what is symbolizable and what is not in the enigmatic messages brought to the child. If you like, it measures out the traumatic quantity.

Secondly, aside from any quantifying aim, the constancy of the drive's push is only approximate and valid for a determined time lapse. Against the idea of absolute constancy, one could pose the hypothesis of a neo-creation of sexual 'energy' based on the same lines that governed its original genesis.

But there is another economical aspect which remains very important, and that is the distinction between modes of functioning: primary process (of so-called free energy) and secondary process (of so-called bound energy). It is possible to imagine that the circulation in question – free and bound types, or more or less free or bound types of circulation – could be conceived following a non-physicalist model and refer to what one could call the circulation of meaning or information in communication circuits – with perhaps the accompanying paradox that it is also necessary to talk about the circulation of non-meaning, that is, the non-symbolized.

Finally, still within this problematic of psychic economics, I come back to Freud's postulation of the independent existence of affect and representation based on incontrovertible clinical facts. On the one hand, this independent existence is worth translating in terms of the circulation model I've just evoked, and, on the other hand, it's worth modulating it according to the particular case. The more an affect is qualified, the less mobile it is; the less qualified it is, the nearer the specific process draws to the primary process. But one can only asymptotically postulate a discharge (anxiety) or an absolutely unbound (*delié*) displacement of affect.[8]

I intended to relate the drive to the transference. That would necessitate a lengthy expansion, so I will be content just to point out the scope of the issue. In my view, transference is characteristic of the analytical situation and of other specific intersubjective constellations which have in common the reproduction and renewal of the primal seduction situation. This is how I interpret Lacan's formulation of the 'subject who is supposed to know', which he proposed as a suggestion rather than argued for in detail. In the beginning, the subject who is supposed to know is the adult for the child; so much so, that one can say that the primal situation of the drive is already both a transference and a transcendent relationship. A transcendence within its own terms (*en deça*), as there is an emptiness of signification (*signifiance*) or a lack of signified (*signifié*) which constitutes the enigmatic character of the adult message. A transcendence and transference beyond their own terms (*au delà*), as every movement of symbolization consists in adding new signifiers in order to displace, transpose, and thus bind together the original and most traumatic signifiers. Transference – in the analytical sense – can be nothing else but the pursuit or renewal of this movement of symbolization. In this sense, far from being a sort of role-play or disillusion-game that some wish to find in it, transference would be the reopening of the primal transference, and, in turn, its fate could be nothing else than to be itself transferred (the 'transference of the transference' is a formulation I have rediscovered in Wilhelm Reich, though he probably doesn't give it the same meaning).

I also promised to return to my two initial questions: must one 'do' something with the drive? and what is the status of the theory of the drive? Well, the very content of what I've proposed offers some avenues. First of all, 'what to do?'. It cannot be denied that this kind of question (what for?) is inseparable in its 'representation-purpose' from an adaptive aim. This is the adaption of a concept to a finality, even if this were purely technical and did not claim to imply 'value'. Has the question 'what for?' grounds for existing in the sexual field? Isn't it important to ask oneself first of all what the drive can do with us and how we can deal with it?

As for the status of the theory, this can't be separated from the function of knowledge and of infantile theorization in the birth of the psyche (I recall again the term 'infantile sexual theories'). There is no question at all of devaluing the theory, as people often want to by making it an avatar of fantasy, while performing a devaluation of fantasy in its own right by seeing it just as fictional, and only emphasizing its unreal aspects . If you really wish to follow me, you must suppose that analytic theory at its most general level (notably this theory of the drive or of the object-source) must show us how, in what conditions, with what results, and failures, and at what price, the subject 'theorizes' and metabolizes the enigmas which directly present interhuman communication. In a certain way, therefore, analytic theory is a metatheory in relation to the fundamental theorization operated by the human being: not first of all to appropriate nature cognitively but to bind anxiety in relation to the traumatic effect of the enigma.

This means that analytic theory has no way at all of imposing itself on, or even interfering with this process of individual symbolization as it is operated from the beginning and as is claimed to be pursued by clinical treatment. The theory says that there are grounds to help patients to 'theorize' in their own terms, with the elements left over from their individual history. The theory of the drive – a drive finding its source in the object-representations of every individual – is an inducement to maintain analytical theory at a distance from clinical practice and its process of transference.

Notes

1. 'La pulsion, pour quoi faire?' The French contains these two meanings whose ambivalence Laplanche subsequently explores. Important in structuring this ambivalence is the infinitive verb 'faire' (to do), which cannot be carried over into English.

2. The French word 'repulsion' (repulsion) contains the French word for 'drive' (*pulsion*). The use of this term appeals therefore to the repression of drives by theory and extra-mural psychoanalysis.

3. Laplance refers here to the distinction between experience as tentative or searched for (as in *Erfahrung*, *Experiment* or *Versuch*), and experience as lived in the past (as in *Erlebnis* and *Ereignis*) [*New Foundations for Psychoanalysis*, p.249].

4. 'Or il y a un "os" qui s'oppose a ce reflux...' 'Os' literally means a bone, but here is

employed in a colloquial sense: 'C'est un os bien dur à ronger' means 'it's a hard bone to gnaw', or, to use a similar English expression, 'it's a hard nut to crack.'

5. Freud refers to his theory of the neuroses as his 'neurotica' in his letter to Fliess of September 21, 1897 (Freud/Fliess Correspondence, p.264).

6. 'Propping' or 'leaning on' (*étayage*) is Laplanche's suggested translation of Freud's term 'Anlehung'. Strachey translates this by 'anaclisis', a neologism that has been consistently and heavily criticized (cf. *The Language of Psychoanalysis*, pp.29–32; *New Foundations*, pp.144–5).

7. Laplanche refers again here to Freud's distinction between thing-representation (*Sachvorstellung*) and word-representation (*Wortvorstellung*) which has been overlooked by many critics. Failure to note this distinction constitutes an important part of the Laplanchian critique of Lacan's conception of the unconscious (*The Language of Psychoanalysis*, pp.447–9; *New Foundations*, p.53.

8. 'Anxiety' is the *Standard Edition* translation of the German 'Angst', which Laplanche renders as 'angoisse' in French, which is nearer 'anguish' in English; 'dé-lié' – unbound or unlinked – forms a pun here with *délie* – meaning 'supple' or 'nimble', especially when applied to the mind (*un esprit délié*).

The Wall and the Arcade

'For if the sentence is the wall before the original language; the word for word is the arcade'.

Walter Benjamin [1]

I always have problems with the 'title', which I think has something to do with the process of sublimation. I have systematically and repeatedly forgotten the title of these conferences.[2] I was told: this year our conference has a more speculative, even philosophical, subject; you must have something to say about it.

My own title, with which I was quite pleased – I mean that it incited me, and three quarters of the exercise lies in incitement – was successively: 'Translation of an unknown text', then 'Translation of unknown inscriptions' (you will see why I changed it). But I was warned that this title was already heavily 'occupied': *besetzt*, as we say with respect to Freudian terminology, when a French term is already entrusted to translate a certain German word.

'The Wall and the Arcade', my opening epigraph taken from Benjamin, suited me. In a temporary backlash to this, I felt a tendency to say 'The Wall *or* the Arcade' in order to compose too good a title; but there is also the wall *and* the arcade, which together form an arcade through which to pass.

I would like to centre on something I find myself immersed in these days willy nilly: translation. I am grappling more than ever before with the practice of translation by translating the *Gesammelte Werke* of Freud: translation as general questioning, for which the epigraph above from Benjamin provides one orientation point among many others to relate to; translation as the ineluctable model of analysis, when it is a question of the soul's apparatus (Freud's *Seelische Apparat*),[3] of repression, but also of interpretation, sublimation etc.; finally – and my drift leads me there willy nilly – there is translation as a model of the drive and as the drive which impels me. Long before Freudian meditation helped us to progress with terms like 'the drive to' and 'the pleasure to' (indissociable from the pleasure of), the terms the 'drive to translate' and the 'pleasure to translate' have been current in Germanic reflections for almost two centuries.

The arcade? I asked Michel Tourlière to provide an illustration for a book that's just appeared of what might be a 'new foundation':[4] a change of foundations. In sending me back a picture of 'alternative foundations', which could be seen as alternating provisional arcades, thus suggesting an *interpretation*, namely that everything lies in this 'let circulate' (*laissez circuler*) or 'let see' (*laissez voir*) that this very alternation suggests.

For Benjamin, it is the *Wörtlichkeit*, the word for word (which he continues to designate as an 'interlinear' dimension of translation), that is the arcade. How does it go for Freud? Calling *The Interpretation of Dreams* to the rescue, I came across a 'current title' at the end of chapter 7: *Der Zwang zur Zusammensetzung*, 'the compulsion (*contrainte*) to compose', which one can only pair up with our *Trieb zur Übersetzung* (the drive to translate).[5]

In Freud's chapter, the 'compulsion to compose' is the secondary elaboration. Pontalis and I have noted often that this elaboration is neither 'secondary' nor as negligible as one would like to think. In *The Interpretation of Dreams*, I will stop at this passage where Freud compares analytic interpretation with the two ancient methods of interpretation: 'The first of these procedures considers the content of the dream as a whole and seeks to replace it by another content which is intelligible and in certain respects analogous to the original one. This is the '*symbolic*' dream-interpreting; and it inevitably breaks down when faced by dreams which are not merely unintelligible but also confused';[6] and Freud follows this with the example of the famous dream of the seven thin cows that devour the seven fat cows, which is interpreted as seven years of famine following on from seven years of plenty. The second method – which is by far Freud's preferred method – is totally different: this is the *Chiffriermethode*, that is, the 'decoding' method which 'treats dreams as a kind of cryptography in which each sign can be translated into another sign having a known meaning, in accordance with a fixed key...' [7] Obviously, there is an immediate criticism of this: a fixed cipher provides no guarantees. Freud tells us, however, that this procedure can be corrected in a certain way, and this dictionary, this cipher of dreams (*songes*), can become supple and take into account the context, the personality and life-circumstances of the dreamer, etc.; the cipher therefore adapts to the context. Obviously this procedure guarantees neither the proposed fixed cipher nor the multiple cipher. But we will now see why Freud nonetheless by far prefers this method to the first one.

All this seems so old-fashioned that it's worthwhile staying with this issue for a while. First of all, even if this may seem to digress, I would like to stress the following passage, which has never been excised from *The Interpretation of Dreams*, in which Freud describes the required attitude of mind for psychoanalysis (or rather self-analysis), as 'an uncritical self-observation' (*kritiklose Selbstbeobachtung*) (S.E., 4, p.101). This is a long way from our statement of the 'fundamental rule' (that enjoins the analysand to say everything that occurs to him), because it ignores the prescription of a certain attitude of mind on the analyst's part previously described here as 'equally suspended'; so , o.k., from the analysand's point of view, this is a rule which includes, by implication, what will later be required of the analyst. I therefore can't resist quoting this passage which seems to join up what's previously been divided between analyst and analysand into a primal unity (which is nothing more than a sort of primal self-analyzing , or the primal self-analyzing as suggested by Mannoni or Anzieu): '[What is in question, evidently, is] the establishment of a psychical state which, in its distribution of psychical energy (that is, of mobile attention), bears some analogy to the state before falling asleep and no doubt also to hypnosis' (Freud, S.E. vol. 4, p.102).

So what principally does this equal division between analysand and analyst add up to? Nothing other than to cut up the dream narrative completely and systematically (attention to the word for word connections). I re-read this passage: 'Our first step in the employment of this procedure teaches us that what we must take as the object of our attention is not the dream as a whole but the separate portions of its content... Thus the method of dream interpretation which I practice already differs from the popular, historic and legendary method of interpretation by means of symbolism and approximates to the second or 'decoding' method. Like the latter, it regards dreams from the very first as being of a composite character (*Zusammengesetztes*), as being conglomerates of psychical formations' (S.E., 4, p.104).

We all know that we don't get very far like this, and for the very best reasons. First, Freud agreed that it was difficult wholly to apply this model, for reasons that ultimately relate back to the notion of the 'whole' or 'all' (*le tout*): *the whole or all* of time, because most often we don't have the material time to analyze in depth, and we incessantly move from one dream to another; the whole or all of the analytic session, where the dream is included in another 'whole' from which there is no reason to detach it to form a specific separate object; the whole of what one calls the analytic relationship, the whole or all of the transference, all of the process... despite everything, I ask myself if all these good reasons relating to *Zusammensetzung* (construction, putting together) – don't really just serve the less worthy aim of leading us back again to the 'whole' (*en masse*), and thus distance us from analysis as *Lösung*, i.e. untying, and as *Entbindung*, i.e. unbinding and as the labour of birth.

This stubbornly defended outpost against fragmentation sends out echos even to the very late text 'Constructions in Analysis' (1937). Certainly, in this piece, constructions are fully installed as an essential element in analysis; but they are also installed at the same time in opposition to the privileged term *Deutung*, or interpretation, which is henceforth to be confined to the linkage between one element and another, in other words, the *Wörtlichkeit*, the word for word. Of course, this last term is not Freud's but Benjamin's.

Isn't this just saying that the construction – no matter whether it's from the analysand or analyst or whether its made inside or outside the session or whether by Freud or by one of us – actually follows a necessary route that also goes against the grain of analysis, against this *Verfahren* (way of proceeding) which constitutes the Freudian method, that is, a means of getting on, of proceeding.

There was an objection to Freud's refusal of 'psycho-synthesis', and you know how he replied – and my comments here don't contradict this. Synthesis? It is so obligatory; we are so pushed towards it; everyone is so constrained by it; and everyone grabs on to it all the time; so much so that we scarcely need preoccupy ourselves with it…

*

I take a break here to turn to Benjamin and to his article 'The Task of the Translator' (*Die Aufgabe des Übersetzers*).[8] I found several formulæ here which served as incitements and rebounds, but, as I'll show presently, this is only one point, a star in a huge firmament, which we French people are only just beginning to conceptualize. I'm thinking here of the firmament of German thought and its approach to translation. A book like Antoine Berman's *L'épreuve de l'étranger* (1984) gives us some idea of it, though obviously in a very condensed way. Benjamin participates in the great 'anti-ethnocentric' movement (to use Berman's recent term) – or what I call the 'anti-auto- or self-centred' movement of translation (*le mouvement anti-autocentrique de la traduction*):[9] a movement that doesn't want translation to be self-enclosed and reduce the other to the terms of that self, but rather a movement out towards the other. Amongst the many authors that could be cited in this context, I take up this passage by Pannwitz which is cited by Benjamin: 'The fundamental error of the transferer (the *Übertragende* and not the *Übersetzer*) is to take the contingent status of his own language as solid and fixed instead of letting himself be violently moved by the foreign language… He must enlarge and deepen his own language by means of the foreign language; we have no idea how far this is possible and to which degree every language can be transformed…'[10]

We have no idea how far this is still *foreign* to the kind of 'French-style' translation Germans have noted since the 18th century; how we have remained ethnocentrist, and how continuously, with the very best intentions, we have stuck to the method of 'how would we say this if we had to say it ourselves'. This conception strays way over the borders since… one of the best examples of a 'French-style' translator was Freud himself; Freud the great translator of John Stuart Mill and Charcot who advocated reading a whole page or passage of the original, then closing the book and writing whilst asking the question 'how can we say this in German?'

Obviously Freud was deeply influenced by French culture in this; but this global approach to the text took him a long way away from his own psychoanalytic method!

To take up the following question: does translation, whether it be of a text or analytical translation, amount to appropriation or disappropriation? Appropriation is certainly the easier option; but is disappropriation conceivable without mysticism or a certain romanticism built around the 'loss of self', even in the case of a technical translation which has no jargon or bizarre turns of phrase?

To make come to oneself or to head out towards the other? Is there a third option: to prolong the movement forward? In any case, this is the option proposed by Benjamin, according to which authentic translation ought to be nothing but a moment in the very after-life of the work; the *Trieb zur Übersetzung* (the drive to translate) doesn't come from the translator, but from the work itself.

But don't these three approaches of the translator suggest three similar and possible approaches to psychoanalysis and three possible ways to conceive of the transference?

In some ways, Benjamin displays a certain romantic vitalism that needs to be approached with a cool head (*Nüchternheit* – sobriety) and above all with the Freudian method; as – let's emphasize it – Freud distinguishes himself from all hermeneutic traditions by proposing a method, a means of proceeding. The cipher method is fine as long as its not a dictionary but a procedure and process. With regard to Benjamin, I'll give you here a few breakthroughs, a few arcades, which have struck me as being evocative. I am not saying that these are purely and simply truths, but things, so to speak, that give one something to think about. What's alluded to here is the translation of *Dichtung*, the great *Dichtung*;[11] but, after all, isn't it also a question of *Dichtung* with Freud as well?

There's a primary metaphor in Benjamin of the tree and the forest:

'Translation doesn't envisage itself like poetry as plunged, so to speak, in the forest of language, but outside it, opposite the forest without entering it; it calls and penetrates the original in this unique place where the echo in its own language can resonate with a work in a foreign language'. I would prolong this by saying that there's a sort of third possibility between 'being plunged in the forest' and being in the position where 'the tree hides the forest'. In effect, the word for word possibility is in a way the tree hiding the forest. There's quite an original image here: we don't enter the forest (the too familiar use of our own language); we also don't press our nose up to one single tree (such as the lover of reality in Plato); here we are then at the edge of the forest, where *every* tree detaches itself to try to cause a *resonance* from tree to tree of something that echoes the original.

Another image that struck me was the *tangential relations* between text and translation. Benjamin says that translation is not determined by the text in an absolute parallelism, but in the way that a tangent has its course determined by the point of tangency. Obviously, there is considerable depth to be explored here, and probably a mathematician could tell us a lot to stop us from venturing too far; nevertheless, this reminds me of the sketch that I myself have given of tangency, notably the drawing I call the 'tub' (*le bacquet*), and in this idea, analysis can be described as a movement like a helix, through which it's possible at certain moments to pass into other orbits – in other words, it's a tangential departure.[12]

Furthermore, one finds in Benjamin the image and even the term 'unbinding', the *Entbindung* that was so important to Freud: there is an ultimate element beyond meaning, a 'symboliser' (*symbolisant*) that translation *unbinds* from its meaning in order to make a 'symbolized' (*symbolisé*) from it.

Over and above these images and their personal impact for everyone – because, after all, comparison is not an argument – I would like to enter into what seems to me to be the ultimate question raised by Benjamin, though it's not just his question. What is translatable and what is not? This is linked to a second debate which gives us a better view of the first: what is it to translate a translation, and is it possible to translate a translation? What does this mean, and does it still make any sense? Here, according to

Benjamin's terms, it's possible to distinguish between what he calls on the one hand the view (*le visé*), that is, in a certain way the flattest level of meaning; and, on the other hand, the aim (*la visée*), which at one moment he calls *der Gehalt*, the intrinsic value that does not contain meaning but a poetic content. Well, the first here, the flattest meaning, is what seems to be by definition translatable. Let's say it's the text as a vehicle for information. This is what Strachey peddled as a translation of Freud when he lacked inspiration; and this Strachey translation now actually forms the basis of American psychoanalysis. What about the aim, then, the *Meinung* or *intentio*, which Benjamin asserts is different in every language? So much so that two apparently simple and unequivocal terms like 'bread' and 'Brot' have certainly the same view (*visé*) – let's call it the same referent – but that the aims (*visées*) can in no way be superimposed from one language onto the other. However, for Benjamin, to say 'in every language' doesn't imply a purely subjective aim for an individual, even if it was a collective-cultural one, because he equally talks about it as an intrinsic value. The intrinsic value is the more specific, which introduces precisely the task of translating and the obligation to translate. The obligation to translate, its inevitable *Trieb* (drive), doesn't come from meaning; the drive to translate – and here I use my own terms – comes more from the untranslatable. Once more, it's an obligation that does not come from the receiver. It's an imperative which is brought to him by the work itself. It's a categorical imperative: 'you must translate because it's untranslatable'. It's here exactly in this task that the images of tangency, of the word for word and the arcade, mesh in.

I will cite now the precise passage from which I've taken my epigraph on the wall and the arcade: 'Therefore it is not the highest praise of a translation, particularly in the age of its origin, to say that it reads as if it had originally been written in that language ('*particularly* in the age of its origin' precisely because several centuries later the characteristic of the *great* translation would be that it had become the language itself; think of Luther who created the German language *through* his translation). Rather, the significance of fidelity, as ensured by the word for word, is the great desire to bring a complement to the language starting from the original work. True translation is transparent and does not cover over the original;

it does not block its light, but allows the pure language, as though reinforced by its own medium, to shine upon the original all the more fully. This explains the pre-eminent success of the word for word in the transfer of syntax (I translate *Wörtlichkeit* by 'word for word' and not 'literalism' or 'literal rendering' [*Zohn*] as everything, even syntax, plays around the priority of word over proposition), and demonstrates precisely that the word and not the proposition is the primal element of the translation. For if the sentence is the wall before the language of the original, the word for word is the arcade' (Laplanche's comments in brackets).[13]

Now, to return to our basic discussion, what about our second level, the translation of translation? It's a secular debate and perhaps both opinions are equally valuable: the first opinion is 'there is no translation of translation' and the second is 'only translation is translation'. To give away the secret this second proposition can only basically hold up if it is admitted that every text is already a primal translation of something. Conversely, it seems to me that Benjamin doesn't situate himself on the side of the primal but rather the side of the future, so for him there is no translation of translation. There is no translation of translation on the level of the view (*visé*). To turn again to our set scapegoat, Strachey: it is possible to translate Freud from Strachey's translation, but this is of absolutely no interest, and loss will be inevitable, even as far as the quantity of meaning is concerned. The most notable example of this was the other A. Berman who translated Freud from the English.[14]

What then of *der Gehalt*, that is the intrinsic value which *drives* us to translate? Here again for Benjamin there is no translation possible, because on the second level, movement cuts out despite all efforts. I can do no more than to cite one or two sentences here as I did before, because the text is difficult and I am not sure that its obscurity should always be venerated. This is how Benjamin puts it: 'more precisely, one can define this essential core as that which is not translatable again in the translation (even though this is what drove us to translate). It is not transferable just like the poetic word of the original, because the relationship between intrinsic value and language is totally different in the original and the translation (even if it were an inspired translation, as in the case of Luther who was mentioned earlier and others like Amyot).[15] If, in the original, intrinsic value and language form a determined unity like the fruit and its skin, the language of the translation envelops its intrinsic value like a royal robe with large folds. Because it signifies a language superior to itself and thus remains inadequate, forced and foreign in relation to its own intrinsic value.'[16]

I can't give a better illustration of what Benjamin wants to say than by referring quickly and ironically (you'll see why later) to Hölderlin's translations of Sophocles. These translations formed a major reference point in the contemporary debate as a model of a certain absolute and, as you may know, dated from around 1804 – the pre-madness or the beginning of madness stage in Hölderlin's life (or the 'detour of madness and work' as I formerly called it), that is before the repetitive stage which then lasted for several decades after.[17] At this time, Hölderlin on the one hand published some 'Remarks on Antigone' and 'Remarks on Oedipus', and on the other hand published some translations from ancient Greek, Pindar and also Sophocles' *Oedipus Rex* and *Antigone*. This is published in French in the series 10/18 with a very beautiful preface by Jean Beaufret as well as a just about acceptable translation of the 'Remarks on Oedipus' and the 'Remarks on Sophocles'. Then we are offered in this little volume the opportunity to compare a passage of Sophocles with Hölderlin's translation of it: Sophocles' text is on the left page and Hölderlin's translation is on the right... What's remarkable is that both the translation of Sophocles and the translation of the translation of Hölderlin are given in French!

A while ago I said that there was apparently nothing 'below' these two terms of the view (*le visé*) and the aim (*la visée*); there was nothing primal (*originaire*). But nonetheless he does have a third term. I would now like to turn our attention to these 'two' and 'three' terms. For Benjamin, in addition to the inspired text and its (no less inspired) translation, the third term is at certain moments perhaps the original + the translation. At other moments when Benjamin appears more messianic, the third term announces a 'pure language', the language of languages, where the aims (*visées*) of two languages and perhaps all languages are reconciled and rendered whole. Despite appearances, you can see that there is something here that is analogous to Freud: a *Grundsprache* (fundamental language) which is not a

Ursprache (primal language). It doesn't go backwards but forwards, so it's a messianic *Grundsprache* which, we should add, is asymptotic.

The difference between two terms and three terms seems important to me. Two terms don't allow for an orientation. Two terms – the translated and the translator – are either surrendered to a centring on the translator which we've called somewhat narrowly 'ethnocentrism'; or they are surrendered to a centring on what's to be translated, which can in the extreme lead to a refusal to translate. What can we see of this in psychoanalysis? I believe that one can see the same debate sketched out in analysis, and that we face precisely the same problem of the two terms. In this way, it's equally evident in a Jung or a Viderman that the presence only of two terms allows only for a subjective hermeneutics. It's said that between two points you can draw a straight line, but you can also draw an infinity of curves of a certain kind. You can only draw one curve through three points, and draw just one circle. Even so, there must be a third term so that translation (and interpretation) exit from their subjectivity. Benjamin proposes that we put the third term in front in the future, and obviously I don't side with this openly proposed messianism. Do we then place the third term behind in the past? To introduce in another way this notion of 'behind', I would like for a moment to use what I call the Chouraki parable.

You know that André Chouraqui is one of the modern translators of the Bible. Moreover, although Jewish, he's translated both the Old and New Testaments. Moreover too, he is actually working on the Koran, which shows the ecumenicism of this very fascinating man. What he does with the Old Testament is already quite remarkable. It's very open to criticism at certain moments and inspiring at others. I can't go into the detail of these innovations or his way of scouring from the biblical text the multitudes of translations which have covered it over. When he tells us that the water spring (source) and the eye are conveyed by the same word in Hebrew, of course we feel obliged to think that it's the spring that runs dry in the desert.[18] But it's not the water spring that spouts out of the side of a mountain, but the spring that appears precisely as a *water-eye* in certain places in the desert. So when Chouraqui re-translates that water spring into an eye, I find it perfectly convincing. At other moments, it is a little far-fetched, but we know full well that the far-fetched will become convincing in a few decades (see the Benjamin quotation above). This is just to introduce Chouraqui, but what really interests me about him is something quite different: his translation of the *New Testament* starting with the following fact. There are actually Hebrew and Greek versions of the *Old Testament*, which was translated into Greek before the time of Jesus Christ by the 70 (translators of the Septuagint). However, we only have a Greek text from which to.translate the *New Testament*, the Gospels and their sequels. Now what tempts Chouraqui is to translate with the supposition that the authors of the *New Testament* were immersed in the language worlds of Hebrew and Aramaic, though he never postulates that the Greek Gospels were themselves translated from Hebrew. In this way, he re-translates the Greek whilst aiming the translation through the Hebrew (*dans la visée de l'hébreu*). In this way, I talk of his translations as parables; parables which elicit even more interest for what they want to re-translate. It's not a 'text' that he wants to discover beneath the given text. What collapses for Chouraqui is the idea of a complete text which could have been lost. What's lost are certain points, words and specific inscriptions. In other words, there is no text behind the text, and this is why I corrected my provisional title, and shifted it from 'Translation of an Unknown Text' to 'Translation of Unknown Inscriptions'. In a certain way it could be said that he translates the Greek to re-inject the repressed (that's the only way I can put it), that is to say, to re-inject the non-translated in the Greek in order to take the translation further, and to re-translate by reintegrating something that had been discarded or repressed.

Now what's fallen by the wayside or been discarded are words, or the word-for-word. Chouraqui moves from word to word, when, for example, he tries to find a Hebrew or Aramaic term behind the Greek word 'makarioi'. This leads him to de-translate something to be able to re-inject some non-translated into it, which obviously surrenders him up to a new and necessary *Zusammensetzung* (composition); all the *Zwang* (compulsion) drives him to it.

I shift my direction again to talk about something apparently different which I call the 'proof of the unconscious', which of course relates to the 'proof of the existence of God.' The proof of the unconscious is by procedure, just like the proof of the existence of God. Every 'proof' of the existence of God is given pages in Descartes, and there is no syllogistic form there. It's the same for the unconscious: it's a demonstrative or exhibitive procedure which shows us we have arrived at conviction in the necessity of the unconscious – and not only of its existence! Just like Descartes, who was never satisfied simply to prove God as a word, but had to 'produce' (*produire* – pull out of it) a certain essence, even if it might be negative – we also, when we speak of 'proof of the unconscious', we're also obliged to say something else about it, and add a certain content that is more substantial than just saying: 'there is an unconscious'.

There are four proofs for me. The first is the most known and recognized, and one on which we all base ourselves: the analytic *experience*. It's the Freudian and our everyday experience, and one which we should take in the sense of *Erfahrung* (experiential knowledge): an experience that one feels as opposed to a (scientific) experiment, whether this be an experience within the session or an extra-sessional one. This is the whole of psychoanalysis since the *Traumdeutung* (*The Interpretation of Dreams*, 1900), the *Introduction to Psychoanalysis* (Introductory Lectures, 1916–17) which begin with bungled actions (do we need to be reminded?), *The Psychopathology of Everyday Life*, 1901), and all the big 'psychoanalyses'. We know that this proof tells us little about the nature and being of the unconscious. It's a proof that there is some unconsciousness: one can't get away from postulating that some of our words and acts don't place their reason, cause or motivation at our disposal (and let's leave these things hazy); but theoretically this doesn't take us very far.

Even so, I think that this experience already shows us something more. What I want to say – and I tried previously to develop these ideas in a paper I wrote with Serge Leclaire entitled 'The Unconscious' (Laplanche & Leclaire, 1960 [1972]) – is that, even on the level on which psychoanalysis is happy to *unveil* the unconscious, it still says a little more than 'there is unconsciousness (obviously taken in another sense than pre-consciousness, that is, it is non-recallable through group re-memoration). The discussion on the essence of the unconscious can already be raised to the level of that first clinical or experiential procedure, in the sense that it is very difficult to account for the genesis and the structure of unconscious formations other than by a combination: by the combination of two types of wish corresponding to two types of reality. The idea of a compromise-formation notably appeals quite strongly to realism, and it evidently does this just up to the point where it could abolish the very idea of compromise by appealing to another perspective.

I would like to call the second kind of proof *deductive* proof. I have provided a general outline of this in the framework of what I've recently called the 'generalized theory of seduction' (*New Foundations,* 1987). This deductive proof is based on the first (clinical or experiential) one in so far as there must be (and it's enough that there are) adults who have some unconsciousness so that we can show the formation of a repressed unconscious in the child. This second form of demonstration ends up in the following: because of the asymmetrical situation of this seduction, some repressed material must necessarily be produced in the child repressed *material* in the sense of the inscriptions of the (adult) repressed, as I described earlier. This is essentially what I've tried to synthesize recently around primal repression and a translation theory of this psychic process that is induced by the primal universal seduction situation (*New Foundations,* 1987).

I'll just mention the third type of proof rather than enlarge on it, simply because it forms part of my present speculative journeying. It's the proof through the dialectic of *repatriation*. By 'repatriation', I refer in a larger and dialectical sense to what Freud articulated in saying that metaphysics ought to be reconverted into metapsychology. I believe there is a cultural movement there, a movement in the evolution of knowledge (*connaissance*) and probably in attitudes to the world, which is equally a repatriative movement of things, causes (in the precise sense of causality), or even the archeology of meaning in the narrowest (technical) as well as broadest sense of the term. This repatriative movement shows us the way to return towards that reality which is precisely the origin of these notions of thing, cause and beautiful archæological 'find' (*bel objet archéologique*); the unconscious thing, the internal alien body, or thing-representation in Freud's terms, or object-source as I designate it.

Finally, the fourth proof, which relates more directly to the concerns of this paper, namely the *practical* proof, or the postulate of practice. I derive this term or I copy it from Kant's term, in the sense that the postulate of practical reason is a proof of God: the moral and free man could not act without postulating God, as well as the immortality of the soul. By analogy, there could be a postulate of practical analytical reason, which for example could be articulated as follows: every interpretative trajectory which links two terms is doomed to be arbitrary if it doesn't relate to a third term, and if it doesn't postulate something which is unconscious.

The old dispute between Freud and Jung about the 'retro-fantasies' – the *Zurückphantasien* as they're found notably at the end of the *Wolf Man* – was not an easy one. We often don't know who is the victor and who is the vanquished. The proof of this is that so many contemporaries continue to struggle with a theory of interpretation involving two terms: the interpreted and the interpreter. You know that Freud only pulled himself out of this by postulating a certain type of third term (as Pontalis and I have amply demonstrated): that of the primal fantasies, of the prehistoric or 'scientific myth' ('Fantasy and the Origins of Sexuality', 1964).

Following my view, this postulation of our practical reason is that of a real unconscious, in the dual sense in which *we* postulate the unconscious, but the *unconscious* also postulates us. This second way of putting it is nothing else than the explanation of the *Übersetzungstrieb* (the drive to translate).

The dual sense and orientation of our formula reminds us that 'translation' (however metaphorically one takes this term) always requires these two movements, but in the inverse direction. We can find what we may call the 'progressive' direction (*direction progrediente*) right at the beginning of Freud's work in the famous letter of December 6, 1896 (Freud/Fliess Correspondence, 1985, p.208): it's a series of translations which constitutes the psychic apparatus: the movement of translation always carries us forward. This model raises again the whole question of the translation of translation. On another level of theorization it also leads to the libidinal 'stages': does the idea of the translation of translation apply to the succession of two libidinal stages? I don't believe it. The other 'regressive' direction (*orientation regrediente*) involves interpretation in the technical analytic sense of the term, which precisely postulates the unconscious.

Are these two directions contradictory? Or are we simply creating ambiguity when we employ the term 'translation' in both cases (like Freud)? Or does retranslation really involve an indissoluble movement consisting of translation, de-translation, or retro-translation?

My own position is that that there is in fact only one 'progressive' translation, and here I'm in agreement with the German tradition prior to Benjamin, and particularly with the Hegelian tradition, though I have not especially looked at texts on this subject. For me, interpretation is a de-translation to allow the field to open up for a new and more inclusive translation. That is what I tried to illustrate with the 'Chouraqui parable' above. We undo some preconscious material – we don't translate it: there's no translation of translation – so that a new preconscious might recover a part of what has been left aside. We can recover there – why not? – the famous image of the draining of the Zuiderzee as an infinite cultural task.

Another issue I would like to raise with you because it's the order of the day for me, is that of *neologism*. I'm presently confronted with this problem in the translation of Freud. We have created, and I have created, a certain number of neologisms in this project. Obviously I've tried not to become a fan of neologisms, and, at the same time, I've tried to refer the process of neologization to some rational enquiry. In the translation of Freud, neologism is also certainly a true word-creation (and one notices that pure creations are very rare), in contrast to what most often is called 'neologizing use', namely the revivification of old terms that have fallen into disuse, or of an abandoned use of a term that's still used. I can thus resolve to use the French term 'succès' in the old French sense of the German *Erfolg* (outcome), where the term doesn't imply that 'succession' must be necessarily positive. But the use of neologisms isn't forcibly turned towards the past. It can also accentuate and prolong an evolution that is already perceptible in the language. With this kind of neologistic creation, I locate myself in the domain of translation as opposed to the domain of pathological neologism, even if I still have to question the relation between the two.

To my mind, neologistic creation must come from the living spirit (*genie*) of the language, and notably must not be borrowed from a foreign language, be it dead or alive. Strachey's introduction of the terms cathexis or anaclisis were in the end not neologisms but false terms arrived at artificially; it would be the same if I stuffed my translation with German terms' I definitively or provisionally refused to translate. On the one hand, neologism must fit in with the living spirit of the language, and, on the other hand, it must come at a place where it is needed, where there is a lack. There is a lack in the target language in relation to the usage of the original language, and bearings can be taken if a table of meanings and correlations is established. It is noticeable that something is missing in French when it comes to translate *Sehnsucht*, which is neither nostalgia nor ardent desire; elsewhere in the series of French terms that revolve around desire, there's room for a derivation that will convey the nuances of *Sehnsucht*.[19]

By definition, neologisms are doomed to appear bizarre and to be criticized ('notably at the moment of their production', as Benjamin said). They are criticized by the users of both languages: the speakers of our own language – because of the strangeness of the neologism – but also by the speakers of the original language, Germanophones in this case, who feel themselves defrauded because one has tried to carry off something of their indescribable *Sehnsucht*.

'If reality is inconceivable', Hegel said in a slightly different context, 'then we must forge inconceivable concepts...'. I think neologisms are meaning-traps. I have forged the following comparison, in which I believe the French term '*comparant*' fits the reality:[20] storks have almost completely disappeared from the skies of Alsace, and the only way to try and get them to return has been to create false nests. Obviously you don't just build these nests anyhow. It's not any sort of plastic bowl that you're going to perch anywhere. It's got to be in the right place where there have already been storks' nests. As far as possible, it's got to be well manufactured and adapted – *well-fitted*, as the English say: something that lasts... and invites the stork-meaning to come and nest there.

By what right can one forbid the translator to choose to create in his own language and 'make resonate the echo' of the foreign (land) and choose instead to subjugate himself to 'proper usage'? Let me throw in a few of our neologisms, without trying to justify them here: *désaide* – a term Gide would not have disavowed – for *Hilflosigkeit*; *désirance* – presently adopted by Chouraqui as indispensable for the first book of the Koran – for *Sehnsucht*; or *refusement* for *Versagung*. I sound like a shop salesman here in the translators' boutique. But that's where I'd like to stay a minute as neologism is something that can provide a model as well as a prototype of sublimation, that is, at the crossroads between the drive and social recognition or valorization. The neologism is launched to be inhabited from two sides at the same time: inhabited by the language aimed at, but also inhabited by the drive that comes from the original language and probably from further than that too.

I'll end this here. You see that I haven't escaped a certain gathering-together, a certain *Zusammensetzung*, though it is of the conglomeration type. I hope nevertheless that you have wanted to follow me with it. I didn't want to systematize it but rather indicate certain points to hang on to – certain auxiliary hypotheses for my present reflections. And because we have to punctuate a discourse with something, I wrote down these few lines: the first sentence is verse, and follows its disposition –

'Und immer
Ins Ungebundene gehet eine Sehnsucht. Vieles aber ist
Zu behalten'

which is roughly this –

Et toujours
Dans l'inlie s'en va une désirance. Beaucoup pourtant
est à retenir [†]

An image in which the schizophrenic Hölderlin struggled to hold things together.

† And always desiring springs out of the unbound. Much however is to be retained.

And then this sort of ironic transposition, which would very much be the task of the analyst, at least in the analysis of neurosis:

> 'Und immer
> ins Zusammengesetzte geht ein Zwang. Vieles aber ist zu entbinden'
>
> 'Et toujours vers le compose s'en va une contrainte. Beaucoup cependant est à délier' ‡

‡ And always a compulsion flees towards composition. Much however is to be undone.

Notes

1. Walter Benjamin, 'The Task of the Translator', *Illuminations*, (Cape, London, 1970), translated by Harry Zohn, p.79.
2. This article is based on a paper given to a conference of the Association Psychanalytique de France (12–13 December, 1987). The title of this conference was 'The displacements of reason'.
3. 'Appareil' in French also means 'appearance', 'display', and 'machine' (as in 'appareil de photo' – camera).
4. The book in question is Laplanche's *New Foundations for Psychoanalysis* (1988/1989). Unfortunately Michel Tourlière's cover drawing, 'Alternation of Foundations' (Alternance des assises) is not reproduced in the English edition.
5. The Standard Edition renders *Zwang* by 'obsession' or 'compulsion'. Laplanche does not follow this in his French translation, but suggests instead 'contrainte', which emphasizes the element of constriction in the compulsion.
6. This quote is from *The Interpretation of Dreams*, Chapter 2 (Freud, S.E., vol.4, pp.96–7). Note that Strachey places 'symbolic' in inverted commas – which are absent in the original German!
7. Freud, S.E, vol 4, p.97; Laplanche translates 'Chriffriermethode' here as 'coding-decoding' method (*méthode de chiffrage-dechiffrage*).
8. An English translation of this can be found in *Illuminations* (1970).
9. *le mouvement anti-autocentrique* – 'auto' in French does not simply imply 'self' but also 'engendered within itself', as in 'automatic'.
10. In this quote, Laplanche stresses the choice of *Übertragende* rather than *Übersetzer* here to show the involvement of *Übertragung* ('transference' in Strachey's translation of Freud) in the whole issue of translation.

11. 'Dichtung' in German has several meanings, ranging from poetry to a single poem to fiction.

12. The 'tub' – *le baquet* – is one of Laplanche's major concepts. Laplanche relates the term to Freud's early model of the psychic process, notably the attempts to account for the elaboration of memory and the production of 'fictions' (cf. *Problématiques* V, p.30ff). The word is chosen both because it describes the transference 'loop': (*New Foundations*, p.156) and because its metaphoric range, which includes Messmer's famous '*baquet*' used in early hypnotism and the 'black box' model of mechanical memory.

13. I have used Zohn's English translation here (Benjamin, op.cit., p.79) except where it differs markedly from Laplanche's translation and the original.

14. Anne Berman translated some of Freud's work into French from the Strachey translation (cf. Bourguignon et. al., 1989, pp.10–12 & p.86). The contrast is with Antoine Berman mentioned earlier.

15. Jacques Amyot (1513–1593) translated the works of Plutarch and Longus into French.

16. The comments in brackets are Laplanche's references to the text cited.

17. cf. Laplanche's *Hölderlin et la Question du père* (1st ed. 1964, 3rd ed. 1984).

18. In French, 'source' – water spring – also means 'origin' (an important term for Laplanche!). This dual sense is played with in the following discussion.

19. Laplanche's neologism for 'Sehnsucht' – *désirance* – has caused considerable controversy in France.

20. The term *comparant* in French relates to the previous 'comparison' (*comparaison*) but connotes a older legalistic meaning: a *comparant* lined up before the judge or the tribunal and waited to be identified as the criminal.

21. The quote is from Hölderlin's poem *Mnemonyme*.

Notes on Afterwardsness[1]

I want to stress first of all that the whole problem of *Nachträglichkeit* (afterwardsness) also *forms* itself through afterwardsness. I also want to say that it's because of the French reading and translation of Freud that the concept of afterwardsness has become important. If, for example, you take the index of Freud's *Gesammelte Werke*, you will find that neither *nachträglich* nor *Nachträglichkeit* are mentioned. In the *Gesammtregister*, which dates from much later – 1968 in fact, so it comes after the publication of *The Language of Psychoanalysis* – actually has one or two entries under the adjective 'nachträglich', but these are not very significant examples. If you also look in the indexes of the work of Freud's main disciples, you'll find the same negative result. It's therefore in France, and in close relation to the problems of translation, that the importance of *Nachträglichkeit* has made itself felt. First of all, it's importance was noted by Lacan, who in 1953 drew attention to this concept in a precise but restricted way. He did not look at the broader implications of the concept for Freud's work. He focussed only on its importance in the *Wolf Man* case, and missed out completely its use in the period 1895–1900. It was left to Pontalis and myself to draw attention to this general importance of the concept – first, in 'Fantasy and the Origins of Sexuality' (1964) and then in *The Language of Psychoanalysis* (1967). I have continued this elaboration of the concept in my own work, in the *Problématiques* (1981/88) and in the *New Foundations*

(1987). I am presently working on an article on 'The Afterwardsness of Nachträglichkeit', which will eventually form a chapter in a book I am writing on time. In this, I give a detailed account of Freud's use of the term, and the way in which it differs from my own, so here I will content myself with only presenting the general lines of my argument. I'll develop my argument along three general lines: first, what happens to Freud's concept; second, the issue of its translation; and finally, what is my own conception of afterwardsness. Here again I must stress that one can examine carefully what Freud said without actually adhering to his argument – and that's certainly my position!

First, Freud's view of afterwardsness. He used the terms 'nachträglich' and 'Nachträglichkeit' over a great period of his working life, in fact from the time of his correspondence with Fliess, through *The Interpretation of Dreams*, and *Little Hans* to the *Wolf Man*, and indeed well beyond that. So it's possible to see the development of these terms – which never actually became fully-fledged concepts – in the general context of his work. They never anyway became fully-fledged enough for Freud to dedicate a whole article to the concept of afterwardsness. We can see the youthful development of the term afterwardsness in Freud's correspondence with Fliess. Several things become apparent here. First, the use of the adjective 'nachträglich', which is taken from current usage, is used by Freud in several ways. We can roughly divide these uses into three: first, there's the sense of 'ulterior' or 'secondary' – it relates secondary consciousness to a primary one. Strachey and Masson usually translate this by 'subsequently'. So it assumes the purely temporal meaning of 'later'. The second use follows the direction of time from the past to the future, and the third use inverts it from the future towards the past. The second use from past to the future is very much tied up with the seduction theory: it's a question of the deposit of something in the individual which will only be reactivated later, and so will only become active in a 'second time' – that's the seduction theory. One should point out that this seduction theory was very mechanical, because Freud never thought that one could reverse temporal direction. One can use the time bomb example to illustrate this: the first memory is like a time-bomb which is triggered off by something outside it. There is no sense here of retroactivity. But there's a third use which does convey the sense of retroactivity. There are a number of passages concerning things which are registered in a first time then understood retroactively. These are relatively rare in Freud.

I'll limit myself here to making a few contextual remarks about these three uses. In the choice between a determinist conception that proceeds from the past to the future and a retrospective or hermeneutic conception that proceeds from the future to the past, Freud always chooses the former. Indeed, he never even attempts to reconcile the two conceptions. I refer here to the letter to Fliess of 4 October 1897 in which he relates an episode of his self-analysis and comments: 'A harsh critic might say of all this that it was retrogressively fantasised instead of progressively determined. The *experimenta crucis* must decide against him' (Freud/Fliess, p.270). My other contextual point concerns the appearance of the substantive 'Nachträglichkeit'. As you know, this word is relatively rare in German. It is remarkable that this substantive only appears in one letter to Fliess of 14 November 1897 (ibid., p.280). This letter comes after the so-called abandonment of the seduction theory, at a moment when Freud becomes even more determinist – determinist in the sense that the future and the present are both determined by the past. This letter is entirely focussed on the organic determinism of repression and therefore on the phylogenetic origin of ontogenetic development. It's on this level of the determinism of the development of individual sexual stages by phylogenetic sexual stages that Freud poses afterwardsness, so evidently there is no question of reversing temporal progression. So you can see that things are not all that simple. Whereas we may wish to see at best a double and even contradictory use of 'Nachträglichkeit', we actually have a use that is heavily determinist.

Now you could criticize this view for being too heavily based in texts before 1898, so I'll give you brief illustrations of Freud's consistent rejection of the reversibility of temporal direction in later texts. There are three important texts here: *The Interpretation of Dreams*, *Little Hans*, and the *Wolf Man*. In the progression of these, Freud becomes increasingly caught up in a rhetorical exchange with Jung to defend his view that there is a real primal scene – 'real' in the sense of really experienced. Freud made some concessions, but he never wavered in his conviction that what comes before determines what happens after. It seems to me therefore totally wrong to try to assimilate Freud's concept of 'Nachträglichkeit' with Jung's notion of 'Zurückphantasien' (retrospective fantasy).[2]

Now to my second point: translation. Alternative translations are offered for this term as for many others. Either one decides that this term must be translated according to the context; in other words, it must be 'interpreted'. In this case, we could not have a single term in either English or French for 'nachträglich/Nachträglichkeit'. This approach is well illustrated by Strachey who translates 'nachträglich/Nachträglichkeit' by a whole series of terms according to the context: 'by deferred action', 'subsequently', 'in a deferred fashion', 'subsequent', 'after-effect', 'deferred effect', 'deferred nature of the effect', 'later', etc. As long as one wishes to 'interpret' in this way, and impose meaning on an essentially open text, a unitary translation is impossible. Let's now take the example of two translations of 'Nachträglichkeit' which seem to be in competition: 'retrospective attribution' proposed by Helmut Thomä, and 'deferred action' classically proposed by Strachey. I'll take two groups of words to illustrate: in the *Studies on Hysteria*, Freud talks of the 'nachträgliche Erleidigung der Trauma'; and, in the letters to Fliess, Freud writes 'Phantasien sind Dinge früh gehört erst nachträglich verstanden'. In the first phrase, it's totally impossible to translate 'nachträglich' by 'by retroactive attribution', which would produce the absurd translation: 'the liquidation of the trauma by retrospective attribution'. It's equally absurd to translate the second phrase by: 'Fantasies are things which were heard previously and only understood by deferred action'. You can see in these two examples that interpretative translations fail to convey the whole context in which Freud employs the term 'nachträglich'. So either one decides to split up and divide the term in translation, or one chooses a term that will allow the reader to stay with Freud's term and reinterpret it for themselves. That's why I propose a translation that is not interpretative: I suggest the term 'après-coup', and 'afterwardsness' in English. In all cases in Freud, it's possible to use either 'afterwards' or 'afterwardsness'.

I now want to talk about my own conception of 'Nachträglichkeit', and to stress that I differ from both the Freudian and hermeneutic conceptions.

To introduce this, I would like to take a passage from *The Interpretation of Dreams* which has not been commented on by other critics (cf. Thomä & Cheshire, 1991): this is the famous 'Knödel' (dumpling) dream which Freud introduces to 'explain the factor of "deferred action" (Nachträglichkeit) in the mechanism of the psychoneuroses' (Freud, SE, 4, p. 204-5). This text is important because it shows that in 1905 Freud still considered 'Nachträglichkeit' as an important concept that needed to be explained to his students. In this anecdote one finds reference to the two possible temporal directions involved in afterwardsness. The first direction is evoked when the adult man who sees the child at the wet-nurse's breast retroactively imagines all that he could have drawn erotically from that situation if only he had known. So this is a true example of 'Zurückphantasien' (retrospective fantasy) and of hermeneutics: he reinterprets the function of breast feeding in terms of his present situation. This is a totally Jungian conception. The other temporal direction is equally present, as one cannot forget that, according to Freud, oral sexuality is not purely invented by the adult. He thinks that the child at the breast erotically enjoys sucking, which he describes moreover in the *Three Essays on the Theory of Sexuality* as the primary oral erotic experience. In this context, it is also the oral sexuality of this man which is awakened by this spectacle of the child at the breast. So there are both progressive and retroactive aspects involved here. Here I would like to intervene in Freud's account to give my own point of view, which is in no way a choice between these two options. It's neither opting for the hermeneutic position nor Freud's deterministic one. What Freud scotomizes or does not wish to see in this example is the wet-nurse. He only takes into account the two interlocutors centred in the subject: that is, the man-baby, and the adult man; one sucks the breast and the other experiences erotic pleasure. Freud completely forgets here the wet-nurse and her own sexuality. He has completely forgotten his seduction theory, and his insight in the Leonardo study into infantile seduction by the mother. He treats the breast as an object for the child, and not as an erotic zone for the nurse. There is a breast here for the subject, that is, that comes from the side of the other, which also brings from its side something erotic along with the milk. So if one introduces a third term into this scene that is, the nurse and her own sexuality – which is only at best vaguely sensed by the baby – then it is no longer possible to consider afterwardsness in dual terms. The third term is then passed to the child from the adult: this is the nurse's message to the child.

The second thing I would like to add to transform the concept of afterwardsness is the idea of translation. In my view, afterwardsness is inconceivable without a model of translation: that is, it presupposes that something is proposed by the other, and which is then *afterwards* retranslated and reinterpreted. On the one hand, therefore, there's my introduction of the notion of the other, and, on the other hand, there's the translation model. So we then arrive at this idea: even if we concentrate all our efforts on the retroactive temporal direction, in the sense that someone reinterprets their past, this past cannot be a pure or factual one – a 'raw given'; it contains rather in an immanent fashion something that comes before – a message from the other. It's impossible therefore just to hold a hermeneutic position on this – that is to say, that everyone interprets their past according to their present – because their past already has something deposited in it that needs to be deciphered, which is the message of the third person.

To conclude, therefore, I would like to say that Freud's concept of afterwardsness contains both great richness and great ambiguity between a retrogressive and progressive directions. I want to account for this problem of the directional to and fro by arguing that, right at the start, there is something that goes in the direction from the past to the future, and in the direction from the adult to the baby, which I call the implantation of the enigmatic message. This message is then retranslated following a temporal direction which is sometimes progressive and sometimes retrogressive (according to my general model of translation).

Notes

1. These notes are taken from a recorded conversation between Jean Laplanche and Martin Stanton at the Chateau de Pommard on Sunday December 1, 1991. In this, Laplanche refers extensively to an essay he is working on: 'The Afterwardsness of *Nachträglichkeit*' (*La Nachträglichkeit dans l'Après-Coup*). Neither this, nor indeed these notes, are yet published in the original French.
2. Laplanche here criticizes recent attempts to assimilate Freud's use of 'Nachträglichkeit'

into the hermeneutic tradition, notably through parallels with Jung's notion of 'Zurückphantasieren' (Thomä & Cheshire, 1991). Thomä and Cheshire also fail to distinguish between Freud's concept and Laplanche's concept of 'afterwardsness'.

Biographical Sketch

Jean Laplanche was born in Paris on 21 June 1924 into a family of Burgundy wine-producers who have owned the Château de Pommard since the French Revolution. Laplanche has kept strong connections with Burgundy, and divides his time between Paris and Pommard. He began his secondary education at the Collège Monge at Beaune, then moved to the Lycée Henri IV in Paris to prepare for the entrance exam for the Ecole Normale Superiéure (ENS). During this time, the Second World War broke out and he became an active member of the resistance movement in Paris and Burgundy. In 1945, he entered the ENS as a philosophy student and studied under Maurice Merleau-Ponty and the eminent Hegel scholar, Jean Hippolyte. At the end of these studies, in 1951, he took the state exam, the *agrégation de philosophie*, and received highest commendations. While still a philosophy student, he won a visiting scholarship to Harvard, so spent the year 1946–7 in the United States. During this year, he developed his interest in psychoanalysis, as well as in cultural anthropology. On his return to Paris in 1947, he began psychoanalysis with Jacques Lacan. He decided to become a psychoanalyst, and Lacan advised him to study medicine. He began his medical studies in 1951, and completed his MD in 1959. As part of this he wrote a thesis on the German poet Hölderlin's 'schizophrenia', which was published in 1961 as *Hölderlin et la question du père*.

In 1950 he married Nadine Guillot, who has shared his cultural and intellectual interests, especially in art and psychoanalysis. During the 1950s, he played a prominent role in French intellectual life, notably as one of the founders, along with Cornelius Castoriadis and Claude Lefort, of the political journal *Socialisme ou Barbarisme* (1949–65). This produced a radical left critique of the Stalinism of the French Communist Party and a critical reformulation of Marxist theory.

At the 6th Colloquium of French psychologists at Bonneval in 1960, he presented a paper with Serge Leclaire on 'the unconscious' in which he criticized Lacanian formulations for the first time. In 1962, Daniel Lagache offered Laplanche a teaching post at the Sorbonne, and suggested to him that he collaborate with Jean-Bertrand Pontalis, a fellow Société Française de Psychanalyse (SFP) member and philosophy teacher, to write *The Language of Psychoanalysis*. Lacan regarded this project as 'too scholastic'. During the crisis and eventual dissolution of the SFP (1963–5), Laplanche distanced himself from the Lacanian position and, when the SFP dissolved itself in January 1965, joined the Association Psychanalytique de France (APF).

In 1964 he published with J-B Pontalis the path-breaking essay 'Fantasy and the Origins of Sexuality' which has been influential in disciplines such as Film Theory, Literary Criticism and Cultural Studies (see its reprinting with accompanying essays in these fields in Victor Burgin, James Donald, Cora Kaplan (eds.) *Formations of Fantasy*, Methuen 1986). In 1967, again with Pontalis, he published *The Language of Psychoanalysis*, a theoretical and critical vocabulair of psychoanalytic concepts and terminology that has become an authoritative reference book for psychoanalytic theory internationally.

In 1968, Laplanche helped found the new psychoanalysis and psycho-pathology programme at the University of Paris VII – Censier. This programme now takes 200–300 students a year. In this context, Laplanche pioneered a doctoral research programme in psychoanalysis (which does not include an analytical training). The doctoral programme now takes 50 students a year.

In 1970, *Life and Death in Psychoanalysis* presented a critical archæology of Freud's theory in the areas of sexuality, the ego and the death drive. This was followed by the five volumes of the *Problématiques* (1980–7), which contain essential critical revisions of the conceptualization proposed by

The Language of Psychoanalysis, as well as a clear elaboration of the Laplanchian theory of seduction. Finally in 1987, he took account of his position to date in *New Foundations for Psychoanalysis*, which proposed fundamental revisions of psychoanalytic theory and practice.

At present he is scientific director of the team that is translating the complete works of Freud into French. As a part of this, he has written a 'reasoned terminology' (*terminologie raisonnée*) which takes account of his critical revisions of *The Language of Psychoanalysis* and relates the linguistic to the conceptual problems posed by translating Freud. Finally, he is presently working on a book on time, which will elaborate further the issues of temporalization raised by 'afterwardsness' (*Nachträglichkeit*), seduction and translation.

Bibliography

Laplanche, J (1961), *Hölderlin et la question du père*, Paris, PUF.

(1970), *Life and Death in Psychoanalysis*, trans. J. Mehlmann, Baltimore MD, Johns Hopkins 1976.

(1979) 'A Metapsychology put to the test of Anxiety', *International Journal of Psycho-Analysis*, vol. 62, 1981.

(1980a) *Problématiques I: L'angoisse, Paris, PUF.*

(1980b) *Problématiques II: Castration-symbolisations*, Paris, PUF.

(1980c) *Problématiques III: La sublimation*, Paris, PUF.

(1981) *Problématiques IV: L'inconscient et le ça*, Paris, PUF.

(1984) 'To situate sublimation', trans. R. Miller, *October*, no. 28, Spring.

(1987a) *Problématiques V: Le baquet: transcendance du transfert*, Paris PUF.

(1987a) *New Foundations for Psychoanalysis*, trans. D. Macey, Oxford, Blackwell 1989.

(1989a) 'Terminologie raisonnée', in *Traduire Freud*, ed. Bourguignon et al.

(1989b) 'Temporality and Translation', *Stanford Literary Review*, Fall 1989.

Laplanche J. and Leclaire, S., 1960 'The Unconscious: a psychoanalytic study', trans. P. Coleman, *Yale French Studies*, no. 48, 1972.

Laplanche J., and Pontalis, J-B., (1964) 'Fantasy and the Origins of Sexuality', *International Journal of Psycho-Analysis*, 49, 1968.

(1967), *The Language of Psychoanalysis*, trans. D. Nicholson-Smith, London, Hogarth 1973.

Notes on Contributors

Andrew Benjamin is a senior lecturer in Philosophy at the University of Warwick and author of *Translation and the Nature of Philosophy* (1989), and *Art, Mimesis and the Avant-Garde* (1991).

Elizabeth Cowie is a senior lecturer in Film Studies at the University of Kent. She co-founded and co-edited the feminist journal *m/f* (1978–86) and is the author of a forthcoming book on women, film theory and psychoanalysis.

John Fletcher is a lecturer in English at the University of Warwick and co-editor of *Abjection, Melancholia and Love: the work of Julia Kristeva* (1989).

Martin Stanton is a practising psychoanalyst, director of the Centre for Psychoanalytic Studies at the University of Kent, and author of *Sandor Ferenczi: reconsidering active intervention* (1991).

Index